H·O·P·E

ALSO BY EMILY MARLIN

Taking a Chance on Love

H·O·P·E

NEW CHOICES AND RECOVERY STRATEGIES FOR ADULT CHILDREN OF ALCOHOLICS

EMILY MARLIN

PRODUCED BY THE PHILIP LIEF GROUP

1817

HARPER & ROW, PUBLISHERS, NEW YORK
Cambridge, Philadelphia, San Francisco, Washington
London, Mexico City, São Paulo, Singapore, Sydney

Grateful acknowledgment is made for permission to reprint the following:

"Characteristics of Alcoholic and Healthy Families" on page 6 excerpted from *The Adult Children of Alcoholics Syndrome* by Wayne Kritsberg, © Health Communications, Inc.

COA Quiz on page 254 reprinted by permission of *Alcoholism & Addiction Magazine*.

Children of Alcoholics Screening Test on page 256, © 1983 by Dr. John W. Jones, reprinted by permission of Camelot Unlimited.

Eating disorders questionnaire on page 264 from *Fat Is a Family Affair*, © 1985 by Judy Hollis, reprinted by permission of Hazelden Foundation.

AA Preamble on page 266 reprinted by permission of AA World Services.

"The Twelve Steps and the Twelve Traditions" on page 266 reprinted by permission of AA Grapevine.

"Detachment" on page 267, © 1980 by Al-Anon Family Group Headquarters, Inc.

"What Are the Signs of Alcoholism?" on page 257 reprinted by permission of the National Council on Alcoholism.

FIRST EDITION

Designer: Helene Berinsky
Copyeditor: Margaret Cheney
Index by Alberta Morrison

Library of Congress Cataloging-in-Publication Data

Marlin, Emily.
    Hope: new choices and recovery strategies for adult children of alcoholics.

    Bibliography: p.
    Includes index.
    1. Adult children of alcoholics—United States. 2. Alcoholics—United States—Family relationships. 3. Alcoholism—Treatment—United States. 4. Alcoholism—Psychological aspects. I. Philip Lief Group. II. Title. [DNLM: 1. Adaptation, Psychological—popular works. 2. Alcoholism—psychology—popular works. 3. Alcoholism—therapy—popular works. 4. Family—popular works. WM 274 M348h]
    HV5133.M37   1987   362.2'92   86-46158
    ISBN 0-06-015769-0

87 88 89 90 91 RRD 10 9 8 7 6 5 4 3 2 1

Dedicated to my parents, Orville and Emily Marlin,
and to my sibs, Mary, Pete, and Mike

CONTENTS

PART III
REAFFIRMING THE FUTURE

ACKNOWLEDGMENTS

Keeping it simple, I've decided to write a gratitude list to acknowledge the people who were enormously helpful to me in the writing of this book. The specific contributions they made, unquestionably significant and much appreciated, are not nearly as important to me as what they gave of themselves. For these gifts of support and affection, I am deeply grateful to:

Janet Goldstein
Charlotte Henshaw
Dorothy Kellett
Philip Lief
Bob Markel
Kevin Osborn
Peg Parkinson
Wendy Pratt
Sandy Shapiro
Iris Topel
Robin Wise

and the ACOAs who shared their secrets with me.

SURVIVAL IS NOT ENOUGH

STRATEGIES FOR RECOVERY

Most of the people who come to my office for psychotherapy are the adult children of alcoholics. Although I did not set out to specialize in working with ACOAs, more and more of them were referred to me for therapy, in part owing to my years of experience in the field of chemical dependency and my long-held admiration for the various Twelve Step programs, such as Alcoholics Anonymous and Al-Anon.

It is my impression that I am not alone in this experience. Other therapists also report seeing more and more ACOAs. This apparent upsurge in the number of adult children seeking therapy does not indicate a dramatic increase in the ACOA population, but rather a dramatic increase in public awareness. Many adult children of alcoholics are only now beginning to recognize and identify themselves as ACOAs. And, as our knowledge of the effects of alcoholism on the family has rapidly expanded, many therapists have learned to ask their patients questions designed to elicit information about the presence of alcoholism in their families.

The ACOAs I see are usually seeking treatment—in individual, group, couple, or family therapy—for a variety of problems that relate to their having grown up in alcoholic households. They very seldom identify that background as the source of their troubles, however. Instead, they describe themselves as anxious or depressed, and they tell me they are having problems with the people in their lives. These problems are evident in unhappy relationships, or in difficulties at work, or in compulsive behavior of their own.

For many of my patients, the problems of today are the unsolved problems of yesterday—their current difficulties usually have a great deal to do with unfinished family business—unresolved conflicts and hurts encountered in their childhoods. Finishing this unfinished business then becomes the primary goal of therapy, and it usually involves confronting skeletons in the family closets: more often than not, the skeletons are (or were) alcoholics.

Almost never do my clients come right out and say, "My father (or mother) is an alcoholic." They say instead, "Sometimes (s)he drank too much." Because of what I know about the disease of alcoholism, and the denial that accompanies it, when a client says someone "drinks too much," I make an assumption that the person being discussed is probably an alcoholic. I don't say that straight out, of course, but I do begin to listen closely for anything that might indicate that my client grew up in an alcoholic household. With therapy focused in this way, the client and I often discover that much of his or her fear, anger, confusion, insecurity, or guilt springs from surviving a childhood with an alcoholic parent.

I have learned about the special problems of adult children of alcoholics in the twenty years I've practiced as a psychotherapist. Most of my information has come directly from working with adult children of alcoholics. A second important source is my own experience: I too come from an alcoholic home. The experience is not as rare as we once thought it was: according to a February, 1985, Gallup poll, nearly one out of four people reported that alcoholism had been a problem somewhere in their families.

A third and very important source of my knowledge has been the self-help organization known as Al-Anon/ACOA. My professional colleagues and I would know much less than we do about the particular problems of ACOAs were it not for this pioneering group.

Not all children who grow up with an alcoholic parent (or parents) are affected in the same way, of course. Some apparently reach adulthood without any psychological damage or glaring deficits of one kind or another. Others who are much less fortunate become alcoholics, or marry alcoholics, or both. Still others are pseudo-survivors: they appear to be unscathed but are actually covering up considerable emotional pain.

Adult children of alcoholics are *not* all alike. Even siblings, who grew up under the same roof, within the same alcoholic family, often develop strikingly different characters. Although they share the common circumstances of growing up with an alcoholic parent, their perceptions of their childhood situation, and their experiences within it, are not the same. For instance, an older brother might be heading off for college by the time a parent's alcoholic drinking begins to surface, while his little sister might still be quite young. Each will have a very different experience of their parent's drinking. And different sensitivities and temperaments can also create a variety of adaptations and anxieties among ACOAs. A big sister, for example, may throw herself into her work to avoid thinking about family troubles, and become an "A" student; her younger brother may be unable to concentrate on anything but family troubles and therefore do poorly in school.

But, although the nature and extent of their suffering may differ, children of alcoholics—like the alcoholics themselves—suffer from the disease of alcoholism. Grandchildren suffer, too: nonalcoholic parents who are themselves adult children of alcoholics pass down their own childhood feelings, fears, anxieties, and attitudes. And children who grow up around alcoholic grandparents are often strongly affected, even though the disease of alcoholism itself has skipped a generation. For this reason, everything in this book that applies to adult children of alcoholics (ACOAs) applies equally to grandchildren of alcoholics.

As ACOAs, we should be careful not to label ourselves as "sick" simply because we share many of the characteristics or problems frequently attributed to those who grew up in alcoholic homes. Everyone has problems and, in fact, many adults who did not grow up in alcoholic homes experience the same tensions, feelings, and fears that we do. Many of those who draw comfort, strength, and hope from attending Al-Anon/ACOA meetings are not themselves adult children of alcoholics. Yet, because they recognize our experiences as similar to their own, they too can benefit from similar recovery programs—and from this book.

All people, whatever their backgrounds, are influenced by their pasts. Conflicts and coping mechanisms are replayed over the course of their lives.

Adult children of alcoholics, however, are especially vulnerable to the pull of past experiences and past survival tactics. Many of us continue to function, as adults, under the painful influence of the families in which we were raised. Often, we continue to be plagued with feelings of hurt, anger, fear, humiliation, sadness, shame, guilt, shyness, being different, confusion, unworthiness, isolation, distrust, anxiety, insecurity, and depression. Only when we begin to experience and acknowledge this emotional pain in our present lives do we recognize the need to change and the need for help in dealing with our difficulties.

ACOAs often describe themselves as overresponsible, controlling, compulsive, obsessive, workaholic, dramaholic, people pleasers, self-defeaters, failures, perfectionists, and procrastinators. We say we do not know how to be intimate, how to have fun, or how to be assertive. Extremely critical of ourselves, we have a hard time acknowledging our successes and strengths. We are much more likely to do things because we feel we should rather than because we want to. We express more interest in taking care of others than in taking care of ourselves. We usually accentuate the negative and eliminate the positive.

But ACOAs can change.

You can recover from the effects of alcoholism. The first, and most difficult, step in the recovery process requires you to admit that a problem exists, to recognize that past and present pains are inhibiting your chances of finding comfort and happiness in your life. Until you have stopped denying that anything is wrong, you will be unable to address the true nature of your problems. After you have acknowledged the problem, however, you can begin to make the changes necessary for recovery. Recovery requires introspection; you will need to trace the origins of your painful feelings and fears. If you grew up in an alcoholic home, Part I of this book will help you break through your denial and understand the origins of your present pain and fears. You will learn of tools that you can use to examine your personal family history—and better understand the effects of alcoholism on your life.

In addition, the self-tests in the back of this book can help you determine the exact nature of your problems and the specific kind of help you may need. The Recommended Reading will direct you to books in areas of particular interest: alcoholism, sexual abuse, eating disorders, and family systems. And the Resource Organizations will guide you to organizations and associations that can help treat your specific problems.

Because recovery is a lifelong process, you will need to make a strong and earnest commitment to recovery. You cannot expect to recover overnight from the consequences of years in an alcoholic environment. You will need to make a lifelong commitment to try to change yourself for the better with each new day. For adult children of alcoholics who make this commitment to change, there's good news: help

is available. A great variety of self-help groups and professional therapies can assist you in your efforts to make the changes you want to
make in your life. In a sense, this book can be seen as a combination
of self-help and professional therapy: the people interviewed have
shared their personal experience, strength, and hope in the belief that
it may help you find your own recovery path. And my advice as a
therapist will, I hope, help you choose the right path.

In Part II you will find a detailed exploration of the major tasks
involved in recovery from family alcoholism: mourning past losses,
overcoming past fears, forgiving yourself and others, and putting the
past behind you; rediscovering and nurturing your feelings, your vulnerabilities, and the childlike joy, trust, and spontaneity frowned upon
in alcoholic households; giving up unrealistic perfectionism and your
attempts to control others as well as yourself; and building a positive
sense of self-worth by recognizing your strengths instead of dwelling
on real or imagined faults. You will learn new strategies that will allow
you to form more satisfying, more intimate relationships with others
and to live a happier, more fulfilling life. You will be presented with
new choices of attitudes, thoughts, and behaviors that can contribute
to your recovery.

Part III of this book will show you how you can further your recovery by rebuilding relationships with parents and siblings. You will see
that participating in an "intervention"—whether or not it succeeds in
getting the alcoholic in your family into treatment—can contribute to
your own recovery. You will also discover how your personal recovery
can enhance—and be enhanced by—the important challenge of parenting.

Adult children of alcoholics want to find a way to free themselves
from childhood fears, the hidden anxieties that interfere with the joy
of living. As children, we fought losing battles against the family "secret" of alcoholism. Until quite recently, most of us suffered our defeat
in silence. We were afraid to tell our secrets.

This book is about ACOAs who are now able to share their secrets.
It is about their search to find the help they need and deserve. Adult
children of alcoholics survive. But survival is not enough. More and
more ACOAs are realizing today that survival gave them a chance to
exist, but it has not given them a chance to live. I hope this book will
provide them with that chance.

REEXAMINING
THE PAST

· 1 ·

"PERFECTLY NORMAL"
—
GROWING UP IN
AN ALCOHOLIC HOME

GROWING UP "NORMAL"

*"Whenever I saw something that I didn't have,
I decided that must be normal."*

■ ■ ■

"My family was normal." "I grew up in a normal household." "My childhood was pretty normal." This is how typical adult children of alcoholics begin describing their families. We would like very much to believe that our parents weren't alcoholic, that our families were just like all the others in the neighborhood.

FEELING DIFFERENT

Yet, while clinging to the concept of normal—or typical, average, or ordinary—adult children of alcoholics usually also talk about having felt "different." Our families weren't at all like the ones we saw on television—they weren't the Cleavers or the Brady Bunch or the Cosbys.

How were we to know, as children, that things were far from normal when everyone in the family was trying so hard to keep up the pretense of being typically all-American? How were we to know that feeling different had a great deal to do with the big family secret—the one

3

that everyone kept and never told? Family alcoholism is the secret that everyone knows—and pretends not to know.

Every member of the family masks the secret of alcoholism with the illusion of normality. In alcoholic households, each person—from the youngest child to the most senior member—works very hard to keep up the image that everything is all right, that they are just like other families. And, as the disease progresses and life becomes more unmanageable, the impulse to disguise it becomes even stronger. The perception of normality—of not being different—can act as a reassuring and stabilizing force in any child's life. And to the child who is denied this reassurance this "normal" image seems even more important.

"All my life I wanted to believe my family was normal. But I didn't know what normal was," admitted Susan, a young woman who wants to stop feeling so self-critical and negative. "All I knew was that everyone else had it, and I didn't. The best I could do was to try to imitate the families that seemed normal to me. I would visit other kids' homes and take in every detail. Whenever I saw something that I didn't have, I decided that must be normal: kids who had their own room, clean clothes in every drawer, team pennants hanging from their walls. I never had any of these things. In fact, I slept in the same room with my grandmother until I was thirteen, and when I finally did get my own room, it was no bigger than a closet—and it didn't even have a door, so I never had any privacy at all.

"I still don't know what normal is, and I still have to fight the feeling that whatever I have isn't enough. I live with this battle all the time. I feel that I have to work twice as hard as anyone else because I'm only half as good.

"I always think people will think I'm strange. If people like me, my first reaction is to think there must be something wrong with them, they pity me, or they're humoring me. I'm afraid to get close to people because I know that when they find out who I really am, they'll be appalled and run away.

"I've spent my whole life trying to figure out what normal really is, and I'm starting to realize that almost everyone else is looking for the same thing. Ultimately, I think we'll discover that the whole concept is false. There is no such thing as 'normal.' And what I think is normal may not be at all normal for you.

"All the same, it still keeps coming up. Tomorrow night, for instance, my co-op board is meeting in my studio apartment—you know, I still don't have a bedroom. Anyway, I started looking around the apartment this afternoon and I suddenly felt that my home wasn't good enough, that everyone else must have a better place than I do. Before I knew it, I'd put myself in the position of an outcast, just the way I felt growing up with my mother's alcoholism. I spent my childhood trying to be like everyone else and here I am still doing it.

"I have to keep reminding myself that I don't have to imitate other people the way I used to. Everyone in my family always tried to act 'normal'—to be like someone else—but I'm trying not to do that anymore. I know that looking outward for what's normal isn't important; I have to look inward. I've learned that those 'things' I used to think everyone else had won't make me happy."

Like many of us, Susan feels puzzled and troubled when dealing with questions of normality. Children in alcoholic homes grow up having litttle or no idea what is normal and are only certain that they aren't. It is easy to become preoccupied with the notion, and envious of others who seem normal in comparison.

WHAT IS NORMAL?

"Normal" is not a very helpful word in describing a family background —particularly that of an alcoholic family. It makes more sense to describe families as either functional or dysfunctional. However, it is important for us—as ACOAs—to remember that no family is perfectly normal, functional, or healthy, just as no family is totally abnormal, dysfunctional, or unhealthy. Alcoholic families are by no means the only kind of dysfunctional family. Families shattered by divorce, mental illness, suicide, chronic diseases other than alcoholism, or the sudden death of a family member often interact and behave in ways similar to alcoholic families.

"I can really relate to my friends who grew up in alcoholic homes," Tess told me. "Talk about guilt and shame. My sister, who is mentally retarded, lived at home and I never wanted to bring school friends by. She was such an embarrassment—drooling, talking gibberish. And I felt so guilty for not being more sympathetic. My mother took care of her around the clock and my father, brother, and I got very little of her attention. Poor martyred woman, she didn't have any energy left after looking after Ginnie. We stood in awe and fear of my mother; she directed us all.

"She was too tired to ever go out, and the rest of us were too mortified to be seen with Ginnie, so we stayed home all the time. My mother wouldn't hear of getting a babysitter. All of our lives centered around Ginnie's condition, but no one ever complained. She was the poor little princess. We didn't have much of a family life at home and we didn't have a life outside either. We never went anywhere or did anything."

Like Tess, many non-ACOAs identify with the characteristics attributed to children of alcoholics. Problems common among ACOAs are not necessarily unique to ACOAs. Others may share these difficulties and they too can benefit from this book and from the self-help groups and various therapies that we as ACOAs find helpful.

Although Tess had no alcoholism in her family, the patterns of behavior that arose around her sister are strikingly similar to those that develop in an alcoholic family. And patterns of behavior—healthy or unhealthy, functional or dysfunctional—emerge in every family. Each individual family, whether alcoholic or not, lies somewhere along a continuum from severely dysfunctional to highly functional. Two families, each of which has an alcoholic parent with similar drinking patterns, may differ significantly in other respects. One family might band together with a certain degree of warmth and nurturing, while the other might withdraw into a cold remoteness. These patterns of behavior within a specific family determine where it lies on the continuum.

Dr. Wayne Kritsberg has set forth the characteristics of the extremes of this continuum in *The Adult Children of Alcoholics Syndrome: From Discovery to Recovery*:

Unhealthy Family	Healthy Family
1. Rigid rules.	1. No rigid rules.
2. Rigid roles.	2. No rigid roles.
3. Family secrets.	3. No family secrets.
4. Resists outsiders from entering the system.	4. Allows outsiders into the system.
5. Is very serious.	5. Has a sense of humor.
6. No personal privacy, unclear personal boundaries.	6. Members have right to personal privacy, develop a sense of self.
7. False loyalty to the family, members are never free to leave the system.	7. Members have a "sense of family" and are permitted to leave the system.
8. Conflict between members is denied and ignored.	8. Conflict between members is allowed and resolved.
9. The family resists change.	9. The family continually changes.
10. There is no unity, the family is fragmented.	10. There is a sense of wholeness in the family.

In functional families, members treat one another with respect and love. Sensitive to feelings and considerate of needs, they share a sense of security. Family conduct is usually predictable, behavior is reasonable, and parents are responsible. Children grow up feeling nurtured and protected. And, as Virginia Satir has pointed out in *Peoplemaking*, "In a nurturing family, it is easy to pick up the message that human life and human feelings are more important than anything else." In functional families, the standards of expected behavior are firm yet flexible. Family rules, implicit or explicit, take into account individual differences but are basically consistent.

Every family operates in a variety of ways aimed at keeping the whole working. And if one person gets sick or has serious problems, the whole family organizes itself around whatever seems to be wrong in an attempt to make it right. In most families, for instance, if one parent broke a leg and was forced to stay in bed for several weeks, the other parent and the children would take on the injured parent's responsibilities in order to keep the system running as smoothly as possible.

PRETENDING TO BE NORMAL

In an alcoholic family, this attempt to preserve the system demands that everyone play the game of "let's pretend we're normal." But it gets very difficult to sustain this game. In a normal family, one or ideally both parents are in charge. In an alcoholic family, however, no one is really in charge since the parents are often either physically absent or emotionally unavailable. Because of their individual turmoil, parents may not be able to set appropriate, consistent family rules. In alcoholic families, more often than not, rules are either nonexistent or extremely rigid. In either case, children in alcoholic families usually get strong messages that they shouldn't trust anyone outside the family, shouldn't talk about what's going on inside the family, and shouldn't have feelings of their own. Family life is often chaotic; at best it is unpredictable and confusing.

If you grew up with an alcoholic parent (or parents), it is likely that neither of them, in their narrowly focused lives (the alcoholic obsessed with alcohol, the nonalcoholic obsessed with the alcoholic), was able to give you a strong sense of self-worth, express affection, or help you solve problems. Perhaps they were frequently angry, insensitive, nonnurturing, unprotective, or neglectful. You may have been physically abused or terrified by the threat of violence and abuse. Children in alcoholic families don't always get the attention, affection, love, and understanding they need in order to grow up feeling safe and secure.

You may have grown up feeling unloved, fearful, and alone. And you may still feel that way.

"The first time I knew there was a problem in my family was when I was about seven years old," said Joe, a fifty-year-old Marine who recently became aware of a strong and persistent feeling of rejection. "My mother sent me to the store for a loaf of bread and everything seemed fine when I left the house. But, by the time I got back, there was a real brawl going on. My parents were screaming at each other, my father was breaking up the house, and my sisters and brothers were crying. I was so frightened that I hid behind the ironing board until things calmed down.

"My mother told me to tell the neighbors that we were having a party. I knew it wasn't a party. My mother threw her wedding ring out the window in the middle of the fight and we spent the whole next day looking for it.

"Then, after my brothers had grown up and moved out of the house, my mother snatched me up from my bed in the middle of the night and took me and my sisters to another state. There was no warning, no talk about her leaving our father, no goodbyes.

"There were seven people in the family, but I never felt it was a family. Something was always boiling. There was lots of action, but no consistency or affection. I was the youngest, and when my parents finally divorced, I was the only one still at home. Neither of them asked for custody of me. That proved that I didn't matter to either one of them. That's the way I always felt."

Joe describes feelings of confusion, rejection, and fear characteristic of children in alcoholic homes. Although he knew something was wrong, he didn't understand until much later in his life that his parents' violent behavior was closely related to their alcoholism.

If you grew up in an alcoholic home, you too may have tried to pretend it was a party when you knew it wasn't. Your childhood world —inconsistent, unreliable, and incomprehensible—probably left you feeling unprotected, fearful, and isolated. And most of us don't realize, until we feel and examine recurrent pain or fear in our adult lives, an examination often aided by professional therapy or self-help groups, that perhaps our families weren't so "normal" after all.

GROWING UP IN DENIAL

"My mother had convinced all of us that he was a typical father and that we didn't have any problems."

■　■　■

As children, most of us unfortunately knew very little, if anything, about alcoholism. We may not have known, for example, that we were denying something, and that denial is characteristic of the disease of alcoholism. Denial in this context means a denial of reality—an attempt to justify, hide, or safeguard drinking. Alcoholism has been described as "the disease that tells you you don't have a disease." But it also tells the rest of the alcoholic's family that he or she doesn't have a disease.

"I only remember seeing my father drunk a few times," recalled Ernie, an intense, driven young man in his mid-thirties. "He was in the Air Force and everyone drank. He drank every day and it seemed to us kids that he only had a few martinis before dinner. Then one day he joined AA, got sober, and went to meetings for fifteen years.

"When we were young, my mother had convinced all of us that he was a typical father and that we didn't have any problems. And to this day she still doesn't believe he was an alcoholic. She claims he just went to meetings because he was attracted to the social and spiritual aspects of the program.

"My younger sisters have only recently told me stories of how he'd go out drinking by himself and how afraid they were he would get in an accident. But at the time they didn't tell anyone how afraid they were. Still, according to my mother and older brother, Dad wasn't an alcoholic, he just liked to go to AA meetings. I should have known that didn't make much sense, but I guess I didn't want to face up to the fact that my father was an alcoholic either. Dad died a few years ago and I'm sorry I never discussed it with him. He told me he was an alcoholic so I believed him.

"When I first came to an ACOA meeting, I completely identified with what others were saying. I knew he had to have been alcoholic. I started to remember his drinking days and I realized how much easier it was for me to see him as the war hero he wasn't rather than as the alcoholic he was."

If a parent doesn't behave the way the stereotypical, falling-down drunk does on television or in the movies, most kids will rationalize, minimize, or deny that drinking causes serious family problems. Just as alcoholic parents make up excuses for drinking, children make up reasons too. They're also in denial.

But families of alcoholics have not been alone in adopting this attitude of denial; for too long, few families—alcoholic or not—were educated about alcoholism. Society has also been in denial. By conservative estimates, there are over twenty-eight million children of alcoholics in this country. And, until only a few years ago, this population was largely invisible. Even now, not many schools, religious institutions, or health facilities have chemical-dependency education programs. Furthering our childhood denial, many of the adults who could have helped us—teachers, counselors, scout leaders, and others—may have had alcoholic skeletons in their own closets. Thus, even in the rare cases when we were able to give them hints about our problems, their own denial might have interfered with their ability to recognize and deal with the reality of alcoholism in our families.

This denial of reality usually involves everyone who cares about the alcoholic. As an alcoholic's drinking intensifies, denial increases. To conceal the alcoholism, everyone affected comes up with explanations, justifications, rationalizations, and fabrications—anything to protect the alcoholic and compensate for the calamities that may result from his or her drinking.

Denial feeds on family loyalty. Children want to see their parents as heroes: they want them to appear strong and healthy. Even when alcoholic behavior becomes cruel or grossly inappropriate, children will try to excuse or protect their parents. Most children of alcoholics feel that talking about the drinking would be betraying their parents—they would feel guilty about revealing the family secret to their friends or other adults. They have a strong need to defend their parents at all times. And that protectiveness usually continues long after childhood.

"I remember my mother drinking from about the time I was eight years old," said Vivian, a forty-four-year-old professor. "She had been divorced for a few years and married a man who owned a bar. She spent most of her time there and left me at home to take care of my younger sister. I always felt she loved us, but we just couldn't rely on her. I blamed her drinking on my stepfather. Even today, it's hard for me to say my mother is an alcoholic.

"Eventually she got out of that marriage and married another alcoholic, so it was easy for me to believe she drank because of the men she got involved with. I would like to think she wouldn't have turned to drink if she had chosen healthier men. But that isn't true. Her last husband, her fourth, didn't drink. I remember visiting her one summer about ten years ago. She was out in the garden all day and every once in a while I'd look for her and she wouldn't be there. Meanwhile she seemed to be getting more and more sloshed. And then I finally realized she was sneaking off to the bar down the street. It wasn't until I was about to leave that I noticed how drunk she was. My stepfather drove me to the bus stop and in the car he said, 'Your mother's an alcoholic.' I said, 'I know.' That's the first time I admitted to myself or anyone else that she was an alcoholic."

Children have just as much trouble admitting how they feel to their brothers and sisters. Children of the same family—even children who sleep in the same bed—usually avoid discussing what terrifies them about the behavior of an alcoholic parent. They feel that if they don't talk about it, it may not really be happening—or maybe it will go away.

Children also think they won't be believed. After all, they're only kids. So, even if things seem really crazy at home, they almost always feel certain that no one will believe them anyway. This often gives them the out they are looking for. Even when directly questioned, for instance, by a family therapist or a concerned schoolteacher about a parent's drinking, a young person will tend to deny it.

Few families try as hard as the dysfunctional ones to make things work. In spite of the denial, they sense something is wrong and try hard to make it right. But they're at a decided disadvantage because they don't usually know what the real problem is.

In the name of loyalty and love, children cover up alcoholism in the family and bury their feelings about it. They deny the disease, defend the alcoholic, and dismiss their own knowledge of what is going on in the family.

Alcoholism may be in the family experience, but the word is seldom in the family vocabulary. Even if they know that alcoholism is at the root of family difficulties, they seldom know how to solve the problem or how to ask for help in solving it. It's like having an elephant sitting in the living room: Everyone notices it, but they walk around it—and nobody mentions it at all.

BREAKING DOWN DENIAL   Overcoming this pattern of denial is the first—and most important—step toward recovery. When in doubt, check it out, because it's extremely difficult to be objective about yourself. It takes a lot of energy to keep up appearances, to create a forest so that people won't see the trees. Take "The COA Quiz" and the "Children of Alcoholics Screening Test," included in the Self-Tests for

ACOAs at the back of this book. If you are an adult child of an alcoholic, these tests will help you break down any lingering denial.

GROWING UP PERFECT

*"I thought that if I was very good
he wouldn't drink so much."*

▪ ▪ ▪

Children who grow up in alcoholic families develop a strong attraction to fantasy. When we were growing up, fantasies provided an antidote for the very real pains we had to endure. Illusions and delusions kept us in the safety of our own heads rather than in the real—and very unsafe—world of the alcoholic home. And no fantasy attracted us more powerfully than the illusion of perfection. Because we often felt responsible for the alcoholic's drinking, we tried as hard as we could to be perfect. And, in our make-believe worlds, achieving perfection seemed perfectly plausible.

"My mother always gave me the impression that I was the only one who could get my father to stop drinking," remembered Jane, a thirty-year-old nurse. "She told me I was his favorite, that he would listen to me. She made me feel totally responsible. I thought that if I was very good he wouldn't drink so much. I thought if I didn't upset him, he wouldn't go out to the bars at night. So I tried my best to be the perfect daughter, but it didn't seem to do any good. Every night he would go out anyway, and he kept on drinking."

It's very frightening for children to find themselves living in a chaotic situation. And as children we took the blame for much of the chaos—including the alcoholic's drinking. At one time or another, either parent—the nonalcoholic as well as the alcoholic—may have blamed us for the drinking. And, knowing little about the disease, we willingly shouldered this blame. Indeed, we often felt that whatever went wrong in the family was our fault.

Children have a strong need to feel powerful and often overestimate the impact of their thoughts and actions on other people, even more so when they live in a turbulent situation. Children of divorce, for instance, almost always think they caused their parents' separation. In our alcoholic homes, we believed that we could magically fix everything simply by changing our own behavior. And when the family situation failed to improve, we assumed we were to blame for all the terrible things that happened. These guilt feelings and self-blame only strengthened our urge to be perfect.

SHOULDERING RESPONSIBILITIES

In our quest for perfection, we learned to take responsibility for ourselves at a very early age. To remain blameless, we had to be perfect; we had to be whatever and whoever anyone wanted us to be; we had to avoid being a burden to anyone. To make everything run more smoothly in the alcoholic home, we shouldered responsibilities not only for ourselves, but for our brothers and sisters too.

Our willingness to shoulder responsibility was encouraged by our parents' inability to concentrate on the tasks of parenting. When they were confronted with a child's needs, their increasing preoccupation —with alcohol or with the alcoholic—made them seem helpless to meet those needs, or resulted in promises to take care of things "sooner or later." Unfortunately "sooner or later" often became "not at all."

We reacted by being overly responsible. We were put in the position of protecting, rather than of being protected. By pretending to be grown-up, by taking care of others, we tried to keep our fears from overwhelming us. Children need supervision; and when we didn't get it from parents, we frequently learned to supervise one another. Often, because we got so good at it, we ended up taking care of our parents as well.

"My mother was often sick, hungover from pills and alcohol, so I took care of many things around the house," recalled Pamela, who suffers from a very low self-esteem because she cannot live up to her own perfectionist standards. "She depended on me much more than I depended on her. I had all the grown-up responsibilities.

"I've always been the superresponsible person in the family. I'm the one who always jumps in to take care of things—nobody ever took care of me. And even now it's hard for me to admit that I need to be taken care of sometimes, too. I never let anyone know how frightened and alone I feel."

GROWN UP TOO SOON—OR NOT AT ALL

Most children of alcoholics seem to grow up too soon. In taking on so much responsibility, we learned to act mature even when we didn't feel like adults. And our parents frequently reinforced this "maturity" because it made life easier for them. The child who behaves very responsibly, takes charge, and does a job well is most likely to get praise from overwhelmed or sick parents—and from people outside the family too. Almost everyone—parents, teachers, religious leaders, coaches, and in later life employers and co-workers—fails to see this overresponsible behavior as a cause for concern.

People outside the family are much more likely to pay attention to individuals who are highly *irresponsible*, that is, to the adult children of alcoholics who never grow up at all. Although most adult children of alcoholics behave overresponsibly, some of them—especially those who come from large families in which many older siblings acted as caretakers—avoid responsibility like the plague. They procrastinate, always hoping that someone else will take charge. However, those adults who never grow up often suffer from the same perfectionism as those who grow up too soon. Adult children of alcoholics who don't grow up give up on trying to achieve perfection for themselves, and instead try to manipulate others with passivity and irresponsible behavior. The idea is to push other people to become the perfectionists they don't feel they know how to be. For those of us prone to irresponsibility, it's safer not to act grown up at all.

IMPOSSIBLE STANDARDS

Whether we grow up too soon or not at all, as adult children of alcoholics we can be very, very hard on ourselves. We set up impossible standards based on our rigid ideas of what is right or wrong, based on what is acceptable and what isn't, based on what will incur blame and what won't. And when anyone—including ourselves—fails to live up to those standards, we refuse to make allowances.

We can't just be strong, we have to be the strongest of the strong. To aspire to anything less than perfection is totally unacceptable. We have to be the best. And, through force of habit, we dwell on our failures, instead of our achievements. Even when we admit to ourselves that we may have done well, we still think we should have done better. And this perfectionism too often convinces us that we are never good enough.

Most ACOAs find it difficult to recognize their many strengths. The positive qualities and inner resources so readily apparent to others—including therapists who, like me, regularly work with them—go unnoticed by the adult children of alcoholics themselves. If you have a hard time recognizing your own strengths, Chapter 12 will help you take stock of your positive characteristics.

GROWING UP IN CONTROL

*"I thought I could control his drinking
by not speaking to him."*

■ ■ ■

Controlling behavior and perfectionism often go hand in hand. Our desire for our own perfection drives us to try to control everything about ourselves and our lives. And our desire to make everything right —as children in the alcoholic home, and later outside the home— compels us to try to control others. We don't just want to perfect ourselves, we want to perfect everyone else too.

The conflict, confusion, and chaos in the alcoholic home made it seem necessary for us to try to exert control over ourselves and others, simply in order to survive. We had to stay in control in spite of, and because of, the terrible fear that any minute everything could spin out of control. Even the extra responsibilities we took on—for our brothers and sisters, for example—were an attempt to stop the chaos from closing in on us.

We also took seriously what we believed was our responsibility for the alcoholic's drinking. And this led us to try almost anything to control his or her behavior.

Jane, the nurse who had tried to stop her father's drinking by being the perfect child, told me she had tried other methods too. "When I was in high school I thought I could control his drinking by not speaking to him. I stopped talking to him for about a year. I was trying to punish him. I wanted to make him feel so guilty that he'd stop drinking. Of course it didn't work. All it did was make him cry all the time when he was drunk because I ignored him. Then I'd end up feeling sorry for him and guilty myself.

"When that didn't work, I tried yelling and screaming at him. I even threw his liquor bottles at him. I would telephone Al-Anon in front of him and tell them my father was an alcoholic. Nothing worked. He went right on drinking.

"Trying to control him carried over to my personal life too. At school I'd pick the kids who were messed up and I'd try to help them get straightened out. I had my own lonely hearts' club band. All the kids I befriended had tragic lives. They were worse off than I was, so, in my typically controlling fashion, I tried to make their lives better."

The fear of losing control in the alcoholic family often turns us into very controlling people outside the family too. When we were growing up, we had to maintain control of our feelings and behavior, and we had to try to control others in the family as well. We used survival tactics just to get by, and control was the number one defense.

We also used control as a defense against anxiety—anxiety that things would get worse, or that things wouldn't get done, or that things would stay the same. Being in control gives children of alcoholics the idea—however false or misguided—that they can make things in the family better. We like to think we can be responsible enough to solve the family problems. We come to feel we have to take all action, because no one else will. As a result, most of us learn to distrust others, to depend only on ourselves.

Attempting to be reasonable in a totally unreasonable situation may not be such a bad idea, but survival tactics learned *inside the home* quickly became bad habits *outside the home*. At home, we *overfunctioned*, trying to manage unmanageability, hanging on to the notion that we could do it alone, and do it just fine. We thought we knew what would make things right, but to put our "perfect plans" into effect, we had to make other people do what we wanted them to do. And while we might have been able to marshal siblings into a clean-up crew at home, our friends at school could only have resented our insistence on trying to organize them too.

Our desire to seem just like everyone else also fed our need to control ourselves and others. The alcoholic family, wanting to appear normal, tries to look normal, but usually fails miserably; it's very hard to keep up pretenses. And the more chaotic things get, the harder we try to control them. Unfortunately, nothing ever seems to work.

For most of us, control is still a very big problem. We've tried our whole lives to be in control, having had so little security in our childhood, and we may still feel an urge to manage others. If you are fighting an urge to control, the emotional tightness and anger that come with this urge can act as strong warning signals for you. Control simply doesn't feel good, and if you start to feel angry, it often means you aren't getting your way. When people aren't under their control, it makes controllers very angry. The more in touch we are with our feelings, the better able we are to let go of our need to control.

· 2 ·

THE CHILD WITHIN
——
HIDDEN FEELINGS,
HIDDEN FEARS

Children in alcoholic homes direct their efforts to control, to make everything perfect and ordered, as much inward as outward. Just as we denied the disease itself, we denied—and probably continue to deny —our fears and feelings. We thought that to admit our emotions would diminish our perfection. And so we tried to control our own feelings, masking our vulnerability. We may even have used self-control in a self-protective attempt to ward off feelings of emptiness, of aloneness —emotions that reinforced our sense of being different. In suppressing our fears and feelings and in taking on adult responsibilities at an early age, we denied all of our natural, childlike qualities—a denial that haunts us in our adult lives.

Inside every adult child of an alcoholic is a frightened child who is terrified that things will go out of control. Trying to keep everything anchored, this wounded child—a child damaged, but not destroyed, by family alcoholism—keeps all of his or her fears and feelings well hidden.

Many ACOAs who experienced serious emotional pain in their childhood homes refuse to acknowledge this emotionally wounded child. Having grown up too soon, we carry the pain of not being able to acknowledge our feelings into our adult lives. Today we may believe that sad feelings represent a force that will pull us back into the hopeless, helpless days of our childhood. To hide our inner fragility, we

17

may deny, or repress, or project our feelings. We retreat from the threat of discovering that insufficient parenting prevented us from getting the support we wanted, needed, and deserved when we were children. And this wounded child within continues to deny and repress our "threatening" emotions.

HIDDEN FEELINGS

Feelings—our own and others'—frighten us. Not only do we avoid our own painful memories, we often avoid emotional intensity in our adult lives. Frequently the wounded child within an adult prevents him or her from feeling anything. Many of the ACOAs I have spoken to describe a numbness rather than actual feelings. When one of my clients speaks of emotional numbness, I attempt to draw out his or her true feelings, emotions that have been blocked from consciousness. Although the feelings exist, buried deep within, they have been so thoroughly suppressed that this dull numbness may provide the only hint of their existence.

Adult children from alcoholic homes who seem to have grown up to be normal, functioning adults are often unaware of deep layers of anger and grief. Some of us, often with tremendous energy and pronounced cheerfulness, completely avoid giving the impression—even to ourselves—that we are actually living with a great deal of sadness. We try to gloss over grief and convince ourselves, and the people around us, that we are "just fine."

If you get anxious around people who freely express their feelings, particularly angry or negative ones, you may need to develop a sense of personal security—a sense of security that can only come with the recognition and protection of this hidden child. Only then will you be able to experience, trust, and share your innermost feelings, the feelings you never before permitted yourself to admit.

"I recently attended an ACOA workshop which helped me recognize the child within me," said Kay, a decorator in her forties. "The workshop included a visualization exercise which helped me to see myself very clearly at the age of four. Conceptualizing myself, I saw a helpless, frightened, angry little girl. It made me realize all the childhood losses I'd experienced: I wasn't properly cared for, I didn't get affection, and I didn't have any fun. My mother's message was, 'You do the housework first,' and, of course, the work was never done—there was never any time for play. The atmosphere was heavy and somber.

"At the workshop, I was absolutely amazed that I was able to get in touch with the child within me for the first time in my life. I never before gave any credit or validity to that child. I strongly denied that any part of me was ever young. I had always prided myself on being grown-up. Finally getting in touch with that inner child was very freeing for me."

Most adult children of alcoholics still find it difficult to acknowledge the hurting child hidden inside the "perfect" children we pretended to be. But that child within must emerge if we want to recover from alcoholism in the family. In addition to the visualization exercise mentioned above, you will find other specific exercises in Chapter 10 that can help you parent your own child. First, though, you need to acknowledge that a wounded child exists inside you, and make a commitment to do everything you can to understand that child. The rest of this chapter will help foster such an understanding.

THE SHIELD OF INVULNERABILITY

Because they had to grow up so soon, most adult children of alcoholics hate to be reminded of their possible fragility and vulnerability. They pretended they were super-strong for so long that they were unable—and may still find it almost impossible—to say things like "I want," "I need," or "I hurt." They grew accustomed to taking care of people and very uncomfortable with letting someone else take care of them.

Riddled with self-doubt, children of alcoholics often feel as if "I'm not enough." We find it difficult to accept love because we probably didn't feel that it was offered to us during childhood, and most of us never learned to love ourselves. Negative feelings constantly reinforced our low self-esteem and insecurity, convincing us that we were undeserving of love and affection. It was hard for us to trust anyone, inside or outside the family, because of all the mistrust we picked up in unreliable home situations. And our fears of abandonment may still be so great that we sometimes imagine we are being abandoned even when we are actually being loved. After all, our fantasies always feel safer to us than reality. All these feelings prove that we *were*—and *are*—

vulnerable, but at the same time they prevent us from admitting it. And these negative feelings make it very hard for children of alcoholics to imagine that other people are vulnerable too.

Raised in houses of denial, we felt ashamed at the possibility of being exposed, of being seen for what we really were, of being imperfect. Other people seemed threatening to us, urging us back into stances of denial. Children in alcoholic homes, who look at themselves with an extremely critical eye, counting and recounting all of their faults, find it very hard to believe that anyone would accept them if they revealed themselves as truly vulnerable. We find it unthinkable that we could be accepted for our whole selves and not just the parts we think are attractive to others. After all, many of us can't even accept *ourselves* for what we are.

Children of alcoholics don't allow themselves to seem vulnerable or needy because they're ashamed of not being in control at all times. Trying to act self-sufficient and self-satisfied, we actually feel afraid and alone. An illusory shield of invulnerability can cover up a multitude of insecurities; it allows us to hide our real emotions, but it often makes us unapproachable too. It distances us in personal relationships.

If you still have trouble expressing your own very human frailties you may need to work on allowing yourself to be more vulnerable. It's not easy for ACOAs to ask for help, to share fears and weaknesses with other persons, to let people know we are just like everyone else in the human race; but it is essential to our recovery.

HIDDEN FEARS

Fears unfold early in homes with one or more alcoholic parents, and they continue to haunt grown children long into their adult lives. Some of the fears commonly expressed by adult children of alcoholics are fear of outsiders, of authority, abandonment, insanity, criticism, and confrontations.

Parental alcoholism doesn't affect everyone exactly the same way, of course. You may have experienced more or less fright than others, but almost all of us grew up in houses of fear. However, because we tried so hard to maintain the illusion that nothing was wrong in the family, our childhood fears seldom surfaced until much later in our lives. To cover our terror as children, we may have acted self-sufficient, withdrawn, or belligerent. And, because we tried to ignore or suppress it, what frightened us in childhood haunts us as adults. Eventually, our pasts catch up with us.

If you grew up in an alcoholic family, you can now begin to address these fears that plagued you in the past, the fears that may still arise in your personal and work worlds today. It is important to understand that your fears resulted from circumstances beyond your control. When you were young, you simply didn't have the inner resources, the emotional strength, to deal with these feelings. The desperation of trying to keep things under control in an alcoholic home suppresses many fears and feelings. As you learn about some of the unresolved fears of other adult children, you may finally feel safe enough to express your own fears. Once you begin to acknowledge your fears, you will be paving the way to resolving them. For it is through a process of acceptance and eventual letting go that we are able to overcome and transform our fears.

As you read about the hidden fears of ACOAs, imagine how each one applies to your own childhood. Do you recognize yourself in the circumstances presented? Can you identify with the experiences shared by other adult children of alcoholics? Do these fears still haunt you? What problems do they create in your life today?

THE FEAR OF BEING FOUND OUT

"I would run home and try to make it look like she was just sick or very tired."

■ ■ ■

The desire of children of alcoholics to appear "normal" and the denial it fosters makes them afraid that other people will discover what they themselves really don't want to know. Just as alcoholics try to cover up their alcoholism, nonalcoholic parents and children join in this conspiracy of silence by also covering up for the alcoholic. Children and adults alike build a wall of denial to guard against the discovery of a problem that they may view as a moral failing.

"We were always on guard in our house when my mother was on one of her binges," recalled Barbara. "My younger brothers would just try to stay out of her way when she was drinking, but I always felt it was my responsibility to protect her.

"My father would explode whenever he came home and found my mother passed out or stumbling around drunk. So after school I would run home and try to make it look like she was just sick or very tired. I'd wash all the glasses and throw away the liquor bottles, spray the house with disinfectant, and try to get her into bed.

"Whenever the phone rang I'd leap to answer it; I didn't want my father, or anyone else, to hear her slurred voice and know she was drunk. He often called in the late afternoon to see what kind of shape she was in, and if he thought she was drinking, he would say he had to work late. When I answered, I'd say she was fine, or she was outside, or she was taking a nap. I didn't want him to get all crazy and either not come home at all or come home ready for a big fight with her.

"I'd cover up for her at school too. I wouldn't even tell her about parent-teacher meetings, because I didn't want her to go there drunk and embarrass me. At the last minute, I'd tell my teacher that she had the flu or had to take my grandmother to the doctor, or something like that.

"My mother had this old plaid bathrobe—she practically lived in it. To this day, twenty years later, I have such a feeling of revulsion whenever I see a robe like that. My husband bought me one like it for Christmas last year and I really got hysterical. Poor guy, he had no idea that it would upset me; it's just a robe, after all. But it brought back too many awful memories of the way I had to cover up for her."

The disease itself wasn't the only thing we wanted to keep hidden as children. For example, because we didn't want to cause further problems, we probably refused to admit (to ourselves or anyone else) our parents' inability to take care of us the way we needed to be cared for. But, most importantly, we didn't want anyone to know that we felt inadequate, fearful, often overwhelmed. We were afraid that if we took our fingers out of the holes in the dam walls—if we admitted our true feelings and fears—we'd be engulfed by the flood of emotions. In fact, the reason our secret childhood fears continue to haunt our adult lives is that we kept them as well hidden as the sickness in the family.

FEAR OF RIDICULE AND REJECTION

"We felt sure that everyone was laughing at us."

■   ■   ■

Children of alcoholics are sensitive to criticism; we were often afraid that people would make fun of us, or reject us, because of an alcoholic parent's inappropriate or embarrassing behavior. Often deeply ashamed, we worried that an alcoholic parent's behavior would reflect on us—as a blot on the whole family.

"I grew up in a small town in the South where my father was the veterinarian," recounted Richard, a recently divorced physician. "Everyone knew him, so everyone knew when he was sober and when he was on a binge. He would be sober for months on end and then he'd suddenly go on a spree.

"He was the nicest guy in the world when he was sober and everyone liked him and looked up to him. They humored his drunkenness, though. No one seemed to think he needed help. People would say things like 'Even when he's dead drunk, he's better than any other vet in the county.'

"But when he was on a drunk people knew to stay out of his way. He got very nasty and violent. We felt very embarrassed and knew everyone made jokes about his drinking. People seemed to take it for granted that he was unreliable, but my brother and I were humiliated by it. We were always disappointed when he wouldn't show up for our school plays or soccer games. We felt sure that everyone was laughing at us because we weren't even good enough to get our father to come out and watch us perform.

"We never knew what to expect. Once he was drunk for a solid year. The whole town knew he was out of commission: people just stopped talking about him or asking for his services. It was like he had died, but we knew—and everyone else knew—that he wasn't dead, he was just dead drunk."

As the disease progresses, drinking incidents (and accidents) become commonplace, and the alcoholic parent's behavior becomes increasingly obnoxious or menacing. Knowing that other people notice such behavior usually creates severe embarrassment for children. Even if mom's slurred speech or dad's repetitive remarks did no more than raise the eyebrow of an outsider, we were ultrasensitive to any indications of disapproval. And, when one of our parents actually did make a scene, our humiliation was complete.

All children feel judged, to some extent, by their parents' behavior. Because alcoholic behavior is often noticeable and sometimes outrageous, as children we were very sensitive about what other people would think of us. We supposed that if someone looked at an inebriated parent and saw a "no-good drunk," we would be seen as "no-good children."

FEAR OF TRUSTING

"She never told the truth and
was always trying to hide her drinking."

. . .

"My stepmother was an alcoholic and I remember her drinking from about the time I was six," said John, a fifty-year-old father of three grown children. "I didn't really mind her drinking because that's when she would leave me alone and my father would pay some attention to me. When she wasn't drinking, he'd ignore me and she'd pick on me all the time. She never told the truth and was always trying to hide her drinking. I never took her seriously or trusted her.

"I grew up not trusting anyone. I thought everyone lied the way she did. It's still hard for me to trust people, especially women. I always assume ulterior motives. And I certainly don't trust people in authority. I'm sure that comes from my parents saying, 'We're your parents. We're doing what's best for you.' They really weren't and I knew it.

"Group therapy has helped me to see that not everyone is dishonest; it's helping me to trust people a little. Before, I never wanted anyone to get close to me. I felt I was better off operating by myself."

It's hard to learn how to trust when you hear so many mixed messages in your own home. You may have been told, "We're your parents —we're doing what's best for you." "Use your own judgment—but we know what's right." These are the kinds of messages that many of us received as children of alcoholics. Our parents sounded as if they wanted us to make our own decisions, but often in fact they decided for us. Even when our parents said they knew what was best for us, we often knew they didn't. And we found it impossible to learn trust and autonomy from these mixed messages, which left us feeling confused, suspicious, and insecure. Children are usually very perceptive; we knew a great deal that our parents never suspected we did. We were often angry and resentful at not having been told the truth and at not being treated honestly and openly.

Constant deceit and disappointment hardly breed trust. As children, we quickly learned that our parents didn't always say what they meant or mean what they said. They frequently made promises that they then didn't keep. So how could we develop the ability to trust when we felt we couldn't count on the very people we most wanted and needed to count on, our parents?

FEAR OF ABANDONMENT

> *"I was always afraid one of them would*
> *walk out and never come back."*

■ ■ ■

Many children of alcoholics are never sure when their parents will show up and when they won't. You may have heard your parents promise to be home at dinnertime or to pick you up after school. But many of us learned that such promises didn't necessarily mean much. Though you may have gotten used to parents who didn't arrive as scheduled, it's nearly impossible that you adjusted to the underlying fear that they wouldn't show up at all. And the fear of being left alone can be devastating to a child.

Even when our parents could be depended on to be physically present, though, our abandonment fears didn't disappear. "My parents were always home but never really there," remembered Sallie, a single woman in her mid-twenties. "They didn't physically leave me, but I felt as if I was totally ignored. I always felt alone. My father would come home drunk, and my mother would spend the rest of the night fighting with him.

"Finally, at about midnight, my mother would suddenly realize I was there and would say, 'What are you doing up at this hour?' I'd go to bed but lie awake worrying that one of them would leave. I was always afraid one of them was going to walk out and never come back."

Alcoholic parents (and their spouses) are often emotionally unavailable to their children. They can be so preoccupied with their own problems that they forget, or ignore, the individual needs of their children. Your parents may have alternated between periods of smothering attention and times when they didn't seem at all interested in your needs. This kind of inconsistency creates confusion and mistrust. And the insecurities that result from such mixed messages can only intensify our fears of abandonment.

FEAR OF DISAPPROVAL

> *"Everything I ever accomplished was a*
> *fruitless attempt to win his approval."*

■ ■ ■

All children seek parental approval, but for the children of alcoholics approval and disapproval become directly connected to the alcoholism. Children often feel as if their behavior causes or controls when and how much parents drink. And they also feel responsible for the nondrinking parent's moods. They find themselves walking on eggs almost all of the time.

As children, we were often afraid that what we did would escalate the drinking, or provoke anger and rage. This made us feel responsible and guilty. We were afraid that if our parents were angry at us because we had somehow failed them they would drink more. We didn't understand that alcoholics drink more because they are alcoholics. We didn't understand that our alcoholic parents drank because, once they were physically addicted to alcohol, they could not *not* drink.

"I always felt my father disapproved of me," Lynn, an ambitious law student, told me. "He is a workaholic who drinks very little. But after even one drink his personality changes. He has a terrible temper, and I was always afraid of getting him angry.

"Everything I ever accomplished was a fruitless attempt to win his approval. I graduated from college with honors after a horrible history of drug addiction, and I kept waiting for him to say he was proud of me. He never did. He doesn't know how, and I've finally come to understand that it has nothing to do with me. He simply can't give very much of himself. He's incapable of bestowing praise on anyone. But at the time I felt it was some failing of my own."

This fear of disapproval may lead to extremely critical self-judgment in adulthood and reinforce the perfectionist tendencies of most ACOAs. You probably judge yourself much more harshly than any outsider would, and as a result you demand too much of yourself. If this is the case, you will need to learn how to regard yourself more leniently and fairly. Chapter 12 will help you accomplish this.

FEAR OF ANGER AND CONFRONTATION

*"My brother threatened to shoot him
if he didn't stop hitting my mother."*

■ ■ ■

Children of alcoholics are almost always afraid of anger—our own as well as other people's. Exposed to dangerous domestic arguments, we grew afraid that uncontrollable rage would erupt from every heated discussion. We were just never sure that a small scene wouldn't become a very big one. And being outside the battle—watching siblings or parents raging at one another—could be just as frightening for us as being in the middle of it. We felt powerless, not knowing whether to duck out or dash in.

"I hate confrontations," admitted Terri, a writer bothered by episodes of severe depression. "Even loud disagreements make me want to leave the room. I get very frightened when people at work get into arguments. I want to run and hide. I don't want to be part of any controversy.

"My father was a very abusive drinker. He was quite mild when he wasn't drinking, but after a few bourbons he became a madman. He never hit me, but he beat my two brothers, and he was always slapping my mother around.

"I remember the last time he ever put a hand on my mother. They were having a terrible fight. My oldest brother was sixteen and he ran upstairs and came back down with my father's loaded shotgun and threatened to shoot him if he didn't stop hitting my mother. My father just froze, and he never hit her again. I think he realized, even in his alcoholic stupor, that my brother was big enough and angry enough to blow his brains out."

The explosion of murderous rage that Terri saw in her brother is not uncommon among children of alcoholics. In an alcoholic home, anger moves in a vicious circle. The fear of confrontation causes most family members to suppress their hostile feelings. But, because all anger is bottled up tightly, whenever it emerges, it comes with a boom. Often, the only anger we witnessed—or expressed—was in uncontrollable bursts of rage. And these scenes only strengthened our already powerful fear of anger.

FEAR OF IMPENDING DOOM

"When he was sober he would bring me gifts,
but when he was drunk, I was a 'whore.' "

■ ■ ■

No child can predict what will happen when a parent starts drinking. Alcoholism creates personality changes, and most children don't understand the Dr. Jekyll and Mr. Hyde results. They're just afraid that something terrible may happen. For most of us, this sense of impending doom is still very strong. We grew up constantly feeling wary, knowing that the best of times could quickly and unpredictably become the worst of times. And we carry this persistent anxiety into our adult lives; we are always waiting for the other shoe to drop.

"I was my father's favorite," Linda, a seemingly self-assured gym instructor, told me. "When he was sober he would bring me gifts and tell me he loved me. But, when he was drunk, I was a 'slut' and a 'whore.' I was only sixteen and had never even been out on a date.

"I remember one night he was carrying on like that while I was washing the dinner dishes. He was drunk and outrageous, screaming at me and calling me dirty names. I felt like killing him or myself with the butcher knife I was washing. Murder or suicide seemed like perfectly reasonable alternatives at the time.

"I was furious at him for being so hateful and angry at myself for having murderous thoughts. Half of me was the little girl who still remembered how much she loved her father, but the other half of me wanted to kill him."

No matter how bad things seemed in an alcoholic household, we were constantly afraid that things would get even worse. And they frequently did. The threat of someone's losing control or someone's getting hurt were realistic fears; we grew afraid both for ourselves and for other family members. Even if you or your family were never actually subjected to physical or sexual abuse, the loudness, profanity, and verbal abuse in an alcoholic household can be very frightening. It can be extremely painful to have to submit to a verbal attack, or to hear a parent or sibling vilified.

The insistent possibility of drinking accidents also feeds feelings of uncertainty. Even as children, we knew that drunks got into physical fights and got beaten up; we knew that drunks got into cars and got killed or killed other people; we knew that drunks could fall down stairs and break their arms or legs—or necks. Children generally love their parents and they don't want to see them get hurt. But we also knew that *anything* could happen when a parent started drinking. And that "anything" terrified us. Unprotected ourselves, we were also unable to protect others.

FEAR OF INSANITY

*"I was in a panic, but a small part
of me didn't want to die."*

■ ■ ■

It's not unusual for children in alcoholic homes to think they must be crazy. There is generally an enormous discrepancy between what children perceive and the messages their parents give them. Because the alcoholic family is usually heavily steeped in denial, children have a difficult time knowing what is real and what isn't. It's no surprise that children in such a family would question their sanity.

"When I was fifteen I was convinced I was going crazy," remembered Marcia, an artist who has won several prizes for her drawings. "I was so sick of the lies, the threats, the abuse. I couldn't handle my father's drinking and I was tired of trying to convince my mother that things were really bad.

"I seriously thought about suicide. I had a bottle of pills the doctor had given me because I was so nervous. Killing myself seemed like the only way out. I was too frightened to run away from home and I was scared to death I'd kill my father.

"I was in a panic, but a small part of me didn't want to die. I called a teacher at school who had been very nice to me. He told me to throw the pills down the toilet and to come in and see him the next day.

"I felt relief and a tiny ray of hope. The next day I met with him and the principal and they decided the family should get some professional help. So my mother and I went into therapy, but my father refused to go because he 'didn't have any problems.' Again, it was my problem. I was the one who was nuts.

"The therapy didn't last long because my mother was in so much denial. She just kept trying to convince the therapist that she was a successful career woman and a good mother and things weren't that bad at home."

If you encountered the same kind of typical parental denial that Marcia did, the experience could only have reinforced your sense of craziness. Children feel helpless when confronted with their parents' power; they seldom consider that they might be right when what they believe directly contradicts their parents. Until she sought help as an adult, Marcia never realized that she might have been the strongest and sanest person in her family. It's not crazy to acknowledge the chaos and inconsistency of an alcoholic home; what is crazy is trying to pretend that all that chaos is normal.

Sometimes the intense fear of insanity, coupled with the pain and hopelessness of growing up in an alcoholic household—feelings that often linger in our adult lives—can bring on a suicidal depression. If you have suicidal thoughts today, follow Marcia's example. Although it was extremely hard for her to do, asking for help probably saved Marcia's life. Suicidal thoughts cannot be ignored; they should act as red flags, alerting you to the seriousness of your hopeless feelings.

If you are feeling suicidal, you need to get help immediately. Call your family physician, your best friend, or the nearest hospital that offers a walk-in mental-health emergency room. (Most hospitals now provide this service; if your hospital doesn't, the emergency-room staff should be able to direct you to one that does.) Or make a call to your community mental-health center or the suicide hotline now listed in most local yellow pages. The person you speak to can provide you with immediate comfort and direct you to professional help.

NAMELESS, UNSPECIFIC FEAR AND ANXIETY

"There was always an underlying current of tension in the house."

■ ■ ■

Children in many alcoholic homes feel afraid without really knowing what they're afraid of. Nothing is out in the open, nothing is really talked about, and nothing seems secure. Children, like adults, fear the unknown; and all the secrets in an alcoholic home create many unknowns. It's small wonder that ACOAs often come to therapy with feelings of acute and chronic anxiety.

"I was always a very angry child and never knew exactly why," remembered Jan, a young photographer from the Midwest. "I became an angry adult, and only recently decided I was tired of being angry. When I started to let go of the anger I realized how frightened I was. Anger covered up my fear for many years.

"My mother didn't like me. When she drank, she'd single me out for her wrath. My siblings were never abused the way I was. Later, I always gravitated toward people who rejected me just the way my mother did. I'd set people up to be abusive to me—then I could hate them. Only recently have I been able to admit that I wanted my mother's love all those years she was beating me up. I stayed angry rather than admit that that's what I always wanted."

The alcoholic home is a very confusing one for children because parents don't or won't explain what's going on; often they don't know themselves. Faced with so much unexplained tension and activity, we grew up never knowing quite what to expect. And this inconsistency and confusion, added to the other fears we had accumulated, created anxiety and dread in us that we may still find difficult to pin down.

"My parents didn't really fight, but there was always an underlying current of tension in the house," says Bill, a young publicist. "My father spent a lot of time at his club, and my mother spent a lot of her time watching the clock and waiting dinner for him.

"Every once in a while she would suddenly sweep us all up and into the car and drive to a motel, where we would spend the night. One minute we'd be home in our pajamas watching TV and the next we'd be out in the freezing cold driving in the dark.

"She never explained what was going on, but we guessed she was mad at him for not coming home. Maybe she thought he would come looking for us, but he never did. The next morning we'd usually go home, but on those nights we never knew whether we were leaving home forever or just for a few hours. In a way it was an adventure, but it also was very frightening."

To make progress on the road to recovery, adult children of alcoholics have to confront their fears. As a child, you may not have even known you were afraid. But, even if you did know, you probably felt that you couldn't find a safe place where you could give voice to your fears. But today there are safe places; you no longer have to feel alone and afraid.

If you are the adult child of an alcoholic, you have probably already come to recognize that in some very real way you gave up your childhood in order to survive. The background of your alcoholic home can't be changed, but your present-day attitudes and behavior can. As an adult, you can learn how to heal the child within you—and get on with your adult life.

· 3 ·

DISEASE AND DIS-EASE

ALCOHOLISM AND
THE FAMILY

Margaret, a restaurant manager in her early thirties, described her background this way:

"I'm one of eight children and we're very close. My parents are alcoholics, but we didn't realize that at the time. They just seemed to be busy with other things when we were growing up, so they didn't seem to have much influence on us. We kids formed an exclusive little club and we didn't let our parents in. The older ones bossed the younger ones around; we made our own rules and got advice and support from each other.

"A few years ago one of my sisters committed suicide—an overdose of pain medication—and that tore the whole family apart. My parents refuse to believe it had anything to do with alcoholism. They don't want to remember that she was on pain medication because she lost a leg in a drunk-driving accident.

"My sister's death made some of us look at our own alcoholism. Both of my parents have stopped drinking, although my father says he only stopped because of his health and my mother says she's dieting. Neither of them will admit they're alcoholics. We all denied the problem for so long that it's become a bad habit with us. And bad habits are hard to break."

Most families—alcoholic or not—work hard to maintain internal stability; every member of the family makes an effort to preserve and protect established patterns of family behavior, and whenever anything threatens this routine, members of the family will band together, resisting any change of the status quo. In alcoholic families, acknowledgment of the problem, rather than the problem itself, threatens the established (albeit unhealthy) routine. In our own systematic way, we tried to normalize the abnormalities; alcoholic families function in spite of dysfunction. Although some of the coping skills you may have developed to keep the family going—such as hard work or keeping a cool head during a crisis—may actually have proved useful and admirable in your adult life, most of these abilities probably surfaced as an attempt to preserve an unhealthy way of life.

ENABLING BEHAVIOR

Nonalcoholic family members have gotten a lot of bad press for doing their part to maintain the stability of the alcoholic family—for being "enablers." Enablers can be children, spouses, friends, co-workers, bosses, doctors, or anyone in the alcoholic's life who unwittingly supports the drinking by covering up for the alcoholic, making excuses for his or her inconsistent and irresponsible behavior. We have been accused of being as irresponsible as the alcoholic because, in taking on his or her responsibilities, we made it easier for the alcoholic to drink. But enabling deserves more compassionate understanding.

The road to alcoholic hell is undoubtedly paved with the good intentions of enablers. The enabling behavior of children, however misguided, is motivated by a strong, sincere, and healthy desire to preserve family unity. But enablers don't see the disease of alcoholism itself as the threat; admitting the problem seems to pose much more danger. They truly believe they are helping the alcoholic when they take care of things that alcoholics aren't capable of handling. Enablers try to make life easier for alcoholics, who can be having a rough time of it indeed. In fact, they only help the disease go unnoticed and undiagnosed. What enablers don't—and in the case of children, probably can't—understand is that in most cases alcoholics have to get worse before they can get better. Unless and until you allow the alcoholic in your family to face the consequences of his or her drinking by letting these consequences fall where they may, the drinking will continue and your entire family will get sicker. It may be painful to stand by while the alcoholic suffers real-life losses—the love of family, a job, physical health—but these losses are often necessary before an alcoholic will face the disease and decide to do something about it. (See Chapter 4 for more on the need for most alcoholics to "hit bottom" before being willing to change, and Chapter 15 for information on doing an intervention with an alcoholic.)

"Enabling" is an unfortunate term because it suggests that enablers are intentionally doing something terribly wrong, willfully aiding and abetting the downfall of the alcoholic. It is extremely difficult not to be an enabler if the person you care about is having a problem that you think you can help fix. It's about as hard for caring family members to stop enabling as it is for the alcoholic to stop drinking. Both behaviors can be habitual or addictive.

From a clinical perspective, the concept that alcoholism is a "family disease" makes sense. But is it fair to label everyone in a sick person's life "sick"? Enablers behave the way they do because they've been taught that is what loving people do. They are neither inadequate nor irresponsible. Families are supposed to take care of their own, especially when members are helpless. Society condones and encourages the superresponsibility of caretakers, particularly when they are women. Women are supposed to nurture, not abandon. And men in our society are expected to "protect" their loved ones. Enablers, therefore, are meeting the standards of society.

The problem for ACOAs arises when, more often than not, the enabling behavior we adopted in childhood continues into our adult lives. Long after we have grown up and left our alcoholic homes, we often choose to marry alcoholics, which allows us to continue playing these familiar enabling roles. The same young child, for instance, who excused her mother's alcoholism by saying, "My mom can't come to the PTA meeting, she has the flu," may find herself, as an adult living with another alcoholic, saying, "Jim won't be able to come to work today, he isn't feeling well."

If you grew up as an enabler in an alcoholic home—and especially if you became involved with another alcoholic after leaving the alcoholic household, you will need to adjust your ways of thinking and behaving. You will have to learn—and accept—that superresponsibility and overprotectiveness hurt rather than help you and the alcoholic. By "not doing for" instead of "doing for" the alcoholic, you will force him or her to confront the consequences of the drinking and increase the likelihood that he or she will have to own up to the problem. Enablers need to step out of society's stereotypical roles.

But you won't be able to stop enabling unless you first stop denying and begin to acknowledge the real problem. You shouldn't feel guilty about your past enabling behavior, though. You acted out of love. You did the best you knew how in the unhealthy environment of the alcoholic home. By refusing to make it easier for the alcoholic to drink, though, you can do even better—for yourself and the rest of your family.

It may come as a serious blow to have done all this heroic coping and then be told, when you finally go for help, that you've been doing it all wrong. But what you were doing was not all wrong. More likely, it was the right thing at the wrong time. Enablers need to be shown why it might make more sense to be tough rather than tender.

Enabling efforts, and the strengths they gave birth to, should not be criticized. In this book—and through self-help groups or professional help—you will learn how to turn your strengths into different, more appropriate, actions; how to distance or detach yourself from an alcoholic without ceasing to love him or her; and how to modify or change your behavior so that it is ultimately in the best interests of both yourself and the alcoholic(s) in your life.

CO-DEPENDENCY

People who live with an alcoholic tend to develop personality traits similar to those of the alcoholic, even when they themselves are not addicted to alcohol. Spouses and children are addicted to the alcoholic in much the same way that the drinker is addicted to alcohol. As the alcoholic became more and more obsessed with the bottle, we became more and more obsessed with the alcoholic. For the alcoholic alcohol is a mood-altering drug; and the moods of other family members change accordingly. Personality changes occur not only in the alcoholic but in other family members as well. Just as the alcoholic has a compulsion to drink, the nonalcoholic spouse and children have a compulsion to protect the drinker.

Most professionals in the field—and others knowledgeable about alcoholism—now use the term "co-dependency" for the condition of family members who are not alcoholics. If you react to a family member with an alcohol problem and focus on that sick person rather than yourself, you are a co-dependent. Your obsession with the alcoholic makes you co-dependent. Sharon Wegscheider-Cruse, a leader in the study of alcoholism and the family, described co-dependency in Choice-

Making as a condition "characterized by preoccupation and extreme dependence (emotionally, socially and sometimes physically) on a person or object. Eventually, this dependence on another person becomes a pathological condition that affects the co-dependent in all other relationships."

In any family, whether people are sick or healthy, family members depend on one another. But in an alcoholic family, or in a family with any kind of disease, individual members tend to become *overinvolved* with one another. Mutual dependency is healthy; but if your dependency has become obsessive, you have a problem. In recovering from our alcoholic upbringings, we must strive to find a balance between dependency and autonomy that allows us to be neither underinvolved nor overinvolved with people close to us.

"I remember one of the first childhood games I played with my sisters," recalled Dixie, a vivacious woman of forty-five, now two years sober and in the process of ending her third alcoholic marriage. "In the children's playroom, we had our own ginger-ale version of our family's fully stocked liquor bar. And we would go into the playroom and start imitating our relatives: crossed legs, long cigarette holders, cocktail glasses in hand. We loved to mimic them; drinking and smoking cigarettes was our idea of sophistication.

"There was co-dependency all around us but of course we didn't see it that way at the time. We used to spend our summer vacations on the Cape with my father's family and I remember his sister as being tipsy all the time. But no one ever even mentioned that she had a drinking problem.

"She loved to go down to the docks when she was drunk and direct traffic coming off the ferry. My sisters and I were always expected to run down to the docks after her, to try to bring her home. We would cajole her into taking us for a walk along the beach. It became fairly automatic: if Aunt Jane wasn't at home when we heard the ferry whistle blow, one of the grown-ups would look around and say, 'Has anyone seen Aunt Jane?' And that was our cue to dash off and try to get her out of the middle of the street."

This rather mild case of co-dependency shows how children can be subtly enlisted to help take care of alcoholics. Like Dixie, we usually got a lot of practice focusing on the alcoholics in our lives, and little practice in focusing on ourselves. And, like Dixie, many of us choose partners in later life who would allow us to continue our habitual co-dependency.

In the alcoholic family, the suffering alcoholic makes everyone else suffer. We treat the alcoholic as if he or she were a baby, the helpless center of attention. And, as long as all of the co-dependents are busy taking care of the baby, we cannot take care of ourselves. The alcoholic has to let go of the bottle to get well; the co-dependent has to let go of the baby, the one with the bottle. Recovery begins with the first person in the family who takes responsibility for himself or herself. When caretakers like us finally start taking care of ourselves, there is hope that everyone in our family will get better.

Today, your "baby" may be your parent, spouse, friend, or child. Even if the alcoholic in your life has achieved sobriety, co-dependency may still affect your relationships. As new roles are adopted, continued overinvolvement can prolong old tensions or create entirely new problems. Reading the following descriptions of the most prevalent characteristics of co-dependency will help you determine to what extent co-dependency still affects your life today. Although co-dependency can exist in nonalcoholic families too, these descriptions concentrate on the co-dependency in alcoholic families.

LOW SELF-ESTEEM

The least functional person in the family, the alcoholic, the sick person, gets almost all of the attention. Other co-dependents, especially children, not only receive very little attention but also begin to feel unworthy of attention. Co-dependents, in focusing their energies on the alcoholic, value themselves less and less. The life of the alcoholic can become the whole life of a co-dependent spouse or child, who thus becomes self-less. Do you find yourself focusing more on your parent, spouse, friend, or child than on yourself?

EMOTIONAL BLACKOUTS

Preoccupation with alcoholics often causes co-dependents to forget their own needs and feelings. As adults, we continue to associate feelings and needs with the helpless child within, and separate ourselves from that child by blocking out painful feelings and memories—feelings which we fear might pull us back into the unhappiness of our childhood years. And, in refusing to acknowledge the child within, we shut ourselves off from feeling an essential part of our inner self. We totally ignore our own needs and interests by concerning ourselves with another person's problems. Do you still suppress your real feelings most of the time? Are you afraid of these feelings? Do you suffer from emotional blackouts?

SAVIORISM

Alcoholics are often surrounded by rescuers. The entire family—children and adults alike—is enlisted in the effort to protect the sick person. The casualty list is usually high. It's a vicious circle: our low self-image prompts us to focus our efforts on behalf of the alcoholic, and our failure to save her or him only increases our feelings of worthlessness. Co-dependents can survive, but without help few of us really learn to live our own lives.

BLURRED BOUNDARIES

In healthy families, clear boundaries—those invisible lines that separate people emotionally—keep individual members distinct and independent yet close enough to enjoy warm, supportive relationships. Parents and children learn to respect, tolerate, and encourage one another's boundaries, honoring one another's needs for privacy, time alone, and mood shifts as well as needs for attention, companionship, and affection. Healthy boundaries are well-defined but flexible; they allow for give and take.

In alcoholic families, the boundaries of the alcoholic and the co-dependents tend to blur. Family members do not accept, encourage, or respect one another's space. As co-dependent children, we didn't know how to establish appropriate distance, or appropriate closeness, between ourselves and our parents and siblings. In our alcoholic homes, boundaries between us and other family members were unclear or nonexistent: we weren't exactly sure where one person left off and another began.

If boundaries between you and the rest of your family blur, you may have taken on the feelings and opinions of your brother or mother without being aware of the transference. Or you may have assumed others felt exactly the same way you did—unable to acknowledge that their feelings might differ.

Edith, a thirty-two-year-old office manager, told me, "I was extremely close to my mother, who was a prescription-drug abuser. In the last five years of her life she became a compulsive gambler. My father is an alcoholic.

"My mother confided in me and used me as a sounding board. If she'd told me the sky was red, I'd have believed it. She was very controlling and kept me very close to her. She'd let my twin brothers go outside, but she kept me at home with her most of the time. She needed me; I wasn't free to develop other relationships.

"I still have problems with boundaries. I allow people to ask more or expect more of me than they should. I also invade other people's space. When people go on vacation at work, I want to rearrange their desks. I lose sleep over other people's problems."

Without boundaries, there's no allowance for individuality or autonomy, which are crucial to healthy growth and development. The over-involvement of members of alcoholic families in one another's lives prohibits independent action. Your father or an older sister may have constantly interfered with your decision-making ability or your efforts to gain independence. Or you may have tried to explain how your little brother felt—without first finding out how he did feel. Even when relationships within the family were fraught with conflict, those of us who were involved stuck together like glue.

"Emotions were totally suppressed in my family," admitted Jean, a twenty-seven-year-old musician. "People never got angry or said how they felt. It was like an invisible straitjacket. You knew you couldn't say certain things. My mother told us how we should feel, which, of course, was how she felt. I really accepted my mother's feelings as my own. Even now she expects me to feel the same way she does about everything."

In alcoholic families, we found it difficult to maintain a separate identity because one family member's stress was simultaneously experienced by everyone else in the family.

These boundary problems often persist long after we've left the alcoholic household. Do you find yourself speaking and feeling for the alcoholic—or for others—in your life? Do you often say "we" when you mean to say "I"? Do you make assumptions about the way someone else is feeling? When you feel energetic, for example, do you assume that the people you're with also feel eager to get up and go—whereas they really just want to sit and relax? If so, you probably still have difficulty constructing healthy boundaries.

ISOLATION

Alcoholic families have boundary problems not only among themselves but also between the family unit and the rest of the world. As family denial gets stronger and stronger, it begins closing the family off from the community. And, as the disease progresses, the isolation usually increases. As the family gets more and more obsessed with its problems, its focus becomes more and more inward. A distance is created and maintained between the family and outsiders.

Jackie, a twenty-eight-year-old schoolteacher, described her experience: "There were six of us in the family, and we were very close. My parents didn't encourage us to have friends outside the family so we always did things as a unit. It kept us pretty isolated from others, and we were very critical of anyone outside the sibling group who tried to get in."

The progressive blurring of boundaries between family members wasn't the only reason our families started closing themselves off from the outside world, though. The characteristic denial of alcoholic family members made us see any outsider as a threat to our being "found out." Our misguided desire to protect the alcoholic from the consequences of his or her disease left us alone—and lonely.

"I have always been very afraid of people and new situations," admitted Carol, who only recently confronted her fear of the outside world. "My father died when I was six and I knew my mother had a serious problem with alcohol when she started having seizures—I was about thirteen. I was an only child and my mother rarely left the house. My grandmother and aunt lived close by and we would see them occasionally but mostly we were home alone. I never had any friends because I was afraid to bring them home, never knowing what condition my mother would be in. And she didn't have any friends so I had no exposure to other people. I was like my mother's guard dog—just sitting around watching to see that she didn't set the apartment on fire or fall down the stairs."

The family further withdraws from the outside world as the disease worsens. Each person's world shrinks as the family concentrates on taking care of the person who seems to need more and more care. The patterns of behavior that isolated us as children don't necessarily stop after we have grown up and left home; old habits die hard. But physically removing ourselves from the unhealthy environment can provide us with a new awareness of these entrenched family patterns.

"I never really noticed how closed my family was until my wedding," Sueann, a young landscape artist, told me. "There were about twenty of my relatives there and they just stayed together and didn't make any attempt at all to speak with my husband's family or my friends. They're very shut off.

"I guess we've always been pretty isolated from other people, never letting anyone from the outside get inside the family circle. All the kids are married now, but we're still expected to come home for every single holiday. And our spouses have never been made to feel welcome by my parents."

You may still feel closed off from the rest of the world. Do you often feel alone and afraid? Do you feel as if no one understands you? Do you usually prefer escaping from people rather than seeking them out? Do you avoid social situations? Do you distrust strangers? If you are still plagued with feelings of loneliness and isolation, group therapy or a self-help group like Al-Anon/ACOA can help you realize that you are not alone.

FAMILY SECRETS

"I think my mother may have had a drinking problem, although to this day no one in the family has ever mentioned it," says Jim, a musician in his fifties. "It's been a secret for almost fifty years. I never saw her take a drink or even act drunk, but whenever we'd come home from grade school she would be lying down in her bedroom with one of her 'headaches.'

"On those rare occasions when my brother and I would dare go into her room, the shades would be drawn and we'd have to go on tiptoe so we wouldn't disturb her. She would be in a horrible mood when she got up, and she'd run around the house trying to put it into order before my dad got home from work. When he arrived, she'd be all smiles, as if she hadn't even been sick.

"Once my brother and I were looking for our baseball uniforms and we found several empty liquor bottles in the bottom of the clothes hamper. Of course we never said anything."

The process of denial ensures that in alcoholic families the best-kept secret—the one that isolates us the most—is that someone in the family is an alcoholic. The family will go to almost any lengths to maintain the secrecy. They don't know what to do about it, but none of them will talk about it either.

But alcoholic families keep other damaging secrets as well. Eating disorders, child abuse, and incest are not uncommon in alcoholic homes. But, like the alcoholism itself, these tragedies are cloaked in silence. And, because this secretiveness can allow these practices to be passed down from generation to generation, silence may be the biggest tragedy of all.

EATING DISORDERS

"I always had a weight problem," says Anna, now in her fifties, "but I didn't see myself as overweight. No one in the family seemed to notice; at least no one ever said anything about it. No one in our house ever acted as if they were interested in what anyone else was doing. I felt that everything that happened to me was my fault. I wasn't getting anything from anyone, and I used food to try and give to myself. I soothed myself and rewarded myself with food."

Alcoholic homes often provide an atmosphere of emptiness that makes nonalcoholic members prime candidates for eating disorders. Daughters and wives of alcoholics are particularly vulnerable to the feelings of deprivation that precede the onset of eating disorders.

"When we get a new patient in our eating disorders clinic I'm not at all surprised to find out she's an ACOA. At least half of our patients are ACOAs," Terri, a weight clinic counselor, told me. "I usually refer all my clients to an ACOA group rather than a support group specializing in eating disorders. Whether they're ACOA or not, they're amazed at how quickly they feel understood. The constellation of family problems and the personality characteristics of people with eating disorders and those of ACOAs are very similar. Beginning a self-help recovery program like ACOA, at the same time they start individual therapy in our clinic, encourages recovery."

Incest victims frequently have problems connected with food. Not surprisingly, they often find it is easier to talk about their eating disorder than past sexual abuse. Many reveal their incest histories in the course of recovery from an addiction like food, alcohol, or drugs.

There are three major eating disorders, although some people may have more than one of them. Compulsive eating, an urgent preoccupation with food, is the most common. A sense of relief, of comfort or release from anxiety, comes along with eating more food than is necessary to maintain health. Anorexia nervosa is a life-threatening condition marked by major weight loss (25 percent or more of the person's body weight), a relentless striving for thinness and terror at gaining weight. It is often accompanied by frantic exercise. Bulimia is distinguished by alternating episodes of binge eating—consuming enormous quantities of food, usually as a way of dealing with extreme anxiety—followed by purging in order to maintain an acceptable body weight and to alleviate feelings of insecurity and self-hatred.

All these eating disorders, in their severe forms, are similar to the disease of alcoholism. The behavior is out of control, is going to get worse, and is dangerous if not interrupted. But, like alcoholism, the disorders can be treated.

There are several theories about what causes eating disorders. Some experts think there is a biochemical predisposition; others believe that family dynamics cause them. The one thing that everyone in the field seems to agree on is that these disorders have nothing to do with food. Issues of control, self-esteem, growing up, and difficulties with important relationships are centered on in treatment. One expert—Judi Hollis, author of *Fat Is a Family Affair*—summed it up by saying that, for people with eating disorders, "Loving food is safer than loving people."

If you think you may have an eating disorder, test yourself with the "Eating Disorders Questionnaire" on pages 264–265 and refer to the hotlines and other resources listed on pages 273–276.

THE DARKEST SECRET: PHYSICAL AND SEXUAL ABUSE

Children who have grown up in alcoholic families have had a variety of traumatic experiences. When alcohol is the primary focus of a family, resolving conflict and solving problems often become very low priorities. Many real or potential problems are buried under the weight of attention given to alcohol.

Domestic violence can result from increased tension, poor impulse control, and lack of boundaries. Children of alcoholics often grow up with the unpredictability of physical assault and the threat of violence. If you grew up in a violent household, whether or not assaults actually took place, whether or not you were a victim or a witness, you felt assaulted. And your childhood fears became adult fears as well. As an adult, you are probably afraid of angry confrontations, although alternatively you may seek out violent scenarios, precisely because they're so familiar.

Some ACOAs carry the fallout from having had an older person— the alcoholic, the nonalcoholic parent, or another relative—sexually assault or threaten them when they were young. If this happened to you, you may have painful memories of feeling scared and powerless. As a child, you felt you couldn't say "no" or tell anyone about it. Even if you did try to tell an adult, too often you weren't believed.

There is no evidence that drinking causes sexual abuse, but the disorganization of the alcoholic family can provide fertile ground for incest. Like alcoholism itself, patterns of sexual abuse and domestic violence are often carried from one generation to the next. The pathology becomes repetitious. Remorse on the part of the abuser and shame and guilt on the part of the abused are common. These incidents close the family off further and further from other people; isolation results from despair.

Feelings of powerlessness, worthlessness, and fearfulness are common among children of alcoholics. But, if sexual abuse and violence were part of your experience, these feelings were magnified. The very essence of family functioning is to keep its members from harm; if you grew up unsafe and harmed, you experienced a tremendous betrayal.

However, while the terms "incest" and "sexual abuse" describe coercive physical contact involving children, these relationships are not necessarily violent. Children who don't get active, supportive parenting may be particularly vulnerable to sexual abuse. If you were deprived of much-needed affection as a child, when an older person approached you sexually you may have experienced the touching— even if violent—as warm, tender contact. Sexual abuse may have offered you a rare sense of specialness, and as such you were less able to resist. You may have felt that if you resisted you would be abandoned by the one parent who was giving you any attention at all. Many sexual-abuse survivors have very mixed and complicated feelings about the person who involved them in these relationships. They often speak of feelings of fear, guilt, responsibility, loyalty, and confusion—all of which make it difficult to disclose childhood sexual abuse. Many incest survivors report that they actually felt closer to the parent that abused them than to the other parent. They often have deep resentments toward the parent who ignored them and condoned or denied the sexual behavior.

If you were sexually abused and have many complex feelings, you shouldn't feel guilty about what happened to you. You were only a child, and you weren't responsible for the sexual abuse. Children tend to feel responsible for incestuous acts, though the responsibility was clearly not theirs. Or children, boys especially, may have deluded themselves into believing that the older relative was simply trying to "teach" them about sex. This belief makes it much harder for boys to realize they were sexually abused.

When abusive incidents occur, children develop survival adaptations, using a variety of ways to defend themselves from feeling worse.

Often they mentally bury the experiences and feelings that accompanied them. Many incest survivors have vague but persistent feelings that something may have happened, but they can't recall the specifics.

"I was walking into our bedroom one day and saw my husband hanging up his belt, and I just started screaming," remembered Betsy, a thirty-four-year-old teacher. "I suddenly remembered my father taking off his belt, saying, 'If you tell anyone, I'll beat you to death.'

"It wasn't until that moment that I was able to remember the incest and the fear. Thank goodness I was in therapy and ACOA when I had this flashback. I felt protected enough to finally admit to myself and someone else that my father had molested me from the time I was eight years old until I left for college."

Incest victims often feel deep hurt and anger toward others—especially the nonabusive parent—who failed to protect them or refused to believe that they were actually assaulted. It is a terrible experience for a child who feels threatened by one parent not to get protection and understanding from the nonabusing parent. They feel doubly betrayed.

"I tried to tell my mother how frightened I was to be alone with my father, but she actually encouraged rather than discouraged it," remembered Ruth, a flight attendant in her twenties. "She always assigned me to the caretaking role. I remember one incident in particular. We were at a family wedding party when my father got terribly drunk and she insisted that I walk him home, which was about three miles away. He stumbled all the way and I was very embarrassed. Then he tried to force himself on me sexually, and I ran back to the reception. In front of everyone, my mother yelled at me for leaving him alone on the road."

Incest victims are, of course, not all females. And more and more men who have been abused are learning that it helps to unburden themselves in safe surroundings—such as incest-survivors groups, private therapy, or an ACOA meeting.

"My mother would come home drunk in the middle of the night and get into bed with me," said Thomas, a thirty-two-year-old carpenter. "Nothing was consummated, but she abused me sexually. I just froze. I hated the fact that she was there but I couldn't do anything about it. I didn't even know I had these feelings until recently. I felt total despair at first and then I developed enormous rage, really murderous rage. It's extremely painful to feel the rage, but I know I have to; and the group meetings for incest survivors are helping me to deal with all this."

Disclosure is essential for the survivors of incest. Self-help groups provide a safe place for incest survivors to tell their secrets, unburden themselves of their guilt, and express their feelings of fear, anger, and betrayal. Many victims report great relief and subsequent recovery when they are at last able to disclose what they have kept to themselves for so long. And, by speaking up about it, incest survivors can finally accept the truth of what happened in the incest situation, realize they were not responsible for it, and feel that they have regained a sense of their own power and identity.

If you have any vague suspicions or doubts about whether you were sexually abused as a child, you may find it helpful to read the "Twenty-four Stages of Growth for Survivors of Incest" on pages 263–264. You will find telephone numbers of crisis counseling centers for victims of sexual abuse, as well as several useful books, in the Resource Organizations.

The intergenerational patterns of anger and violence, the cycles of physical and sexual abuse, can be stopped. In addition to the growing number of shelters that protect victims of either battering or incest, help is now also available for the batterers and sex abusers. Many treatment programs for battered women and for incest victims also offer both individual and group treatment for the abusers as well, helping them see that violent behavior is *never* acceptable and teaching them how to control their uncontrolled anger.

FAMILY RULES

"Breaking with family rules or traditions is tantamount to treason in my family," said Sueann, who spoke about her family's isolation earlier in this chapter. "Last Thanksgiving I was a few hours late because we decided to go to the parade first. Even though we were there in plenty of time for dinner, we didn't arrive at ten in the morning, when we were expected. Not one person spoke to us when we walked in; not even my young nieces and nephews, who had obviously been told we had done a terrible thing."

The rule of secrecy is not the only one that operates to protect an alcoholic family. A full roster of rules attempts to keep the family close and lend stability to a shaky system. At the most basic level, the rules of the alcoholic family, as defined by Claudia Black in *It Will Never Happen to Me!*, are: "Don't talk, don't feel, don't trust." Most of our families had other rules too, rules that also served to perpetuate the characteristic denial of alcoholic families. You may recognize some of these rules from your own childhood:

- Children should be seen and not heard.
- We take care of our own.
- The family comes first.
- You cannot trust anyone.
- We know what is best.
- Don't wash your laundry in public.
- Put on a happy face.
- What happens in our family is nobody else's business.
- Our family right or wrong.

RECOGNIZING YOUR OWN RULES   Your family may have had other rules too. What were the rules that your family lived by? Which of these rules do you still maintain in your own family or in your personal relationships? Have they outlived their usefulness? If so, throw the old ones out and make new rules more appropriate to who you are now and what you would like to accomplish in your life.

Draw a cartoon of your family, perhaps at the dining table, and attribute a familiar rule to each person, a rule that person obeyed. What are they saying or thinking? A cartoon like this can help you reexamine the rules in your family. You may be able to see who made these rules. Who followed them? Did anyone refuse to follow them? Then cross out all the rules, both your own and those of other family members, that no longer apply to your life now. Make a commitment to refuse to live by those rules today. Are there any left?

THE PLAY AND PLAYERS

CHILDHOOD ROLES

In most families, alcoholic or not, members take on specific roles. The labels given to children by other family members often stay with them throughout their lives. Most people know the roles they are expected to play in their families: the good child, the bad child, the serious child, the comedian, the brain, the rebel, the black sheep.

Alcoholic family members adopt specific roles that are often quite necessary to the family's survival. As the needs of the family change, the roles change too. Often one member will play several roles in succession, or may even take on more than one role at the same time.

Many of the ACOAs I've worked with have found it helpful to identify the roles they played. In recognizing the roles and the common fears and feelings these roles masked, they often realize that the old roles are no longer appropriate, and may in fact stand in the way of getting their current needs met. This recognition can provide the motivation to let go of old patterns of behavior that developed as a reaction to stressful situations, to give up outmoded roles and learn new ones.

In *Another Chance: Hope and Health for the Alcoholic Family*, Sharon Wegscheider-Cruse identified the following roles in alcoholic families: family hero, scapegoat, lost child, and mascot. Claudia Black has described similar roles in *It Will Never Happen to Me!*, defining them as the responsible one, the acting-out child, the adjuster, and the placater.

In reading about these roles, consider the ones you and your siblings played at various periods of your childhood. Keep in mind that they overlap at times. As Claudia Black pointed out, "Some children clearly fit into one or more of these four roles. While one child may be an obvious adjuster, another may play both the placating and the responsible roles. Some children exhibit traits of all four roles." Your own role may have incorporated various features of each of the following.

The family hero, usually the oldest child in the family, is the "superchild." The hero, who may also be referred to as the "perfect child," is usually the pillar of the family. But, while family heroes may have many strengths, they also have some weaknesses. They tend to cover up their insecurities and low self-esteem by performing noble deeds. Underneath all that self-sufficiency, they often feel inadequate and fearful.

The scapegoat is the child who always seems to be in trouble. Acting up, impulsive and defiant, scapegoats serve as buffers; they keep the focus on themselves rather than on the alcoholic. An enormous amount of family frustration and anger can be dumped on scapegoats. Underneath these tough-kid exteriors, though, they are usually frightened and lonely. Scapegoats don't feel that they deserve praise; they unconsciously court punishment, and almost always get what they are looking for.

The lost child is the missing person of the family. Rarely seen or heard, lost children lack a sense of identity and neither ask for nor get very much attention in life. Fearful of taking risks or rocking the boat, the lost child wanders through life feeling unimportant, unnoticed.

The family mascot is usually the youngest child. Mascots get all the laughs; clowning around eases family tension and diverts the family gaze from serious problems. Family mascots often have a hard time growing up; acting like silly kids was a clever way to hide the fact that they were the most terrified members of their families. When they weren't being funny, they may have been especially afraid they were going crazy.

The unscathed child may be a fifth category of child, one that doesn't fit into any of the commonly described roles. Unscathed children appear to be relatively unharmed by alcoholism in the family. They function well in the world, are relatively untroubled and appear healthy and resilient.

Perhaps there were important factors in their lives that militated against any serious disturbance. They might, for instance, have grown up before the alcoholism was very far advanced. They might have gotten a tremendous amount of nurturing from surrogate parents (grandparents, neighbors, godparents). Or they might have been born with exceptional character strengths. In addition, some unscathed children are in denial and are not interested in scratching below the surface to see what impact the alcoholism really had on them. Whether they are truly healthy or only appear to be so on the outside (like the family hero), these ACOAs may not seek the kind of support that most of us find helpful.

No matter what role or roles we played as children, most of us shared the same underlying fears, desires, and attitudes outlined in Chapters 1 and 2. All of the roles, for instance, worked to ease the powerful fear of confrontation. At first, the way a child responded externally to these hidden fears defined his or her role in the family, not the other way around. One child tried to smooth things out and avoid confrontation, thereby taking on the family hero role. Another (the scapegoat) accepted full responsibility for any confrontation, becoming a target for other family members' aggression. A third shrank away from any confrontation through attempted invisibility, becoming the lost child. Finally, one attempted to eliminate confrontation by clowning to ease tensions. But the underlying motivation for these dramatically different patterns of behavior is the same, commonly held fear. Originally, these roles were simply outward *reactions* to our secret inner turmoil, masks that we wore to disguise our hidden fears and feelings. Only through repetition and force of habit did these external responses become internalized.

Similarly, whatever childhood role or roles we adopted, most of us carry comparable problems in our adult lives. Whether you were the family hero or the lost child, for example, you probably suffer from a sense of low self-esteem. All of the roles attempt to perpetuate denial by covering up or diverting attention from the alcoholic. And, in playing one or more of these roles, each of us was trying to impose a measure of control on the situation. The family scapegoat, for example, feels no less responsible for family problems than the family hero. Each of us tried in his or her own way to be the perfect child. And in making this attempt we tried on these childhood roles as if they were costumes of the perfect child.

BLACK AND WHITE OR GRAY ALL OVER

People who grow up in dysfunctional homes tend to see things as black or white, as right or wrong. Rigid family systems make for rigid, absolute thinking. Just as family members have particular ways of relating in family roles, they may also have particular ways of thinking.

Alcoholic parents, when they are battling about the alcohol or other problems, make children feel compelled to take sides. Frequently we saw one parent as a saint and the other as a devil. Consciously or unconsciously, we blamed either the alcoholic or the nonalcoholic—but seldom both—for causing the family's troubles.

Those of us who tried to avoid succumbing to this sort of parental manipulation may have ended up seeing nothing but gray. We may have gotten into what felt like a safe middle ground and refused to budge. But whether, as children, we saw things as either black or white or as all gray, our perceptions were formed as an attempt to cope with an inflexible system that produced considerable uncertainty, insecurity, ambivalence, and distrust.

"When I was growing up, I saw my mother as all wrong and my father as all right," related Sara, a psychologist in her mid-thirties. "It wasn't until I was twenty-one that I realized my mother was right—he had an alcohol problem. Before that, I had refused to see that there was anything wrong with him.

"Until then I had blamed her: she was the bitch; my dad was the tortured victim. He always had a back problem, and he worked too hard. It was like having an invalid for a father. Every night he would sit there and sip his booze and get very sad. He was a very passive drunk, a crying-in-his-beer type, and I felt sorry for him.

"I had very serious problems with my mother. We were both emotional, and we fought all the time. My father hated our scenes. He would get up and leave the room if we had an argument.

"When I was an adolescent my mother would try to tell me that he had a drinking problem and I just would not see it. But then one summer we all went to Europe, and I really did see. He would not go into a restaurant that didn't serve alcohol. He had to have his drinks. That was much more important to him than food. He was a real bore, not interested in doing anything or seeing anything. I finally understood why my mother was so frustrated with him. I saw things in a completely different light."

TORN LOYALTIES, AMBIVALENT FEELINGS

The pressure we felt to choose one parent as all good and the other as all bad was complicated by the rapid changes in mood and fluctuations of character we observed in both parents. Most chronic diseases do not cause major personality changes; alcoholism is an exception. Slowly or rapidly, sooner or later, the alcoholic becomes a very different person. Under the influence of alcohol, he or she turns into someone else. It is hard for children to know how to react to these different personalities. Sometimes the alcoholic is more affectionate and permissive when drunk—what child would not prefer that to having a hungover and grouchy parent? Another alcoholic turns mean and abusive when drunk, and the child becomes terror-stricken. Then, when this same alcoholic is sober, he or she may try to make up for the bad behavior with gifts and apologies.

When an alcoholic parent is not drinking he or she may seem very, very good. But, when this parent is drinking, he or she may act horrid. Naturally enough, as children we responded differently to these contradictory personalities that we saw in just one parent. You may have even experienced these conflicting emotions at the very same time. Ambivalently, you could love and hate the alcoholic parent; you could feel pity and disgust at the same time; you could feel angry and sympathetic; you could feel trusting and suspicious.

Even if only one of your parents was alcoholic, you probably had very mixed feelings about the nondrinking parent too. All of us, as children, had loyalties of differing degree to both our mothers and our fathers. Ironically, children who grow up with an alcoholic parent often feel a greater bond with the more helpless partner. You may have blamed the parent who seemed more responsible, the one who was the ultimate (and available) authority in the family, the one who didn't drink. This parent's mood swings could be wide indeed. And the monumental efforts the nondrinker made to be in control when the alcoholic was out of control—the attempts to stifle spontaneity, to discourage the expression of honest emotions, to impose his or her own order on the chaos—must have upset you a great deal as a child. You felt cheated and angry that the nonalcoholic parent was overinvolved with the alcoholic and uninvolved with you.

"I still have mixed feelings about my parents," confessed Janice, a recent grandmother who still hasn't sorted out her feelings for her parents forty years after leaving home. "Each of them tried to convince me the other was no good, and I didn't know what to think. My father left when I was a baby. My mother always said she had thrown him out of the house because he was an alcoholic. When I was in high school I saw him for the first time that I remember. He told me he had left my mother because all she ever wanted to do was go to dances and have a good time. He said that she once took me to a dance with her and had me so bundled up that I started to turn blue. He said he saved me from suffocating and that's why he left her. I still don't know who was telling the truth.

"As a child I remember feeling very sorry for both my parents; they seemed to have such hard lives. They were so unhappy. I felt sad for them. But that didn't make me feel any less angry at them.

"When I was three, my mother married a traveling salesman and went on the road with him. I was left with my grandparents. I loved them and didn't want my mother to come back. When they would try to read me her letters, I would just cover my ears. I guess I really *was* angry at her, but I never admitted it."

Feelings of ambivalence are an integral part of all relationships. But children of alcoholics have difficulty dealing with this ambivalence. Our tendency to "stuff away" any feelings, the pressure we felt to take sides, and the difficulty of knowing exactly who in the alcoholic household to believe encouraged us to repress any complicating feelings of ambivalence—to keep our homes running as smoothly as possible. Growing more comfortable with our own ambivalence, accepting and dealing with the inevitable conflict of torn loyalties, is an important task of ACOA recovery, especially in our intimate relationships.

FAMILY MYTHS

There is so much denial in alcoholic families that all kinds of untruths and half-truths turn into myths that last for years. Until parents or children get some kind of treatment, these secrets remain and the myths persist, preventing us from dealing with the reality of our lives.

"My mother, until her death last year, maintained the family myth that we were a 'good family.' She meant, of course, that my father was a respected pillar of the community, socially prominent and above reproach," remembered Tom, a forty-five-year-old bachelor with two alcoholic brothers. "She steadfastly denied the truth that my father was a periodic alcoholic. Because we wanted it to be true, it was easy for us to believe that each binge was the last, that it wouldn't happen again.

"Not long ago I discovered love letters that my father wrote before my parents got married. I kept finding sentences like, 'I'm sorry about last night. It won't happen again. Please forgive me.' Even then, over fifty years ago, he was drinking too much.

"To her dying day, my mother never once mentioned the word 'alcoholic.' She still thought he was the perfect husband and we were 'a good family.' "

The problems alcoholic families have in creating healthy boundaries causes us to become so emotionally engaged with the other members of our families that each individual's vision of reality becomes a strand of the family myth. After a while, because all of us are living in a state of denial and delusion, no one really knows what the truth is.

Here are some of the common myths that alcoholic families create:

THE ALCOHOLIC PARENT'S MYTHS

- I'll quit tomorrow.
- I don't have a problem; I can stop any time.
- I can control it.
- I'll just have one more.
- I just like to have a good time.
- Of course I can drive—I've only had a few.
- It wasn't the job for me anyway.
- If you had my problems, you'd drink too.
- It's not my fault that I drink.
- Nobody in this family understands me.
- If I got some love and affection, I wouldn't drink so much.
- I'm sorry . . .
- I promise . . .

THE NONALCOHOLIC PARENT'S MYTHS

- Maybe he's not really an alcoholic.
- She can't be an alcoholic—she gets to work every day.
- Maybe he'll learn to control his drinking.
- Maybe next time she won't drink so much.
- How can I abandon someone who's sick?
- I'm sure I can help him.
- It's my fault she drinks.
- Maybe if I change, he'll stop drinking.
- If she loved me, she'd stop.
- Maybe he'll leave me if he gets sober.
- If only . . .
- She promised . . .

THE CHILD'S MYTHS

- If he loved me, he wouldn't drink so much.
- It's all my fault.
- She didn't really mean to hurt me.
- Maybe if I'm good . . .
- Maybe I'm crazy.
- Maybe next time . . .
- I'm strong, I can handle this.
- I don't need any help.
- I'll never end up like that.
- I have to take care of him.
- I make mountains out of molehills.
- If I behave, she won't drink so much.
- If she wasn't so mean, he wouldn't drink so much.
- It doesn't really matter.
- I'll try harder.
- But she promised me . . .

Eventually we grow up and move into our own homes and start our own families. Yet we haven't necessarily escaped the family myths. In fact, we often add a few more of our own to make the family history palatable, and to maintain the denial:

- I had a normal childhood.
- We had the usual number of family problems, nothing serious.

- I don't remember much of my childhood.
- My mother wasn't really an alcoholic, she just drank too much.
- They had a very active social life.
- My parents fought all the time, but it never had anything to do with the drinking.
- My father only drank socially.
- The drinking never bothered me that much.
- I won't let it ruin my life.
- She didn't drink *that* much.
- That was a long time ago, he doesn't drink now.
- I won't let anything like that ever happen to me.

Members of our own families may have felt the same way we did about our parents' drinking, but we rarely shared our feelings with one another. We may have thought we were being supportive of one another, but our support was limited. Even though we all tried hard to be there for everyone else, each of us ended up feeling alone—and afraid. As long as alcoholism was the secret that no one would discuss, honest and open sharing couldn't possibly take place.

"My mother was always telling us we were a wonderful family," recalled Terry, a psychologist and recovering alcoholic in his thirties. "She'd say things like 'We are a very happy family; Dad and I love each other very much and we want to do everything we can for you.' Meanwhile there was so much tension in the house you could cut it with a knife. She was screaming about my dad's drinking and he was sullen. She seemed very unhappy and he seemed very sad. Yet she kept telling us we had a wonderful family!

"My father is an alcoholic, I'm an alcoholic, my sister married one, and my youngest sister doesn't eat. But it wasn't until eight years ago, when my mother died of cancer and my father felt so guilty, that he finally admitted to a problem with alcohol and got some help. I went into AA myself three years later. The family secret was finally exposed; now we're able to be emotionally close to each other."

In addition to the myth that "nothing was wrong," most of us shared another common family myth: "We failed." Certainly that can be a strong and pervasive feeling, but the real truth in the alcoholic family was that each of us probably did the best we could. We tried to keep the family together the only way we knew how.

DISPELLING MYTHS, UNCOVERING SECRETS: THE SEEDS OF CHANGE

Most alcoholic families cannot begin to recover until someone breaks the "don't talk" rule. When someone in the family has a progressive and terminal disease like alcoholism, it gets harder and harder to ignore or disguise the illness. Not only does the alcoholic get sicker and sicker, but the people around the alcoholic get sicker too. It becomes more and more difficult to maintain the delusion that things are okay. But, until the pain of living in the alcoholic environment becomes so intolerable to a member of the family that he or she talks, the secrets will remain underground and the myths will persist.

Certainly as people become more aware of alcoholism as a disease more families will seek help. More alcoholics will get sober and more spouses and children will find recovery programs of their own. The solution of the problem begins with revealing the family secret. The promise and hope are there; the family just has to come clean about its secret. It seems so simple, but of course it isn't. The family has spent a great deal of effort to keep the secret; it takes as great an effort to tell it.

The blurred boundaries and close ties of alcoholic families may have one advantage, though: once part of the system changes, the rest of it must change too. When one person begins to recover, the totality of change that can come about in a family can be perfectly astounding. The change in one person's spirit can catalyze very significant changes at home. A family *can* be healed, emotionally and spiritually. It can be restored, reconstructed, and transformed. But in order for that to happen each person has to take responsibility for his or her own recovery. In a sense, the whole family needs to recover from alcoholism, not just the member who drinks too much.

FAMILY STRENGTH, FAMILY LOVE

Despite their problems, alcoholic families are often courageous and strong. Anyone who has worked with them can attest to their supreme individual and family resilience. They may be damaged but they are seldom devastated; they may be disturbed but they are almost never defeated. Among their members are survivors, individuals who want more than just to get through life—they want to enjoy it.

Alcoholic families are generally very loyal. The loyalty derives, of course, from love. The love may not be acknowledged or expressed, it may be immature or indirect, but it is usually there. Alcoholic families tend, in fact, to love too much, rather than too little. Not knowing how to express love doesn't mean one doesn't feel it. The love may be misguided; at times it may not be "tough" enough. Love may be temporarily suspended; it may even be experienced as hate. But love is there all the same.

When the family allows its love and loyalty to surface, it can be a wonderful resource for meeting the human needs of support, companionship, and security. And the promises of recovery are possible for the family that not only wishes to get well, but insists on getting better.

· 4 ·

DENIAL AND DESPAIR
THE ALCOHOLIC'S EXPERIENCE

For most of us, a disproportionate amount of our time, effort, and attention has already been heaped on the alcoholic(s) in our families. Our co-dependent obsession with the alcoholic made us neglect our own lives in devoting our energies to protecting the alcoholic.

In order for children of alcoholics to get better as adults, we first must realize that we were not responsible for the chaos in our homes, that we had no control over the alcoholic's drinking or the consequences of that drinking. To move toward the realization of powerlessness over alcoholism, we need to gain an understanding of the disease itself.

The disease of alcoholism has a dangerous tendency to recur generation after generation. So, if you grew up with an alcoholic parent, you and your children and even your children's children run a higher risk of becoming alcoholics too. For this reason, and to better understand how this disease affected (and still affects) you, you will find it helpful to increase your knowledge of the alcoholic's experience. In this way, you can contribute greatly to your own good health.

ALCOHOLISM: A PHYSICAL,
EMOTIONAL, SPIRITUAL ILLNESS

When treating patients who refuse to reveal the extent of their drinking, physicians do not always recognize the symptoms of alcoholism.
Most alcoholics go undiagnosed and untreated because they seem to
be leading ordinary lives—until they develop an alcohol-related physical problem. Serious physiological problems like cirrhosis and pan-
creatitis may not show up for many years. Other physical symptoms
may never be identified. And all the while the body is slowly breaking
down, the emotional and spiritual well-being of the alcoholic is also
under attack. Psychic pain becomes a fact of the alcoholic's life; his or
her spirit is being broken.

Alcohol affects the brain as well as the body. It keeps alcoholics
psychologically immature—they blame others for what is going wrong
in their lives. They think they're just fine, that the only problem is that
everybody else won't let them drink in peace, and they have a million
and one "good reasons" for drinking. They fail to recognize that these
are all excuses, not reasons. The reason, and the only reason, they
drink like alcoholics is that they *are* alcoholics.

Alcohol distorts the relationships alcoholics have with those close to
them as well as with the universe at large. As drinking increases, most
alcoholics become intolerant, dishonest, selfish, arrogant, and manipulative. They often feel unloving, unloveable, and unloved. Spiritually
bankrupt, they don't care about anyone or anything except alcohol.

Alcoholics want to be good parents. They want to take responsibility
for themselves and their families, but they can't. As the disease progresses, parenting skills and love of family become increasingly insig-
nificant to them. It is usually not until alcoholics have stopped drinking
and have been in recovery programs for some time that they become
aware of the damaging effects alcoholism has had on the family. They
become aware of their emotional unavailability and are frequently very
sad to learn how much of their children's growing up they missed.

"When I had been sober about three years and my youngest son was
twelve, we were painting the deck on a hot summer day. I went into
the house and brought out a glass of ginger ale and guzzled it down.
He looked at me in absolute panic and asked, 'Dad, that's not beer, is
it?' "

Gene, thirty-eight, continued: "We thought he had not been deeply affected because my wife and I both got sober when he was only nine. But that look and the fright in his voice made me realize how deeply scarred he had been.

"My wife was a nurse and I was a student when we stopped drinking. Because we didn't physically abuse our kids or each other, and because we did most of our drinking and pill taking outside the house, we deluded ourselves about our parenting. We never left the kids alone, except to go to the next-door neighbors after they were asleep. We really thought we were good parents.

"But even without obvious neglect or physical violence, I know we weren't really there for them much of that time. I was emotionally removed and unreliable. Often I'd say I'd be home at a certain time and arrive much later. I definitely gave them mixed messages, being loving and caring one day and angry and withdrawn the next. I was rigid with them too. When they said something I didn't like or agree with, I'd punish them, even though I had always told them they should express their feelings.

"At the time of our drinking and drugging I could see the changes in my wife but not in myself. She was even fired once for stealing medication at the hospital, and I thought she had a mental problem. I could see that she was lost, but I couldn't admit that she was an alcoholic and a drug abuser. And certainly I thought that I just drank a lot. We spent most of our time trying to be in control, so we didn't see the insidious impact it was having on the kids."

Alcoholic parents who do not sober up can never get to look objectively at lapsed relationships with partners and children. The more they drink, the more emotionally unavailable they become. They simply cannot be there for anyone. And this inability to maintain attachments keeps the alcoholics uninvolved, emotionally undeveloped, and isolated. Even after attaining sobriety, alcoholics can take years to repair the damage done to their relationships with family and friends.

"For years at AA meetings I've been sharing my attempts to have a relationship with my thirty-two-year-old son," said Sarah, now fifty. "There were several years when we didn't speak at all. I kept waiting for him to call me. When he didn't call one holiday, I decided I wasn't going to get in touch with him. That ended up hurting me most of all, but my foolish pride and my feeling that he should call his mother kept me in a hurtful rage for a long, long time. Therapy, and talking about it in meetings, finally got me to the point where I could pick up the phone and call him, with no expectations, no strings attached. It was one of the hardest things I ever did; my attitude of 'I don't need anybody' was so strong—and so stupid.

"Anyway, Bill is getting married in a few months, and we talk on the phone almost every day, even if it's just for a hello-how-are-you. I can't tell you how wonderful this is for me, and how grateful I am. We're both struggling to finally have some kind of adult relationship with each other. A big part of my thing has been that I've really always been such a baby. I didn't act like a parent, yet I expected Bill to treat me like one. I'm the one who needs to grow up!"

LOSING CONTROL

In most cases alcoholics are the last to admit that they have a problem with alcohol. They maintain that they can stop drinking any time they want to. And periodically they may stop for a while to prove to themselves and everyone else that they don't need to drink. But the problem is that they cannot easily stop and stay stopped. Sooner or later, unless alcoholics admit their disease and get into treatment, they start drinking again. Alcoholics can control their drinking some of the time; they can't control it all of the time. That is what makes an alcoholic different from a social drinker. One alcoholic explained, "I stopped drinking because I realized I could not stop."

An invisible line separates social drinkers from alcoholic drinkers. When a person cannot always control when, where, and how much he drinks, alcohol controls the alcoholic. It may take many years for alcoholics to reach that line, although some reach it in a surprisingly short time. But, once the line has been crossed, alcoholics can never drink safely again.

It takes most people who have a predisposition to alcoholism about fifteen years for drinking to go from being a habit and a psychological dependency to a full-fledged physical addiction. Social drinkers can go on drinking forever without developing a problem. However, if drinking begins at a very early age, the addiction process can be much shorter. One of my patients, for example, began drinking at age eleven and was in his first hospital for detoxification by the time he was eighteen. Most alcoholics control their drinking much of the time, but they cannot control their drinking all of the time in spite of good intentions and supreme efforts. Alcoholics have periods of controlled and uncontrolled drinking: relatively stable times alternate with wild and crazy times. But eventually alcohol takes over the mind, body, and spirit of the alcoholic.

Some alcoholics drink episodically, while others drink on a daily basis. Either pattern gets them, eventually, into some serious difficulty. They are usually in some trouble in a major area of their lives: they may be having problems at home, at work, or with friends. Their health may be deteriorating; they may be in a great deal of emotional pain. A social drinker who had that many problems would simply quit drinking. But an alcoholic usually doesn't want to quit, he just desperately wants to be able to "control" the drinking. The alcoholic stops drinking, goes "on the wagon" for a time but then falls off. Until the alcoholic can accept powerlessness over the disease, he or she will probably not be able to maintain any significant period of total abstinence.

Alcoholism has three stages—early, middle, and late—all of which have serious impact on the alcoholic and the alcoholic's family. Reading about these stages will help you recognize the progression of the disease and its effects in your own family. Remember, it's not how much a person drinks that makes him or her an alcoholic, but rather what happens to the person under the influence of alcohol. Alcoholics' body chemistry makes them react to the substance very differently from social drinkers.

Early stage. Drinking starts out as use and becomes misuse. What may have been occasional social drinking becomes a pattern of conduct in too many situations. The alcoholic begins to lose control of his or her drinking and denies a drinking problem.

Middle stage. Psychological dependence increases. Problems surface at home and at work, and life starts to fall apart. The alcoholic needs a drink to treat a hangover. He or she tries to control the drinking by changing some things (the brand of alcohol or the time and place of drinking). Denial becomes more vehement as the alcoholic tries to conceal the drinking problem. The alcoholic is full of remorse and self-hate—especially when waking up and finding that, despite all good intentions, he or she got drunk once again.

Late stage. Blackouts increase (they may have begun in the early or middle stages). A blackout is a period of amnesia. The drinker is awake and active, but later remembers nothing about events that took place. Blackouts may last for seconds, minutes, hours, days, and even weeks.

The alcoholic becomes obsessed with drinking—constantly planning the next drink and unable to remember the last. Since every system in the body is affected by alcohol, physical damage begins to show up. Alcoholics drink not because they want to but because they have to. Now physically addicted, they experience withdrawal symptoms if they stop drinking.

In the late stage of alcoholism, alcoholics drink because they are afraid not to drink (fear of the shakes or of doing anything without a drink). Some alcoholics recall that in this stage they could not get drunk and they could not get sober; they were maintaining and medicating themselves with alcohol. The drink that started out as the alcoholic's friend has become a dangerous enemy. Late-stage alcoholics are no longer happy drunks but miserable, sick, guilty, paranoid, remorseful, and despairing slaves to the bottle.

ALCOHOLIC DENIAL

It is only a matter of time before alcoholism gets the alcoholic. The fortunate ones are those who recognize early on that they have the disease. The less fortunate, if they never admit their addiction, go right on drinking and face, at best, an early death. What keeps most alcoholics drinking too much, too often, and too long is their own denial of the problem. Alcoholics deny that there is a reason to stop drinking, and they say they can "stop any time."

Denial is the hallmark of alcoholism. It begins at the very beginning of alcoholic drinking. Alcoholics want to believe that they can control their drinking, that they are merely social drinkers. Even when the drinking is clearly not social, the alcoholic clings to the belief that his or her drinking is not that much different from anyone else's. Even as the evidence of abnormal drinking mounts, most alcoholics ignore the facts. The last thing alcoholics want to acknowledge is that they can't really drink safely—that they can't always tell when they'll be able to control their drinking and when they will not. As they start to lose more and more control, they make heroic but usually futile efforts to cut down on their drinking or go on the wagon. Some turn to drugs, either prescribed or illicit, as a way of decreasing their drinking; they trade one addiction for another. Especially in the case of prescription drugs—which are, in many circles, seen as more respectable, more socially acceptable, than illegal drugs or alcohol—this can result in even stronger denial.

Denial is deadly. As long as alcoholics deny their problem, they think there is no reason to do anything about the drinking, and so the disease progresses. It simply doesn't come to an end precisely *because* alcoholics don't believe they are afflicted. The disease, as described in the "Big Book," *Alcoholics Anonymous*, is "cunning, baffling, and powerful."

As discussed in Chapter 1, those closest to the alcoholic—family members, friends, bosses, physicians—are usually in denial too. Even in the final stages of chronic alcoholism, many of those close to the alcoholic still refuse to acknowledge the addiction. But, while all deniers help keep the disease in progress, the alcoholic, of course, does the lion's share of denying.

"My father was an alcoholic who died when I was seven," Susie, a middle-aged comptroller, told me. "Then my mother started to drink, but she always denied that it was a problem. I lived at home until I was thirty so I could take care of her. The final straw came when I got home and found my mother passed out on the sofa and her brother, who had come to live with us, passed out on the kitchen floor with a bottle next to him.

"That night I packed a suitcase and went to a friend's house. I never went back except to visit occasionally. My mother went downhill fast after I left; the last time I went home I had to get the police to let me in. She had passed out. We put her in a nursing home and she was there for five years, until she died. She was sober, she had no choice, so we were finally able to have some kind of a relationship. I visited twice a week and on holidays took her to my brother's home upstate. We had very nice visits and she wrote to me all the time.

"Every once in a while she would binge out in the nursing home on aspirin and Coca-Cola to get a caffeine high. I always thought these caffeine binges might remind her of her earlier episodes with compulsive, out-of-control behavior, but she never was able to admit her problem was alcoholism.

"Now I have to look at my denial of my own disease too. My own alcoholism really got out of control after my mother was gone. I had incredible fears and anxieties—feelings of impending doom. Naturally, I found the perfect psychiatrist, one who was willing to reinforce my denial. I told him I was missing work because of my drinking, but he said he didn't think that was so bad. I believed him for about a year until finally I couldn't deny it any longer. I knew I was losing control, so six years ago I went to AA. I've had a few slips since then, because I thought I could cure my own alcoholism. I learned the hard way that I couldn't.

"I think I have finally given up my denial. I hid my alcoholism for many years; most people didn't know. My own brother never saw me drunk and I don't think he really believes I'm an alcoholic. But, as long as I believe it, I know that help is available; and I'm no longer too proud or too independent to ask for it."

One way to make a dent in the family disease is to have those concerned about the alcoholic intervene in the denial process. Many alcoholics get into treatment because they are persuaded or coerced by someone who is no longer in denial. Getting an alcoholic sober, even against his or her will, can be the first step in breaking through denial. A sober alcoholic has less denial than a drunk one. Chapter 15 will explain the intervention process that may help you and your family break through the alcoholic's denial.

Occasionally, the alcoholic's denial breaks down before the rest of the family's. Sometimes the pain involved in being an alcoholic becomes so overwhelming that he or she "hits bottom." Confronted with utter despair, realizing his/her powerlessness over alcohol, he/she gives up the denial and gets into treatment. Children, the spouse, and parents may still be in denial themselves and say things to the recovering alcoholic like "You didn't drink that much," or "You were never a real alcoholic, you just drank a lot," or "You mean you can't have even one drink?"

Ben, now fifty-one, describes his wife's denial: "I realized my problem was alcohol long before she did. She was convinced I was only having a midlife crisis. I had lost my job of twelve years, had been hospitalized three times in six months, and was living in a sleazy hotel room. But she still didn't believe I was an alcoholic."

More often, however, the alcoholic is the last one in the family to give up denial. You may be the first person in your family to see the alcoholism in your parents, siblings, children, or yourself. And that vision may be the first sign of hope for the whole family.

· 5 ·

SEPARATING FACT FROM FICTION
—
TOOLS AND METHODS FOR REEXAMINING THE PAST

Adult children of alcoholics can learn a great deal about themselves by studying their family histories. In order to break the cycle of alcoholism as adults we need to understand how our self-destructive patterns of behavior were established. We also need to discover the link between the old events in our personal histories and the problems in our current lives. These old patterns and problems may have persisted through several generations of our families. But we can take positive action now to stop the cycle and begin our own recovery.

The degree to which an illness or a family disruption affects family members depends upon many factors: birth order, severity of the disorder, compensating influences, temperament, age, and the weakness or strength of relationships within the family. Each of these factors influences the impact of an alcoholic family's disorganization on individual family members.

As we've seen in earlier chapters, outdated family rules and patterns of behavior create serious problems in all of our current relationships, intimate ones as well as those with co-workers, friends, and family members. Each person brings his or her own habits and expectations to a new relationship. And people who have rigid rules tend to use them to see how other people measure up to their expectations. This kind of rigid adherence to old rules can wreak havoc on a relationship; no one can fit another person's measurements.

When two people become romantically involved, they bring with them many scripts from the past: patterns of behavior and interaction that were prominent in their families of origin. For example, one of my patients, a young woman raised in a family where the mother and grandmother took charge of everything while her father drank, automatically assumed a similar role with her new husband. She tried to control every detail of their life together and was quite bewildered at her husband's displeasure with the arrangement. She thought that that was a woman's function in the family, that that was how everyone got their bills paid and their weekend activities planned. Frequently people are quite unaware of these scripts and where they came from. But awareness can often help us to understand present behavior that otherwise might seem baffling.

"All at once I realized why my husband and brother were being so competitive and angry with each other," said thirty-four-year-old Lizzie. "First of all, they're both ACOAs and oldest sons in their families. Second, my husband's father was at sea the first two years of his life. When he came home, my husband was no longer the apple of his mother's eyes: his father was. He tends to experience all men as intruding on his space, getting the attention he feels belongs to him. My brother was visiting us for a few days, and my husband kept complaining that I was making a big fuss over my brother and that I was ignoring him. This is an old familiar feeling for my husband; and I think my brother's visit reactivated those old feelings that he wasn't so important after all.

"My brother, on the other hand, had a very competitive relationship with our younger brother. He's very accustomed to being boss—and the bully. He's very unhappy if he's not running the show. So he was hardly thrilled when my husband made all the plans for what we'd do during his three-day visit with us. They had a very difficult time with each other."

Exploring the past may provide you with a context in which to ask questions you may never have asked before, and to find answers that may contradict previous beliefs. It's not merely the chance to write (record) family history but, in a sense, to rewrite it—truthfully. Family lore often evolves from fiction rather than fact; thoroughly exploring your family history will help dispel myths and establish facts. The tools outlined in this chapter often become the vehicles for sharing family secrets and discussing matters that weren't allowed to be revealed in the past.

GENOGRAMS

A family tree, or genogram, that graphically maps your history over three generations is a valuable tool for ACOA recovery. Many of the ACOA patients have found the genogram, developed by family therapist Murray Bowen, helpful in illustrating alcoholic family patterns.

The aim of drawing a genogram is to paint an accurate and understandable picture, and to instill hope for change in your future. The genogram portrays intergenerational family problems but also shows signs of normal family functioning. For instance, the genogram might show that for three generations most family members graduated from college and held public-service jobs. One family may have a tradition of community involvement and service, while another family may have, through several generations, built up a successful family business.

A genogram should cast an accurate yet sympathetic, rather than a harshly critical, view on your family. Many alcoholic families survive against all odds; seeing the many odds can lead to your being more even-minded and generous about yourself. You can view yourself as a survivor and a success. Almost any situation can be viewed in either a negative or a positive way. Certainly the positive view makes infinitely more sense for us as recoverers.

Genograms should be drawn honestly and then looked at in the most objective way possible. It is important to recognize the pleasurable and positive events, as well as the painful and negative events, in your family history. Constructing your family tree should be a healing process, one that validates your past experiences and clarifies your present problems in ways that can open your eyes to the possibilities of change. Drawing a genogram, and collecting the pertinent data for it, will give you a chance to explore details connected with the lives and deaths of your parents and grandparents. It often sheds light on incidents and intrigues—and it can reveal patterns and uncover secrets that have been in your family for several generations.

It can help you see connections you may never before have noticed. For instance, a genogram may show that the early death of an alcoholic father was closely followed by a daughter's early marriage to a young man with a serious drinking problem. It can reveal intergenerational patterns of family conflicts or alliances that help to explain relationships in a new way. It might, for instance, reveal that the oldest son in each generation had a conflicted and distant relationship with his father. Seeing this on paper could alleviate some of the guilt and self-blame felt by a son who is currently involved in a similar relationship. In this way, a genogram can provide you with a better understanding of yourself in the context of your family history.

Formats for constructing genograms vary from fairly simple to extremely complex. The basic symbols are:

□   = Male.
○   = Female.
⊠⊗ = Died. Write year, age, and cause of death next to symbol.
m   = Married. Insert year and place.
—//—   = Divorced.
═══   = Close bond between two family members.
〰〰   = Conflict between two family members.
A,D,E = Alcohol, drug, or eating disorder. Place letter on top of the symbol for that person.
PA, SA = Physical or sexual abuse. Place the letters on top of the symbol for that person.

In addition, you may come up with symbols of your own to represent events or character traits of particular interest to you.

Next to each person's symbol, major events can be written: "1953 contracted polio" or "Army '60–'62." There is usually a "hero" and "scapegoat" in each generation. These or other short character descriptions can go directly under the symbol for that person: "hero," "scholar," "mother's pet," "violent." Since "secrets" are so big in most alcoholic families, it's helpful to spell out the family secrets right on the genogram; it's a graphic way of getting them out in the open. You can make your own list of things you are most interested in learning about your family.

Whatever other information you want to diagram can be added. You might be very interested in occupations and map those out. Someone else might want to see how an illness like cancer or heart trouble repeats in the generations. You may want to concentrate on things like educational levels, moving patterns, marital patterns (many divorces, none, etc.), crisis reactions, etc. Themes, myths, rules, expectations, concerns, isolation patterns, and current whereabouts can all be used to illustrate the structure and functioning of your family.

In alcoholic families it is particularly important to look for "accidents," disappearances and untimely deaths or hospitalizations, and possible signs of the disease in past or current generations. For instance, the genogram of one of my patients showed that one of her brothers had left home at age thirty. While that in itself does not seem like such a significant event, she explained to me that no one had heard from him since and that no one had made any attempt to find him. She admitted that he had had a long history of drinking and going on binges, when he would disappear for weeks or months at a time. But, at the time the genogram was done, he had been away for twelve years!

Another patient's genogram included an uncle who had died when he was only forty-two. Although the family had insisted for years that he had died of arteriosclerosis (clue one), in preparing the genogram my patient also discovered that his uncle had a very poor work history and was considered the "financial failure" of a very wealthy, successful family (clues two and three). This additional information, coupled with the early death, raised my patient's suspicions that his uncle may have had a drinking problem.

Remember to look for subtle clues that might point to the presence of alcoholism in your family history. "Teetotaling," for instance, which at first glance would seem to rule out alcoholism, often signals the presence of the disease in an earlier generation. Although alcoholism often appears peppered throughout a family's history, it can—and often does—skip a generation. If your grandfather, for example, worked very hard to "control" his drinking, it may have been in response to the alcoholism of one of his parents. He may have practiced what many alcoholics describe as "white knuckle" sobriety. Drinking was still a problem for him because he was obsessed with not drinking, a preoccupation that took tremendous energy and may have kept him from enjoying life. In preparing your own genogram, keep your eyes open for the more subtle signs like teetotaling.

SAMPLE GENOGRAM

Jane, a forty-year-old woman who identifies herself as the "black sheep" of her family, prepared the following genogram. An alcoholic who has been sober for two years, Jane also had two alcoholic parents. Both her mother, who died in 1980 of a heart attack, and her mother's mother were diabetic. Her father died of cancer when he was fifty. The family never acknowledged that her parents' deaths had anything to do with their alcoholism. Both of Jane's maternal grandparents were born in Ireland, but they met and married in this country. Both of these grandparents died at relatively young ages: sixty and fifty.

Jane's father, Joe, the "black sheep" of his family, died of stomach cancer in 1970. His three-year imprisonment for assault was the most closely guarded secret in his family. Like Jane, her father was both an alcoholic and an ACOA. But, like his own father, Joe married a woman who, supposedly, was not an alcoholic.

As the genogram on the next page shows, although they battled among themselves, both Jane and her younger sister, Jill, felt very close to their maternal grandmother. Her younger sister also felt strong ties with her mother, feelings which Jane, who had a stormy relationship with her mother, did not share. Jane, the middle child, was close to her brother John, now married and the father of two boys. The family hero, John apparently has no problem with alcohol.

This genogram reveals clear family patterns that Jane found helpful in understanding herself. She could plainly see that alcoholism was present in each generation—on both sides of the family. Other recurring family illnesses were cancer and diabetes. She noticed that a scapegoat, the acting-out black sheep, existed in each generation—and each one of them was an alcoholic.

This is just some of the information you can include in drawing your own genogram. Obviously the genogram cannot answer every question about a family's history, and may in fact raise many more questions that would be interesting to ask. For Jane, though, the genogram gave the first clear picture of her family's history, particularly in terms of the disease of alcoholism.

Sharing with other family members the secrets you discover can contribute positively to their recovery—and your own. You may find it valuable to ask your siblings or partners to prepare their own family trees separately and then come together to compare and discuss them. It's interesting to see how differently events and people are perceived by several members of the same family. This joint process can open up communication and help family members separate family fact from fiction.

It can also be helpful to go over your genogram with someone you trust outside the family: a good friend or a therapist, for instance. Studying the genogram with someone outside the family can often spark questions that might reveal further valuable information. And this kind of discussion often results in demystifying the family system.

It can bring out feelings that family members have long tried to avoid and can pinpoint areas of conflict you may never have noticed before. An unbiased eye can discover previously unseen strengths and weaknesses in each member, as well as in your family as a whole. Most important, having someone outside the family assist in exploring your

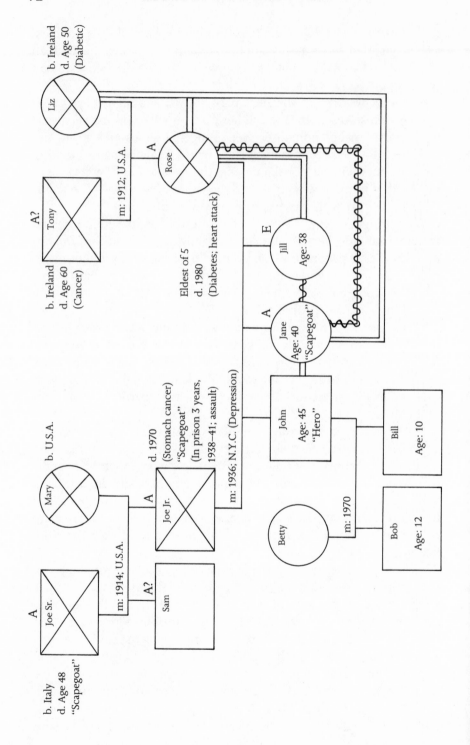

genogram can broaden your perspective and challenge long-held assumptions and beliefs.

FAMILY TAPES

Making a tape recording of relatives talking about their histories is an excellent way to learn more about your past. An oral biography becomes an important family "document" that can be passed down to future generations—it's a living record of the family heritage.

The actual process of recording can be a warm and involved emotional experience for both you and the people you interview. You will probably feel closer and more connected as you learn new things about your family. Family members generally feel closer when they know more about each other. The oral biography session gives them the opportunity to discover a new richness in communication and to uncover family truths together. (Truth is not only stranger than fiction —it's usually much more intriguing.) An interview for a family history can often bring family secrets, like alcoholism, out into the open.

Sharing one's life story is apt to be welcomed and appreciated; few relatives object to the exercise. People are generally flattered that others, particularly their own children, are interested in their experiences and opinions. They also feel better about themselves when they are perceived as authorities on any subject. You may be surprised at how little resistance you meet.

Creating the proper atmosphere is crucial to a family taping. Obviously you should not show up, unannounced and unexpected, with a tape recorder in hand. Adequate preparation is not only polite, it allows your relative to get used to the idea and to start thinking about the past. He or she may need time to decide that your family heritage is worth saving.

If you want to tape an oral biography, you could say something like this: "I've been doing a lot of thinking about our family lately, and I'd really like to learn more about our history. Because I'm sure you know much more than I do, I'd like it if you could share your memories with me so that I can pass along our heritage to my own children someday. I'd love to ask you some questions so that I could get the facts straight. Could I come by someday soon and bring my questions and a tape recorder? That way I could tape our conversation and then make a copy of the tape for you too."

A group interview can be fun too, if you want to interview several family members together. The reminiscences of one person will usually jog someone else's memory of the same event; family anecdotes and jokes will liven up the taping. Humor is almost always a sign of family health, and in family fact-finding, good times are just as important as bad times.

The family tape session is an equal-opportunity exercise: it's just as important for you to share feelings and experiences as it is for your relatives. Family taping can provide the time to say all the things you may want to say but seldom get around the saying. Enhancing communication, the taping exercise can provide satisfying emotional releases for everyone involved. The end result is not just a tape but a mutually better understanding of the way things were, are, and can be. It validates everyone in the family.

Your taping session should be open-ended, but you will find it helpful to have certain questions in mind or written down to prompt thoughts and replies. If you do use a list of prepared questions, it's important not to get locked into asking only those questions. Allowing for spontaneity leads to a pleasurable experience. There should be plenty of time allowed for expressions of anger, joy, sadness, laughter, and whatever other feelings emerge during the taping.

Since these interviews often prove to be emotionally draining, it is important to be sensitive to all participants. Ask only those questions you feel relatively comfortable with; there is something to be said for letting some sleeping dogs lie. For instance, while it might be necessary to get the history of drinking behavior out in the open, it might not be appropriate to ask a terminally ill parent about the illness if he or she clearly doesn't want to discuss impending death. Controversies are counter-productive to family tapings. Oral-biography tapings shouldn't be occasions to fire up or fight old family feuds. Judgmental attitudes are out of place and are not recommended for the family tapes. At the time of taping, for instance, an incest victim should not bring this subject up with the abusive parent. With a great deal of preparation and support, you might find such a confrontation necessary and valuable under other circumstances, but the taping exercise does not lend itself to this kind of discussion.

You might find some of the following questions helpful in getting the taping under way. From these starting points, let the conversation branch off in any direction you all feel comfortable with.

- Where and when were you born? What was happening in your family at that time?

- I would like to know something about your grandparents, parents, and siblings. How would you describe them? What was your relationship with each one when you were young? Now?
- Do you remember any special events in their lives or funny or sad stories about them?
- Did they ever have any problems that may have been related to excessive drinking, like accidents or job losses?
- Did their drinking ever cause you concern? How?
- Did your parents have any kind of physical or emotional problems? What was their drinking like?
- What about the drinking (or drugging) of your other relatives (aunts, uncles, grandparents, siblings)? How did it affect you?
- What was it like for you growing up?
- What do you remember about your school days and work experiences?
- What were the most valuable lessons you learned in your life?
- Were you raised with any kind of religious or spiritual guidance? What did it mean to you then and what does it mean to you now?
- Can you tell me about your married (or single or widowed) life?
- What has given you the most satisfaction in your life? Do you have any unfulfilled dreams?
- Is there anything you feel ashamed about or sorry for? What are your regrets?
- What would you have done differently if you had a chance to live your life again?
- Are there any particular thoughts or memories that come to mind that we haven't talked about today?

You probably will not want, or need, to ask all of these questions in your family tape. The material will most likely flow without a great deal of structure. Remember that the process is much more important than the specific answers to questions; the feelings should be as revealing as the facts. It's nice to elicit an educated history—but it's even nicer to feel that the process has brought you closer to one another.

FAMILY PHOTOGRAPHS

Looking at a family album can provide new insights for adult children working on personal recovery; old snapshots are a great source of information and healing.

There are many ways you can look at family photographs. Are the people in them looking or standing in characteristic ways? Is dad always off to the side and looking bored? Is this the way he was in the family? Are there many scenic views with few people in them? Was your family more interested in seeing the sights than in being involved with one another? Was your brother John always holding on to your mother like this? Was he her favorite? Did your sister Sally always duck her head? Was this because she felt isolated from the rest of you? Photographs may not be worth a thousand words, but they certainly are worth scrutiny; they always serve to bring back memories.

An exercise that is usually very healing is for you to find photographs of your parents at the age you are now. Looking at your mother or father at your age and trying to develop a "day-in-the-life" view of what his or her experience must have been at that time can be enlightening, building both sympathy and understanding.

Caroline, an actress in her early thirties, told me: "I thought about my mother's life when she was the age I am now. All the family pictures from that time show her with two small children clinging to her side, but there are very few pictures of my father. In more ways than one, he was really 'out of the picture.' He was drinking very heavily, spending little time at home. And my mother kept going into the hospital. At the time it was more annoying than alarming. I used to think she was a hypochondriac. I couldn't see that she must have been suffering emotionally. But I can imagine if I had her concerns at my age I might end up in a hospital too, from sheer exhaustion, hopelessness, and frustration. My father got sober a year later but that last year of his drinking had to be terrible for her.

"I used to feel she was always sick, unsupportive of me. I recently looked at photos of me as a teenager, and I looked very sullen. She'd always ask me about my high school friends and I hated that. I always thought she was too nosy. I'm sure I wasn't a delightful daughter, either. Maybe she was just trying to show she was interested in me.

"Looking at the family pictures helped me to see things differently. I don't feel nearly so critical of her. I feel more compassionate. I understand her lack of energy. The next time I visit, I plan to ask her about what her life was really like when she was my age."

Another possibility is to have a photo session with a good friend—you can both look at photographs of your respective families—pointing out observations and asking questions about what the photographs show. Both of you can discuss your perceptions and the realities of what was going on in each family at the time the pictures were taken.

You could also use the photographs to open up discussions with parents and siblings about your recollections and present thoughts. If there aren't any photographs of a particular period, you might want to ask about what was happening in the family at that point. The lack of photographs can be as telling as the existence of others.

Looking at family photographs often reminds us that there were many good times as well as troubled ones. In reexamining the past to pave the way for present recovery, we have to reexperience *all* our feelings and needs, but sometimes we forget that things did not seem so bad before the family alcoholism got bad. Alcoholism is a progressive illness and it probably took years for the losses of family, friends, jobs, psychological and physical health to occur. Pleasurable feelings about the good times of childhood can be recaptured as well as the painful feelings of loss.

"Several months ago I called my cousin, my best friend when we were growing up, to see if she had any family photos I could borrow," Melissa, a forty-year-old chef, told me. "Since then we've been meeting for dinner every other week—after not spending any time together for over twenty years.

"We're both in therapy now and I'm also in ACOA. It's a lot of fun talking about old times, and it's interesting to see how alcoholism was such a big influence in both of our families. It's also very nice to have her friendship again."

Looking through photo albums can give us a great deal of hope for the present and future. It can help rekindle old friendships and bring back many warm feelings. And these good feelings give us hope by showing us that we do have a foundation on which we can build our present and future happiness.

A PERSONAL JOURNAL

Keeping a journal can help you explore your past, get in touch with your feelings, and chart your personal recovery. A journal is a private book in which you can write about anger, resentment, disappointment, without fearing rejection or retribution. Writing sometimes has the immediate effect of bringing relief and satisfaction. Of course, you can write about positive as well as negative experiences and feelings in your journal. History and hope can both have a place in the journal you keep.

You can write about both past and present feelings and events in your journal. Writing about the past can give you a new perspective on old feelings and events. And writing about the present, how you feel about yourself and others with each new day, can give you a concrete sense of the ways you are changing. In this way, your journal can become a personal record of your progress toward recovery.

P·A·R·T·II

REFORMING THE PRESENT

· 6 ·

A COMMITMENT TO RECOVERY
EMBRACING THE PROCESS OF CHANGE

The process of recovery can be likened to that of restoring old paintings. In restoring a masterpiece, the darkness on the surface of the painting has to be removed very carefully in order to get to the original brilliance beneath. An alcoholic family becomes shrouded in darkness as the family system becomes sicker. In recovery ACOAs must try to regain the brightness that lies beneath their gloomy surfaces. Masterpieces may be damaged, but that doesn't mean they are destroyed. They simply need expert, loving attention—just what we need too.

THE POWER OF PAIN

The emotional scars from growing up in families with chronic illness are frequently quite deep, and continue to be painful long after childhood. But pain, emotional or physical, can serve as a very healthy sign that something is amiss and something needs to be changed. Pain can pave the way for change, major change. Acknowledging, and once more experiencing, old pains is an essential part of the healing process. It can spur us to search for new ways to get out of pain and find some pleasure in our lives.

81

REFUSING TO PLAY THE VICTIM

At some time in our lives, most of us realize that we have allowed ourselves to be victimized by other people both inside and outside of our alcoholic households. No one likes this feeling and, sooner or later, we decide not to play the victim anymore.

"I have to work very hard today not to buy into my late father's philosophy of life, which was very pessimistic," said Rob, a thirty-two-year-old ACOA trying to overcome persistent depression. "He viewed the world as a horrible place where no one would help; you had to resign yourself to misery. He was a very unhappy alcoholic. He never allowed anyone to make his life at all easier.

"He was a bookkeeper in the same firm for over twenty years and never took a vacation, never asked for a raise, and didn't even have health insurance. Even when he was in the hospital dying of cancer all he could talk about was how he had to get back to work.

"I used to have tremendous anger at the company where he worked: he saved them thousands of dollars and he died penniless. But I see now that he let them take advantage of him. He programmed himself to be the victim.

"I identify very much with my father and don't want to end up with nothing the way he did. I think that's why I push myself to get help. I've been in therapy and now I go to an ACOA group. I'm determined to get the help I know I need. I've suffered with depression on and off all my life but I don't want to give in to it and feel as hopeless as he always did. He was definitely a victim; I refuse to be one."

Exploring past pain and gaining an understanding of the reasons why so many things felt "wrong" long ago can help push us toward recovery as adults. If you feel you have not yet gained an understanding of the ways your past has had an impact on your life today, you may find it useful to reread Part I of this book carefully.

A COMMITMENT TO CHANGE

Understanding what went wrong in the past is only the first step in our present recovery. To recover fully, we next need to make a firm commitment to present change, to making ourselves better today. Approaching recovery as a monumental task can prove intimidating and forbidding. But seeing it as a series of small steps can make the road to recovery much more accessible. You can change yourself little by little, day by day. But in order to do so you have to make a commitment to change today.

Shortly after Betsy had graduated from college, her older sister first confronted her with the suspicion that their father was an alcoholic. Betsy first reacted with anger and disbelief. But over time her sister's suspicions, coupled with her own dawning awareness of a possible connection between her father's drinking and her mother's serious depression, convinced Betsy to give up her denial.

"I've always had a rivalry with my sister," Betsy explained, "so the very fact that she was going to Al-Anon and trying to get me to go was reason enough not to go. Five years later I went to my first ACOA meeting only because I was so miserable and my therapy didn't seem to be helping much.

"In the beginning, I was intimidated by how well people could verbalize their feelings and talk about what was going on in their lives. It took me a long time to be able to speak at meetings, and I didn't approach people or take telephone numbers for many months. But I did keep feeling better, so I kept on going.

"I made a commitment to myself that I was going to do everything I could for my recovery. I was going to make it my number one priority. I decided that I was going to fully participate in the program—go to two or three ACOA meetings a week and make new friends.

"It was as if I finally had the courage to take charge of my life: to use the program, as well as group therapy and couples therapy with my husband, to do better. It's been a very busy year and a half, but I definitely feel all this work is paying off. I can now express my feelings to people, especially my anger, in a constructive way. I'm trying not to be so hard on myself since I realize I'm my own severest critic—usually the only critic. I'm much less depressed these days and my depressions don't last so long. My communication with people has dramatically improved.

"I really accept Al-Anon and ACOA on blind faith. One of the slogans is 'Utilize, don't analyze' and that's what I try to do. I know one thing for sure: the program saved my life."

It takes a great deal of will power and focused desire to take such significant steps to better one's life, but Betsy has made a commitment to recovery. She realizes that her background—growing up in an alcoholic home—can never change. But she also knows that she can change her own attitudes and behavior. She now seizes opportunities to make positive changes in her life rather than hiding from them.

WANTING CHANGE

Simply wanting change can motivate us to look for new paths, even though they may at first seem frightening and formidable. The process of change can be frightening, painful, and even overwhelming. Like most people, children of alcoholic parents may resist change. We all tend to hang on to the familiar with amazing tenacity, avoiding change until our backs are to the wall. The unknown is almost always more frightening than the known, and people prefer the discomfort they know to the unpredictable results of change that they can only imagine.

But change can also be challenging, exciting, and ultimately rewarding. Fear goes with the territory, of course, but each small step on new terrain we are willing to take will expand the territory of our lives and fill us with a new joy and satisfaction. Reexamining and relinquishing the past offer real promise for the present and future. Once people see the rewards of adopting new roles, roles that work for them, they begin to accept them. And because change often begets more change, welcoming change today will not only make today better, but it will also pave the way for better tomorrows.

It is universally true that we all want change and yet we all don't want change. That is, we seek it yet we resist it. We also usually want someone else to change, to make things different. But things are only different when *we* make the difference. We have the power to change ourselves, but we can't change anyone else.

We tend to be impatient; we look for the quick fix. Once we decide we want to make some changes, we want them to have taken place yesterday. We start to think we should act as soon as we have an insight. Seeing a problem, we want to solve it immediately.

RECOVERY IS A LIFELONG PROCESS

But change takes time and recovery often proceeds in small steps. An earnest, lifelong commitment to recovery means we have to try to get a little better with each new day. As Lois, an ACOA in individual therapy, explained, "I don't think anyone becomes one hundred percent cured of anything. I have to stay alert every day to avoid slipping back into my old self-destructive habits. I feel I'll always be in recovery. Recovery makes me think of those little ducks that you see in carnival shooting galleries: they keep popping up. You shoot one down and another pops up. But I'm committed to taking care of each new problem as it comes up. I feel like I finally have a handle on my problems and can deal with my fears as they come up."

Recovery is an ongoing process and learning to change usually takes practice. Gwen, a thirty-three-year-old student, described how she practiced speaking up: "I was always very, very quiet. When my father was institutionalized, I was five years old. I was terrified that I might go crazy and be taken away too. I remember my mother telling a neighbor that she had to commit my father and a few days later he was gone. He just disappeared from the family and no one ever mentioned him again. I didn't dare expose myself as fragile so I didn't do anything to call attention to myself. People would always say to my mother, 'She's so quiet—what's wrong with her?'

"Finally someone told me about ACOA and I started going to meetings there eight months ago. I love the meeting and go every week. One of the Twelve Steps is discussed each time. I decided that I really want to participate and be part of this group, so I give myself a homework assignment every week. I read the step carefully and make a few notes. Then, when I get to the meeting, I make myself say at least something about the step, even if it's only a sentence. I actually feel very different when I'm able to do that. It feels good to be part of the group, not just an observer. I can see that I'm gradually beginning to feel more comfortable with people, more relaxed about sharing."

We need to be encouraged to take our time, and come to appreciate the fact that the changes that come about slowly are usually the ones that last. Someone about to change needs to be convinced emotionally as well as intellectually that yes, I am ready to make this change today.

RECOVERY ONE STEP AT A TIME To reinforce the idea that he was responsible for his own recovery, and that it would take time, Joe made himself a list, every day for weeks, of what he'd actually accomplished during the day. He'd taken out the garbage, paid bills, walked the dog, spoken up at a meeting. Then he'd make a list of what he hoped to do the next day, and then the next. As he said, it had taken him years to get sick, so he wasn't going to get well overnight.

"Coming from a family with alcoholism, in poverty, made me feel frightened as I was growing up, and I still have some of those same fears. I've had terrible anxieties about money all of my life. My fear is that I'm going to end up penniless and alone," said Joann, a fifty-one-year-old mother of four college students.

"Most people look at me and think I'm successful, since I have a nice apartment, a good job, and dress well. But, even though I've achieved a great deal, I feel insecure and worry about what might happen. I've worked for thirty years and have never been without a job or a roof over my head. So why do I imagine I'll end up on the street? It's totally irrational, but it's an enduring fear.

"We were poor when I was a kid—in fact, we were on welfare and I always felt very ashamed of that. The day the welfare check arrived, my father would cash it in at the local tavern and stay there until it was all gone. My mother took in washing and ironing so we'd have something to eat. We never knew where the next meal was coming from or when we'd be moving out of the apartment in the middle of the night because we were behind in the rent.

"I have to keep reminding myself of today's reality: I have always been able to support myself, I have a good job and money in the bank. I know I'm not able to enjoy what I have today when I worry so much about what might happen tomorrow."

People generally strive to get what they want, and ACOAs are no exception. When the issue of psychic pain is involved, we have a choice of staying in pain or getting out of it. Most of the ACOAs I've met—both in and out of my practice—exhibit a strong and healthy desire to get out of pain and into pleasure. While we may have a great deal of ambiguity about what pleasure is and how to find it, most of us want to find a way, and usually do, to make our present lives less painful than our pasts.

CHANGING OUR VIEW OF OURSELVES AND THE WORLD

To make the leap from what was to what is often takes considerable renegotiation with one's self-image and the world. This renegotiation involves learning to view the world as a more loving and less hostile place, a task made much easier by sharing (speaking and listening) experiences and feelings with a group of people you trust. And it takes changing the concept of self from negative to positive. Recognizing our own strengths (see Chapter 12), instead of dwelling on our weaknesses, can help us cultivate a more positive self-image.

Growing up feeling worthless doesn't mean we *are* worthless; growing up feeling unloved doesn't mean we are unloveable. Growing up fearful of people, places, and things doesn't mean we have to stay afraid. Growing up with guilty feelings doesn't mean we can't learn to forgive ourselves. Growing up in unmanageability doesn't mean life is still unmanageable. Growing up not talking doesn't mean we can't ever talk. Growing up in a sick family doesn't mean we have to stay sick. It's true that we can only change ourselves—but that's actually quite a lot.

PERSONAL RECOVERY

The ACOAs who achieve the best results are those who put in the hard work necessary to make significant changes. Others can help us make these changes, but ultimately we must initiate change ourselves. By exploring and honestly evaluating our pasts, we can often map out new territory for ourselves. We can use self-help books and exercises to discover new ways of getting our present needs met. Psychotherapy or counseling—whether one to one, couples, family, or group—with a well-trained and experienced person familiar with ACOA issues can lead to significant insights and behavioral changes. Self-help groups like ACOA provide safe, supportive atmospheres for airing family secrets. Reading literature about ACOAs and attending workshops, conferences, and rehabilitation centers can also help us.

There is no best answer. When we make a commitment to recovery, it doesn't matter whether we choose professional therapy, self-help groups, both of them, or any other method to help us make these changes—just as long as we make them. Every individual recovery can be viewed as a personal journey. Each person has to decide for himself or herself which journey seems most appropriate at a particular time. Fortunately, we have many strategies to choose from. Only one thing is certain: once we've begun this journey, we'll never be the same again.

· 7 ·

SELF-HELP GROUPS
──
A SAFE PLACE
FOR A CHANGE

As you have seen, you can take a great number of steps toward recovery on your own. Indeed, the first steps—admitting you have a problem and making a commitment to recovery—must begin with yourself. In addition to all the work you can do on your own, however, you may find more help from group experiences with other adult children of alcoholics and from various types of therapy. Groups, particularly, can be "second-chance families," providing you with an opportunity to work through problems from the past in a mutually supportive atmosphere. In this chapter and the next, you will read about the great variety of self-help groups and professional therapies that can help you in your efforts to make the changes you want to make in your life.

In reading these chapters, keep in mind that not everyone feels the same way about each of these treatment programs. What may seem helpful to one person may not work for someone else. Choosing the path you want to take is a very individual choice; the information presented here will help you make that choice a wise one.

All of the groups and therapies considered in these chapters have one important feature in common: they provide a safe place for you to open up, to take the risk of making yourself vulnerable. Each of them can provide the security and support you may never have received as a child. They will encourage you to talk, to feel, and to trust. They will allow you to break away from the obsolete rules and roles of your childhood. Everyone needs a safe place where they can let down their defenses—these groups and therapies can be that place for you.

"I was at this pretty wild party a few years ago," Sara told me. "There was a lot of heavy drinking and people were taking drugs and I really felt out of it. But I found someone I knew and we sat in a corner talking. One man was circling the room in a hostile way—he kept going up to people and trying to start something. At one point he came right up to me and said loudly, 'Isn't it about time you left?' and then lurched off. I was *petrified*."

Sara smiled faintly at the recollection. "I decided to leave—it was all I could do not to run out of the room. I was putting on my coat in the bedroom when another man, a nice-looking older man, came in and introduced himself before asking, very gently as if he really cared, 'Which one of your parents is an alcoholic?' I was flabbergasted. I asked him how in the world he knew this about me and he said, 'I knew you'd grown up with an alcoholic because you didn't know how to deal with that man's drunken anger.' "

It was soon after that, Sara said, that she went to her first meeting of Al-Anon/ACOA. She had been in therapy for some time, trying to work through the problems of a childhood marred by her mother's alcoholism and her father's physical and sexual abuse.

"For years I went to workshops, trying to get rid of all the pain inside. But nothing worked. It took me a long time to get to Al-Anon and ACOA because I felt that the alcoholism belonged to my family and not to me. I didn't want to have anything to do with it; I didn't want to get close to alcoholism again. But I finally went to a meeting because a friend of mine who had joined Al-Anon a few years earlier kept insisting. And the first time I stepped into the room, I felt I was home. The people there had the same feelings I had always had and never felt I could share with anyone. In every social situation I'd ever been in, I felt like a stranger. At ACOA I was finally one of the crowd.

"It was the only place I'd ever found where I didn't have to be the oldest. I didn't have to shoulder all that responsibility I was so used to carrying. It was a luxury not to have to take care of anyone but myself. I went to three meetings a week."

Sara paused. "I finally learned that you make yourself safe from the inside out, not the other way around. All my life I had been looking for things outside myself to take away the pain and of course that never worked. The program has given me the spiritual foundation I use in my daily life.

"The kind of identification I felt at meetings made me begin to see how these people could have feelings of love for one another. I got a lot of help from the most unlikely people. I came to see that someone can be different from me in every respect and yet share the same feelings and behavior. I could even identify with alcoholics who beat their kids the way I'd been beaten.

"I think I was like many ACOAs who have been so spiritually ravaged that at first they don't want to know they have lost their spiritual life. But the program teaches me that the God of my understanding is in everyone. It is the basis for my being utterly without fear of other people. Before the program I was afraid of *everyone*.

"I know I have to take care of myself. I also know I can't do it alone."

ALCOHOLICS ANONYMOUS

Tom, a thirty-eight-year-old alcoholism counselor, expressed concern about ACOAs with their own substance-abuse problems. "I think some recovering alcoholics who go to ACOA start focusing on their parents' addictions and forget about their own. They find ACOA meetings much more emotional, get bored with AA, and stop going to meetings. I think these people have to be reminded that they need to stick with AA also; they need to try to take responsibility for making their meetings more interesting."

If you think you have a problem with your drinking you can test yourself with "What Are the Signs of Alcoholism?" on page 257. And if you are one of many adult children of alcoholics who grew up to become an alcoholic yourself, you must make sobriety the first task of your recovery. Alcoholics Anonymous can help you achieve sobriety.

Universally recognized as the most successful treatment program for alcoholics, AA is the progenitor of other self-help groups, such as Al-Anon (for the family and friends of alcoholics), Alateen (for teenage children of alcoholics), Gamblers Anonymous, Overeaters Anonymous, and Narcotics Anonymous, all of which base their own philosophies on AA's. All of these have adopted AA's Twelve Steps, reprinted on pages 266–267, as the basis for members' recovery. Although some outsiders regard AA as a mysterious program, its Twelve Steps convey wisdom that most people, whether from alcoholic families or not, can easily apply as guiding principles in their lives.

AA is a voluntary fellowship of men and women who believe that to maintain their own sobriety they must "give it away": to stay sober, they attend meetings in which they share their experience, strength, and hope with other alcoholics—those who are still active drinkers as well as those who have achieved sobriety.

The AA program began in 1935, when two men, a surgeon and a one-time stockbroker, both considered hopeless drunkards, found they could stay sober by helping each other. They began to carry this simple message of their own experience to other alcoholics. The basic principles of the AA program, which now has millions of members all over the world, appear on pages 266–267.

Practical experience is convincing; nothing so much ensures an alcoholic's sobriety as intensive work with other alcoholics. It works when all else has failed.

AL-ANON

All too often, those of us who don't grow up to be alcoholics ourselves choose partners who are alcoholics. If you are living with an alcoholic, Al-Anon can help you deal with the particular anxieties, pain, and problems associated with this difficult situation, and especially with the effects of co-dependency.

Al-Anon, founded in 1951 by the wife of one of the two men who founded AA, is made up of families and friends of alcoholics, who meet regularly in groups.

Virginia, a teacher in her early sixties, told me: "I feel very comfortable at my Al-Anon meeting after only a few times. I'm able to speak and unburden my fears and anxieties and stresses. I no longer feel lonely.

"Our group ranges in ages from twenty to seventy, and everyone is warm, friendly, compassionate, and understanding—they even find humor in their situations. I love the group and can't tell you what it has done for me. It's such a relief to know that there are others who are hurting too, that I'm not alone. It gives me hope that maybe my husband will eventually go to AA. But, whether he does or not, I'm taking care of myself. One of my readings says, 'Healing is as contagious as sickness and when one family member seeks help and overcomes grief, in time others will move forward toward a recovery also.'

"I plan to go to an open AA meeting soon so I can hear the alcoholic's perspective about the illness. Al-Anon is a real life-saver, and I'm hanging on tightly."

Living with the effects of someone else's drinking is too devastating for most of us to bear without help. Therefore, Al-Anon's focus, described in more detail on pages 267–268, is on its members, rather than on the alcoholics in their lives. Some people are disappointed when they go to their first meeting and do not get the "how to's" about stopping someone they love from drinking. But they soon learn that each of us can only be responsible for himself or herself. In Al-Anon family members can get the love and support they need to make changes that will allow them to feel better, not necessarily help to get the alcoholic sober. One of Al-Anon's basic principles is "I didn't cause it [alcoholism], I can't control it, and I can't cure it."

DETACHMENT

Al-Anon teaches its members the concept of "tough love," also known as "detachment," which means letting go of an obsession with someone else's behavior—putting some distance between oneself and the alcoholic. Detachment teaches us to help *ourselves* recover from the adverse effects alcoholism has had on *our* lives.

Theresa, a thirty-year-old artist in Al-Anon, told me: "Detachment was a difficult concept for me to understand when I first went to meetings. It's not the 'cool aloofness' I imagined it to be. It's a way of not reacting and not overreacting. It's not getting obsessed with someone the way I used to get obsessive about whomever I was seeing. I used to be very jealous and overreact to everything that happened. I didn't like being that way and the program is helping me to change. I am back with my boyfriend after a year's separation and it's a completely different relationship now. AA helped me with my sobriety and myself; but Al-Anon really helps me with my personal relationships. I go to a meeting a day, AA or Al-Anon, and have been doing that for three years. I'm becoming the kind of person I always admired and never thought I could be."

Al-Anon reminds us that we need to focus on changing ourselves. We cannot change anyone else in our lives, but in pursuing our own recovery, we will stop behaving and thinking in ways that *discourage* change (e.g., enabling and co-dependency). And, although we cannot force or control another person's recovery, other members of our family, attracted by the changes they observe in us, may begin to make their own changes. Kate, a twenty-five-year-old who has been going to

Overeaters Anonymous and Al-Anon for eight years, provides one of
the best examples of how programs can dovetail. "I recently wrote my
mother a long and caring letter, suggesting she go to an Al-Anon meeting and explaining how important the program has been for me.
After I sent the letter, I was really worried what her reaction would
be, but the replies I got were full of gratitude. Here are her first two
letters:

My dear Kate,

Last night I went to an Open Meeting of Al-Anon. Meeting all those
wonderful people, sharing ideas and discussing the Twelve Steps in detail
has helped me more than you'll ever know. I will work on defects in my
own character, one step at a time, one day at a time, and if I can't handle
one day at a time I'll try one hour at a time. I'm learning to analyze my
feelings of guilt—my neglect in nurturing my children because I constantly (for twenty-eight years) focused my attention on my alcoholic husband and not on my needs or those of my children. I think Al-Anon will
help me work out my guilt, which has been hanging heavily on my shoul-
ders for many years.

The Al-Anon pamphlets that I picked up are helping me understand the
difference between grief and depression. I realize now that every time I
thought I was in a state of depression I was really experiencing grief—the
loss of my husband to the bottle.

Grandma has not allowed herself to be damaged by the alcoholism
because she learned detachment many years ago. I have much more to
say, but it will have to wait until after my next meeting. I must help myself.
I'm more battered than Daddy is and I thank God you helped me find Al-
Anon. Much love,

Mom

Dear Kate,

Last night was my fifth meeting of Al-Anon. I can't tell you how much I
receive from these meetings. I am learning to "Let go and let God." It's
extremely difficult for me to let people (especially your father and
brother) do for themselves. I must stop all this caretaking. I'm going to
learn these lessons if it takes the rest of my life.

I've been doing a lot of reading of the Al-Anon literature and find it
so helpful to me. You're right when you say that sometimes you think
you'll go crazy because your thoughts get so confused. I often feel the
same way but think I too can work it all out through Al-Anon a day at a
time.

Today is my first day back teaching school—how can I ever thank you enough for caring enough to send me that letter that inspired me to help myself? I'm facing a new school term with all the tools I need to help me live with an alcoholic. I love you.

Mom

ALATEEN

Most of us, as children, could have benefited greatly from attending Alateen meetings. In providing concrete evidence that children of alcoholics are neither alone nor crazy and that they are not responsible —they are not to blame—for the alcoholism or for other problems related to the disease, Alateen can diminish the negative impact that growing up in an alcoholic home can have on children.

Of course hindsight is always 20/20. Even if you missed out on this valuable support as a teenager, Alateen can still prove helpful for you and your family. If you have younger brothers and sisters who still live at home, you might want to suggest they attend Alateen meetings to help themselves. And if you married or became an alcoholic yourself, your children will find Alateen extremely supportive—even if both you and your spouse are now sober.

• • •

"When I was about thirteen my father, who was in AA, and my mother, who attended Al-Anon meetings, insisted that I go to at least six Alateen meetings," remembered Ruth. "They said they wanted me to know it was available. I went, reluctantly, but I didn't like the few meetings I attended at all. My parents said that it was okay if I didn't want to continue; they just wanted me to have an idea what it was like in case I decided to go later on.

"Four or five months later I decided to go back on my own, this time for me and not for them. It clicked and I kept going to meetings for the next five years. I really started listening to what other kids had to say and the sharing really helped me understand my own feelings and experiences.

"Alateen helped me the most when my brother started drinking. This was much more devastating to me than my father's drinking had been because my father had already been sober for ten years when my brother started drinking alcoholically. Alateen sustained me and gave me strength to deal with all my brother's broken promises and my own disappointments.

"Being in Alateen made me much more open with my peers, both in and out of the program. I often told other kids about Alateen, but I never pushed them to get involved. I'd say they were welcome to come to a meeting with me and just leave it at that. I figure I probably planted a seed in the minds of many people and maybe they'll go for help like I did, when they feel it's right for them. All in all, I think my years of Alateen gave me a lot of confidence in my ability to cope with life's changes and disappointments."

Part of the Al-Anon family, Alateen was formed in 1957 by the teenage son of parents in AA and Al-Anon. Today there are three thousand Alateen groups worldwide. Alateen, which has a Twelve Step program for recovery just as AA and Al-Anon do, is a safe place for youngsters, aged twelve to twenty, to share experiences, information, and hope.

There probably would be many more Alateen groups if it weren't for the factors of denial and fear that make it difficult for children from alcoholic homes—who often depend on the help of a sympathetic adult to drive them to meetings—to get this effective and free treatment. And even when teenagers overcome these feelings long enough to recognize their need for self-help groups, the family secret often keeps them from telling either parent, alcoholic or nonalcoholic, about their need to get to meetings. Even though the program is anonymous, going to Alateen is a conscious acknowledgment of a problem that neither parent is likely to want to admit to unless either or both of them is in AA or Al-Anon.

ACOA GROUPS

ACOA'S BEGINNINGS: NEW KIDS ON THE BLOCK

Only recently have people who grew up in alcoholic homes begun to identify themselves as adult children of alcoholics. They have come to realize that the confusing and often frightening mixture of feelings they had while growing up was not due to their own "craziness" or "badness." They have discovered often with surprise and relief that they are not alone, that some people really do understand. And for those of us who grew up in alcoholic homes, the people who understand best are other adult children of alcoholics.

Many of the ACOAs I treat have had years of therapy, or have been in personal-growth workshops of one sort or another, but never got the help they needed. Most have been referred to me after trying other therapies that did not specifically deal with ACOA issues. They were seeking positive solutions, but they hadn't yet correctly identified the problem. Most knew "something was wrong," but they couldn't say exactly what it was. They only knew that they had been very sad and lonely children. As a member of one of the first ACOA groups said: "We can now get the kind of help that most of us never knew we needed."

The first Al-Anon/ACOA group was formed in 1976 by a half-dozen young men and women. Though they thought they had grown too old for Alateen, they were uncomfortable at regular Al-Anon meetings because they felt as if they were speaking with their own parents—and it didn't feel safe to express their anger. As discussed in Chapter 3, when we were children we buried ambivalent feelings about both parents, the nonalcoholic as well as the drinker. These young men and women needed to bring their feelings for both parents out into the open, but at Al-Anon they felt uncomfortable talking about their nonalcoholic parents.

Their group, called Hope for Adult Children of Alcoholics, began at the Smithers Building of Roosevelt Hospital in New York City, and it is still in existence today.

Tony A. was invited to his first ACOA meeting in 1977 by one of the Hope group members who had heard him speak at an Al-Anon meeting about growing up with two alcoholic parents. He was also a member of AA, the first to join the Hope group. A few months after his first meeting he made a list of ACOA characteristics that he called "The Problem/Solution."

Tony took the list to his ACOA meeting and read it to the group. Watching their faces, he could see that it was having an impact. One man said, "Hey, that's my laundry list!" The term stuck. The document, which has been used all over the country as a format for starting ACOA meetings, is still known as "the laundry list."

At the time he drew it up, Tony felt it was "inspired" writing because it came so easily to him. He credits its genesis to the "group conscience." You will probably identify with many of the characteristics in the list:

THE ORIGINAL LAUNDRY LIST

The Problem: The characteristics we seem to have in common due to our being brought up in an alcoholic household.

- We became isolated and afraid of people and authority figures.
- We became approval-seekers, and lost our identities in the process.
- We are frightened by angry people and by any personal criticism.
- We either become alcoholics, marry them, or both, or find another compulsive personality such as a workaholic to fulfill our sick abandonment needs.
- We live life from the viewpoint of victims and are attracted by that weakness in our love and friendship relationships.
- We have an overdeveloped sense of responsibility—it is easier for us to be concerned with others rather than with ourselves; this enables us not to look too closely at our faults.
- We get guilt feelings when we stand up for ourselves instead of giving in to others.
- We become addicted to excitement.
- We confuse love and pity and tend to "love" people we can "pity" and "rescue."
- We have "stuffed" our feelings from our traumatic childhoods and have lost the ability to feel or express our feelings because it hurts so much.
- We judge ourselves harshly and have a very low sense of self-esteem.
- We are dependent personalities who are terrified of abandonment, and we will do anything to hold on to a relationship in order not to experience the painful abandonment feelings that we received from living with sick people who were never there emotionally for us.
- Alcoholism is a family disease and we became para-alcoholics who took on the characteristics of that disease even though we did not pick up the drink.
- Para-alcoholics are reactors rather than actors.

The Solution: By attending Al-Anon/ACOA meetings on a regular basis, we learn that we can live our lives in a more meaningful manner; we learn to change our attitudes and old patterns and habits, to find serenity, even happiness.

Alcoholism is a threefold disease: mental, physical, and spiritual. Our parents were victims of this disease, which either ends in death or insanity. This is the beginning of the gift of forgiveness.

- We learn to put the focus on ourselves—to be good to ourselves.
- We learn to detach with love, tough love.
- We learn to feel our feelings, to accept and express them, build our self-esteem.

- Through working the Steps we learn to accept the disease, realizing that our lives have become unmanageable and that we are powerless over the disease and the alcoholic. As we become willing to admit our defects and our sick thinking, we are able to change our attitudes and our reactions into actions. By working the program daily, admitting that we are powerless, we come to believe eventually in the spirituality of the program—that there is a solution other than ourselves, the group, a Higher Power, God as we understand Him/Her or It.
- By sharing our experiences, relating to others, welcoming newcomers, serving our groups, we build our self-esteem.
- We learn to love ourselves, and in this way we are able to love others in a healthy way.
- We use telephone therapy with people we relate to at all times, not just when problems arise.
- The Serenity Prayer is our major prayer:
  God grant me the serenity to accept the things I cannot change, the courage to change the things I can and the wisdom to know the difference.

AL-ANON/ACOA TODAY

Beth, a forty-three-year-old social worker, gave me this description of her first ACOA meeting:

"Last week I called the Al-Anon number in the phone book and they told me there was a nonsmoking ACOA meeting with child care in a church not too far from my house. I was surprised there was a meeting so close on a Saturday morning.

"There were about thirty people there, mostly young women, but about ten men. They seemed to be in their twenties to fifties and were very friendly. The person in charge of the meeting read a welcome and the Serenity Prayer. The topic for that meeting was 'abandonment' and we split into two groups to have discussions. Each person spoke in turn. I 'passed' because I was feeling very self-conscious but that seemed to be okay with everyone. I didn't feel on the spot.

"The meeting was very emotional. There were many themes expressed that most people identified with: suicidal behavior; alcoholic spouses and parents; chemical dependency problems of siblings; family secrets; denial, amnesia, and, of course, abandonment.

"I liked the fact that the topic gave us structure but that we weren't compelled to talk just about abandonment. Whatever anyone had to say was acceptable, and people really listened. It wasn't like group therapy, where there is cross-talk. Each person said what he or she had to say without necessarily responding to what someone else had said. That seemed strange to me at first but then after the meetings I noticed that people went up to each other to give support and directly respond to what had been said. For instance, a nice woman about my age came up to me and said she understood why I 'passed' because she had found it difficult to share in her first meetings but had gradually gotten to the point where she could talk, and she felt much better once she was able to do that.

"A few of the people said they were alcoholics in AA and a few said they weren't, but that didn't seem to make any difference. One man mentioned that he was in Debtors Anonymous and that his sister was in Overeaters Anonymous.

"From the stories people told it was not really clear which parent had been alcoholic, but it was obvious that the general atmosphere of growing up in an alcoholic household was a very sad experience. There wasn't as much anger as there was free-floating grief and feelings about still seeking parental approval and about difficulties 'leaving home.'

"The theme that I identified most with was the emotional absence and unreliability of parents. I never felt my parents would be there for me. I always hoped for that but was usually disappointed. I was so used to feeling abandoned that, even in my adult life, when I left people I invariably ended up feeling as if I were the one who had been left. Quite a few other people had the same feeling and many talked about staying in relationships long after they should have, because they were afraid of abandonment feelings.

"After the meeting, people stayed around to talk in small, informal groups and a few people who were going to the coffeeshop down the street invited the rest of us to come along. About ten people came up to me and gave me their phone numbers. I felt very welcome and at ease by the end of the meeting, and I plan to go back next week. They seemed like a very nice group of people."

The national headquarters of Al-Anon Family Groups reports that there are now over nine hundred ACOA groups registered; several hundred others are in the process of registration. In 1981, there were only fourteen groups—what an astonishing growth rate!

It has been estimated that about ten percent of the people going to ACOA meetings are not the children of alcoholics. They have joined ACOA because of some other dysfunction in the families they grew up with: divorce, mental illness, depression, violence, and so on. They identify strongly with the items on the ACOA laundry list.

Every ACOA group develops its own character. If you don't like the first meeting you attend, there are many others. You may want to look a little further.

"There was too much emphasis on the idea of failure at the meetings where I was going," remembered Betty, a twenty-eight-year-old stylist. "There was no real support for competence. I had to find another meeting that was more upbeat. It pays to shop around. Someone told me I should go to six ACOA meetings before deciding which one was best for me. I can appreciate that suggestion now that I see how different groups can be in the same program."

OTHER ACOA GROUPS

There are also ACOA groups that are not affiliated with Al-Anon. In these groups members prefer to remain autonomous and do not follow the Twelve Step program and Twelve Tradition format recommended by AA and Al-Anon. Although some ACOAs prefer the more informal nature of these unaffiliated ACOA meetings, some feel uncomfortable about the lack of structure. Gene belongs to AA and regularly attends both Al-Anon and ACOA meetings. He had this to say: "I don't like the ACOA groups that aren't a part of Al-Anon and don't follow the Twelve Steps. I don't think they can survive. They seem to work to keep themselves sick. They get into fights about rules or format and that's the end of the group. I think that ACOAs need the Al-Anon structure—the Twelve Steps and Twelve Traditions. At least when there's a big conflict about how things should be run, the Traditions are very helpful to fall back on."

Some ACOA groups develop their own format and others use a format suggested in a special issue of the *COA Review: The Newsletter about Children of Alcoholics* published by Thomas W. Perrin. (The Resource Organizations listed on pages 273–276 include addresses for ordering information.) Perrin has also published a valuable pamphlet describing his own ACOA experience, which is reprinted here:

I AM AN ADULT WHO GREW UP IN AN ALCOHOLIC FAMILY

Once I thought I was unique, different and alone. Certainly, the disease of alcoholism kept me ignorant and isolated. The disease told me not to wash my family's linen in public. I obeyed, and so suffered in silence. I survived the disease of my parents only to acquire it myself.

Knowing only that I was affected by alcoholism, I began my recovery, sometimes in Al-Anon, sometimes in Alcoholics Anonymous. For a long time, there was this nagging awareness that once I had dealt with the problem of the moment, I would have to deal with the alcoholism of my family of origin, and its effects on my character. In spite of the progress I had made in my recovery, I was still getting into trouble, still having difficulty with other people. Peace of mind seemed to last only until I created the next crisis.

Some of the answers were sought in therapy. Sometimes I was told I was sick, sometimes that I was just wrong. Mostly I was told that the answers were to be found within myself. I insisted that I did not know the answers. I wasn't even sure how to ask the questions. It never occurred to "them" that I might be truly ignorant rather than neurotic or crazy.

Then I began to discover other Adult Children of Alcoholics. Slowly at first, we shared our experiences, feelings and behaviors. I discovered in ourselves a common history, despite having been raised generations and miles apart. I was no longer alone!

As my trust began to build, the walls came down, if only for a short time. I learned again to feel the hurt and to cry where before I could not. Some of my behaviors had turned into habits and were causing me difficulty in my job and in my family life. I came to understand that my past and my present formed a pattern. Once I had identified my feelings and my behaviors, I began to understand myself better. I resolved to change myself whenever I could, knowing that it would not be easy to alter the habits of a lifetime.

Here are some of the things I found out about myself and that I am now beginning to change:*

- I guess at what normal is.
- I have difficulty following projects through from beginning to end.
- I lie when it would be just as easy to tell the truth.
- I judge myself without mercy.
- I have difficulty having fun.
- I take myself very seriously.
- I have difficulty with intimate relationships.
- I overreact to changes over which I have no control.
- I feel different from other people.
- I constantly seek approval and affirmation.
- I am either super responsible or super irresponsible.
- I am extremely loyal even in the face of evidence that the loyalty is undeserved.
- I look for immediate as opposed to deferred gratification.
- I lock myself into a course of action without giving serious consideration to alternate behaviors or possible consequences.

* Of the twenty characteristics Perrin lists, the first fourteen were written by him, Janet Woititz, Sue Nobleman, Debbie E., and Rob R., and were published in *Adult Children of Alcoholics* by Janet Woititz (Health Communications, Hollywood, Florida, 1983). The last six items were written solely by Mr. Perrin.

- I seek tension and crisis and then complain about the results.
- I avoid conflict or aggravate it; rarely do I deal with it.
- I fear rejection and abandonment, yet I am rejecting of others.
- I fear failure, but sabotage my success.
- I fear criticism and judgment, yet I criticize and judge others.
- I manage my time poorly and do not set my priorities in a way that works well for me.

In order to change, I cannot use my history as an excuse for continuing my behavior. I have no regrets for what might have been, for my experiences have shaped my talents as well as my defects of character. It is my responsibility to discover these talents, to build my self esteem and to repair any damage done. I will allow myself to feel my feelings, to accept them, and learn to express them appropriately. When I have begun these tasks, I will try to let go of my past and get on with the business of managing my life. I have survived against impossible odds until today. With the help of God and my friends, I shall survive the next twenty-four hours. I am no longer alone.

Self-help groups offer enormous support: through attending their meetings, ACOAs get emotional and spiritual help from other people who have had similar life experiences. To find out when and where meetings are held in your area, telephone your local chapter of Al-Anon, an area alcoholism treatment program, or a community-center information office. In addition to the resources listed in this book, local chapters of the National Council on Alcoholism, libraries, and hospitals can provide you with information on ACOA groups in your area.

Adult children of alcoholics are represented in a variety of other self-help groups. It is estimated that fifty percent of the members of Alcoholics Anonymous and Al-Anon are ACOAs. They may go to these meetings instead of, or in addition to, ACOA meetings. A great number of ACOAs also join groups such as Overeaters Anonymous, Drugs Anonymous, Debtors Anonymous, Narcotics Anonymous, Cocaine Anonymous, and Gamblers Anonymous. Some go to ACOA groups that focus on specific problems, such as incest, sexual addictions, "women who love too much," and so on. The National Self-Help Clearinghouse (listed in the Resources Organizations) can provide information on most of the groups mentioned above.

ASSOCIATIONS AND FOUNDATIONS

In addition to the current explosion of self-help groups geared toward helping adult children of alcoholics, the new awareness of our particular difficulties has given birth in recent years to organizations which, unlike previous alcohol research and advocacy groups, focus specifically on children of alcoholics.

The Children of Alcoholics Foundation was formed in 1982, following the release of a study on children of alcoholics that was prepared for the then governor of New York State, Hugh L. Carey. Based on the results of the study, a number of people—child-welfare advocates, public officials, treatment specialists, and ACOAs—saw the evident need for a nonprofit organization to help this particular group. The foundation attempts to make people aware of the intergenerational link in the disease of alcoholism. It believes in providing effective means to help reduce the pain and suffering borne by those from alcoholic families, and seeks to prevent future alcoholism. It also publishes a directory of ACOA groups, available upon request. The foundation's address and telephone number are listed on page 273. A summary of its fascinating research data on children of alcoholics can be found on pages 269–272.

The National Association for Children of Alcoholics was founded in 1983 to support and serve as an advocacy resource for children of alcoholics of all ages. A description of its findings, goals, and accomplishments appears on pages 268–269. By the fall of 1986, NACOA's membership had exploded to 6,500. NACOA has members in all fifty states, plus Canada, Great Britain, Australia, Saudi Arabia, and Norway.

■ ■ ■

If you want to make changes in your life, a self-help group can help. But it's important to make a commitment to *recovery*, rather than to a particular group. As this chapter has shown, people feel different about the effectiveness of different self-help groups. But some ACOAs even worry that the rapid growth of the ACOA movement may dilute the helpfulness of groups. Terry, in his mid-thirties, voiced these concerns: "I worry that the increase in the children of alcoholics movement is going to get watered down. It's becoming less of a grassroots organization. Initially, there was much speaking from the heart when the movement was small and new. Now that it's bigger and more organized, I just hope people don't get lost in the rhetoric and talk in clichés and slogans rather than express their gut feelings."

Take Terry's warning to heart. Whether you choose to participate in AA meetings, Al-Anon, ACOA, or another self-help group, make sure it is one that allows, and encourages, you to express your gut feelings.

· 8 ·

PSYCHOTHERAPY AND SELF-HELP
WORKING TOGETHER
TO FACILITATE CHANGE

Participating in any of the self-help groups described in Chapter 7 can help us see that survival skills that once protected us can be harmful in our adult relationships. Self-help groups provide us with an opportunity to learn more productive ways of relating to people. As we learn to be open and honest, we can begin to confront feelings we've long repressed or been torn by. Meetings give us the chance to mourn childhood losses, to clean up old family business, and to move forward in our own growth and development.

Most important, groups can provide us with the sense that we are no longer alone, a feeling that can open us up to a new hope for the future. "I hear people talking about the very same things I experienced and I'm also reminded of incidents that I'd forgotten," said Cathleen, a copy writer. "For instance, someone mentioned the noise of her father falling off the couch—and I suddenly heard the thud. Almost every night my father would come home from work, have his dinner, lie on the couch drinking and watching TV until he fell off the sofa. Then he'd get up and go up to bed.

"I also see people at different stages of growth and it makes me feel that I can change too. A few months ago I spoke up and said, 'I feel like I'd rather be dead.' A guy came up to me after the meeting and said, 'I feel great today, but this time last year I felt exactly the same way you do.'"

Self-help groups have definite benefits:

- They cost nothing to join.
- They offer instant proof to new members that they are not alone or unique in their difficulties.
- They address specific common problems.
- They function as resources, providing information and education.
- They encourage positive action.
- Meetings often center on one topic, making it easier to stay focused on a particular subject.
- They are very supportive. Members accomplish together what they might not be able to do alone.
- Fellowship develops among members who consistently show up and in many ways help one another out. Peer support reduces individual isolation—self-centeredness gives way to "we"-centeredness.

THE NEED FOR OTHER THERAPIES

But self-help groups alone may not provide all the help you need. In large cities especially, self-help groups can be quite big, and this may initially intimidate or overwhelm you if you feel very shy and uncomfortable sharing with so many people.

"My objection to Al-Anon/ACOA meetings was that they were too large. For me, there were too many people pouring out all their feelings and there didn't seem to be any kind of resolution. People were dumping a lot of garbage, but no one wanted to clean it up," recalled Jim, a twenty-eight-year-old financial consultant in group therapy.

"My feelings were not entirely negative, though. I liked the fact that other people were feeling as miserable as I felt. But I decided to find a smaller therapy group for adult children, and I've been in the group for three months. Maybe I'll go back to ACOA later on. But right now I feel the small group is what I need."

Sometimes the composition of an ACOA group changes from meeting to meeting, making it impossible to depend on the same people being present on a consistent basis. There are almost always newcomers and absent regulars. And every group differs in its particular flavor. For instance, one group may have a reputation for being a very angry group. For some ACOAs, especially newcomers, this outpouring of rage can be very frightening. Phyllis, a programmer in her fifties, commented: "There are some groups very preoccupied with the anger stage of mourning. I think it can be very negative for ACOAs who either haven't gotten to that stage or who have moved beyond it."

Sometimes in groups without leaders, factions develop and controversies arise about how the meetings should be conducted. This can interfere with the orderly operation of the group. When this happens, a splinter group may form, which splits off and decides to go elsewhere.

Many ACOA, Al-Anon, and Alateen members, either before or after joining their self-help groups, therefore also find it helpful to get psychological counseling—whether one to one or in groups—from therapists who specialize in working with people from alcoholic families. You too may find it beneficial to supplement the peer-group support you get from a self-help group with a professionally led group or with intensive one-to-one therapy. The therapist may serve as a reliable, consistent, understanding role model for a troubled client. The therapeutic process may allow you to make up some of the psychological development you may have missed growing up in an alcoholic home. Therapy can thus be an adjunct to your involvement in one or more appropriate self-help groups.

Professional therapy can help you deal with specific problems and attitudes you'd like to change. But most psychotherapists knowledgeable about alcoholism join me in recommending that group-therapy members not forgo entirely attending appropriate Twelve Step programs or other ACOA groups, just because they're receiving professional therapy. These programs complement psychotherapy and offer supportive aspects not available in traditional group therapy. Between weekly therapy sessions, for instance, ACOAs have access to a twenty-four-hour support system of their ACOA groups: they can telephone fellow members during a crisis, or attend a meeting at which their problem can be aired. Particularly for newcomers, this service, which therapists usually cannot provide, is extremely welcome. The combination of intensive psychological treatment with peer-group support can speed up the recovery process and allow you to get a great deal more than what just one form of treatment can offer.

THE ROLE OF THE THERAPIST

As a therapist I feel I am in the "change business." People who don't want to make changes generally don't appear in my office. The people who do want to make changes and seek out therapy are already starting the process of change. I find it very exciting and gratifying to be involved in this process, even though it can be a painful and arduous journey for the client. Occasionally people ask me whether a therapist's work is very depressing. After all, they say, a therapist has to deal with people deeply troubled by pain and conflict. But, while this is certainly true, confronting the pain is necessarily the first step in getting out of it. And I find that hopeful, not depressing.

ACOAs and other people in psychotherapy are their own agents of change. A therapist can only act as a facilitator; those who benefit the most from the process are the people who want to change themselves. With all the psychological knowledge and techniques that therapists bring to their professional work, the most important things they bring to the client-therapist relationship are a safe place, an open mind, and a kind heart. The most significant tool a therapist has is himself or herself. Who that person is rather than what that person does plays the greatest part in encouraging the process of change.

In my own practice with individuals, groups, couples, and families, the incredible changes I have witnessed and participated in are inspiring. I think it is probably very difficult for ACOAs *not* to change. Our pain, our incredible pain, urges us into treatment and thus helps us get better. Allowing ourselves to feel the feelings and experience the pain is the first step in the change process.

CHOOSING A THERAPIST

If you decide that professional therapy—whether group, individual, couple, or family counseling—might be right for you, I strongly advise you to find a professional who understands the disease and its effect on the whole family. You can question the therapist directly about his or her background in the field of alcoholism, or you may want to ask friends who are also ACOAs to refer you to a knowledgeable therapist.

"My therapist didn't think alcoholism was my primary problem," said Maryellen, fifty-one, who now attends both AA and ACOA meetings. "He didn't think I drank too much. He said that we could work on my depression and then I wouldn't need to drink so much. I stopped individual therapy when I went into detox on my own."

Too many mental-health workers lack the necessary expertise in this important area. There are many possible reasons for this ignorance, but chief among these is the lack of alcoholism training. Professional schools still teach almost nothing about alcoholism and even less about its effect on the family of the alcoholic.

A number of biases may also prevent a therapist from getting the necessary training in family alcoholism: The therapist may not view alcoholism as a major problem and may seek instead to find underlying causation or see it as a symptom of other problems. The therapist may never have had experience with alcoholics (hard as that is to believe) and may have negative attitudes and prejudices about alcoholism. Or the therapist may come from an alcoholic home and still be in denial, unable to deal with his or her own personal feelings about it.

Many therapists still have insufficient knowledge about resources for treatment (residential treatment programs, detoxification centers, Twelve Step programs and specific meetings, interventions, books, or conferences). Others lack an understanding of the philosophy and structure of AA and other Twelve Step programs. For these reasons, some adult children of alcoholics stay in therapy for years without addressing the fears and difficulties associated with their alcoholic backgrounds. If you are seeking therapy for yourself, you have every right to ask a therapist questions about his or her background in the area of alcoholism. If you don't feel confident that the person treating you knows about alcoholism and the family, you are unlikely to develop the trust necessary for successful therapy. It should not be your responsibility to educate your therapist. After all, the therapy is for you, not for your therapist.

THERAPY GROUPS

Psychotherapy groups are led by one or two therapists and are often called "second-chance families" because the group process permits participants to work through old issues that they may never have addressed before because of the alcoholism. Some groups are composed entirely of adult children of alcoholics while others are a mix of people —both ACOAs and non-ACOAs. Some therapists believe that when dealing with issues of alcoholism it is best to restrict the group to

ACOAs. Other therapists believe it's important to combine ACOAs and non-ACOAs, to show that, for all members, many issues are more similar than they are different. In both kinds of group, an integral part of the process is to identify and discuss ACOA issues as they emerge.

HOW AND WHY GROUPS WORK

Like self-help groups, the psychotherapy group can be a powerful facilitator of change. Groups, which generally meet once a week, are usually composed of five to ten members committed to attending the group regularly and respecting confidentiality. Like the family, a group is a system—one that has an impact on each of its components. A good leader, the psychotherapist, protects people from being scapegoated or attacked by inappropriate or hostile comments. It is extremely important that a group leader be sensitive, trained, and experienced, preferably with a background of work in the field of chemical dependency (and ACOA issues in particular).

There are various kinds of psychotherapy groups, and each will be a little different, depending on the personality and training of the group therapist. I have been leading groups for over twenty years, and though other therapists may stress other techniques, my method derives from my education in group social work, psychoanalytic training, family-systems orientation, and from my experience as both a professional facilitator and a patient.

Therapists must establish basic guidelines for their groups. Some suggestions are:

- Keep them relatively small in size, usually five to eight members. Some groups are limited to all women, or all ACOAs, but most are mixed: men and women, ACOAs and non-ACOAs.
- Each new member should make the following commitments: to join the group for at least three months, to honor confidentiality, to discuss the sessions only in the group, not to socialize with group members, to report such social contact to the group if it happens, and to give the group a month's notice before leaving.
- Each member should be responsible for his or her participation in the group. What you put in reflects what you will get out of the group experience.
- Groups should be safe places. I do not allow violence or scapegoating. Honorable listening without making judgments is the basic tenor of the group.

Groups are particularly useful places for you to learn how to break the old family rules of not feeling, not talking, and not trusting. Patterns of isolation break down as bonding (trust and attachment between you and others) takes place within the group. Members become more aware of themselves when they get supportive feedback from people who can tell them how they are being experienced, or perceived, today.

"I've been in group therapy for six months, and I feel it's very supportive. It feels like the close family group I never had," said Brian, a carpenter in his thirties. "I like the idea that there are only eight people in the group. I've been to AA and ACOA groups, but they're so large that I'm not really comfortable. In my therapy group, I'm with the same people every week, and I've developed the trust that makes it possible for me to talk. Other people talk about the same feeling I always had when I was growing up, a kind of fogginess, an inability to really know my feelings. It's a great relief to be with people speaking my own language."

COMMUNICATING FEELINGS

One of the most valuable lessons to be learned in group therapy is to say what you feel when you feel it. This kind of honesty and spontaneity may be new to you because you've always repressed your real feelings. The group becomes a testing ground for you to check out how, when, and where to say things that bother you outside the group. Meetings become practice sessions in developing better communication skills, resolving conflicts, and becoming more intimate. In group therapy, you learn to take risks, to admit your vulnerabilities, to express your emotions without censoring them. You learn to break through your silence, to take the risk of confrontation. Confrontations can produce painful feelings—anger, hurt, and fear—but they also promote feelings of love, support, and joy at being known and understood. Group therapy gives people new insights into their emotions and behavior—and gives them, too, the courage to change.

Members constructively point out what they honestly feel and think about each other. This communication may at first seem foreign to those of us whose backgrounds were replete with mixed messages— or no verbal messages at all. These exchanges result in significant behavioral changes; the process fosters greater individual sensitivity, competence, and autonomy. Groups allow you to develop trusting relationships and identify your patterns of defensive behavior—often by seeing the same behavior in another group member. Sometimes the insight you need to change can come from the "I do that too" identification with another group member.

BANISHING FEAR FROM THE GROUP

If you suffer from the feeling that "I'm not enough," groups can reverse your low self-esteem. By providing you with positive feedback from people you respect and admire, and by treating you with respect, encouragement, love, and support, the group can help you realize how important you are. When group members recognize the positive, rewarding achievements in your life, they can reinforce these experiences and increase your self-esteem. By sharing, and encouraging you to share, negative as well as positive feelings, a group can help you develop more complete, honest, and satisfying relationships.

Laura, a young secretary who is also a member of Al-Anon, ACOA, and OA, recently told me: "My recent vacation made me see how much progress I've made in group therapy. It was the first time I was able to go anywhere and feel free and open with new people.

"In group I learned how to express my feelings and my needs. I learned in group to say things like 'I feel confused about something that happened today. Can you give me some input? I'm not sure my reactions were appropriate. This is what happened. . . .' On vacation I was able to run things by my best friend who was with me. There was a big scene at dinner one night and I thought I had been attacked by someone. Her perception helped me to see I had misunderstood and overreacted. That helped me let go of the kind of anger I used to hold on to for weeks. It helped me to see that I could practice what I learned in group: to reveal my feelings and to ask for help and get it."

Many of the members of my groups have said that the group experience has provided them with:

- Nurturance
- A feeling of belonging
- Healthy competition
- Competency and power
- Intimacy
- Acceptance of self and others as "good enough"
- Improved communication
- Problem-solving skills
- Forgiveness

The group experience can help ACOAs resolve some of the fears that prevent us from having close relationships: for example, the fear of acting impulsively or being out of control, the fear of abandonment, the fear of becoming vulnerable, etc. Through sharing these fears, members help each other see the ways they perpetuate their childhood fears, where they came from, and, eventually, how to let them go.

INDIVIDUAL THERAPY

Because some ACOAs are initially fearful of groups, many of them start recovery in individual therapy. This one-to-one process, as it leads to a trusting relationship with a psychotherapist and a degree of comfort in expressing feelings, often paves the way for subsequent group experience.

Individual therapy, like any kind of therapy, is a courageous undertaking. Many people mistakenly feel they must be "sick" if they need counseling with a psychotherapist. But in reality only the strongest, bravest, and healthiest people generally ask for help.

The process of psychotherapy can prepare you for more openness in your daily life. A good therapist will challenge and support you as you attempt, sometimes painfully, to become totally honest in expressing your individual truths. The therapy situation can provide you with a safe atmosphere and tools for personal growth. Change will come about as you confront old myths and discover new truths in the nonjudgmental, supportive environment of the psychotherapy office.

"I started individual therapy because I wanted to find a healthier way to deal with things in my life," recalled Gwen. "I didn't want to continue just reacting to daily events. I wanted to be able to make healthier decisions for myself, to find out how to be comfortable in my own skin and in social situations.

"Therapy helps me pinpoint what I need to work on. I have to focus on myself and therapy gives me this unique opportunity. In the rest of my life, even in ACOA groups, I tend to focus on everyone else. That's my old COA tape.

"Probably the best thing that I've gotten out of my individual therapy so far is trust. I'm learning how to trust other people, but even more importantly, I'm learning how to trust myself. This process of self-awareness is making me feel generally okay; it allows me to feel that whatever I do I'm okay. The kind of unconditional support I get in therapy is something I never got in my home. Therapy is teaching me how to mother that child in me that I feel never got enough mothering. I no longer resent my parents for not being able to give it to me. They didn't have the emotional resources they needed either. But I am getting much better at taking care of myself.

"The feeling of safety and trust I have in my therapy helps me to be more trusting and open outside the sessions too. I can test out my feelings with my therapist and then I can express them to other people. It's good practice.

"I'm also seeing the old issues from my childhood repeated in my present life. That can be really scary, but it also makes me more willing to make the necessary changes to avoid repeating these self-destructive patterns. It's painful to look back, but therapy gives me a safe place to do it. It's the safest place I have.

"In ACOA and group therapy certain people sometimes frighten me. I'm still not comfortable being with someone who may be sicker than me. It makes it hard for me to focus on myself and openly express my feelings.

"I'm not putting down those groups, I still get a lot out of them, but somehow individual therapy prepares and protects me from situations I am still unable to really handle. It's very comforting to know that my individual sessions are strictly for me and I don't have to worry about other people."

Many people mistakenly think that psychotherapy has to be a long-term process. For many ACOAs, though, short-term psychotherapy that supplements their participation in ACOA groups may be all that is necessary. When a therapist is familiar with the effects of alcoholism on the family, therapy can move along at an impressive pace.

You also may not need psychotherapy at all. Sometimes self-help groups can provide the kind of therapeutic experience that makes any additional recovery aid superfluous. Some of your friends may try to convince you that because therapy has helped them it can help you too. They may be right; they may be wrong. Unless you feel totally out of control—for example, if you behave violently, or drink alcoholically, or have strong suicidal urges—trust your instincts when considering therapy. If you don't feel you need it, don't allow yourself to get talked into any kind of therapy by an overzealous person trying to sell you the bill of goods that suits that person. Keep an open mind, but remember that what is right for one person may not be right for you. Or it may not be right right now. You be the judge.

FAMILY THERAPY

Marital-couples counseling and family therapy are other modes of treatment that can be very helpful to ACOAs. Family-therapy professionals may be doctors, psychologists, social workers, or pastoral counselors who have supplemented their mental-health education with specialized training and courses in family therapy. The principles and methods of family therapy can be especially effective in:

- Resolving emotional conflicts
- Modifying perceptions and behavior
- Facilitating better communication
- Handling family crises
- Educating the family

Family treatment focuses on the expectations and interactions of everyone in the family, not just one member. Family therapists believe that each family member acts upon, and is influenced by, every other member's behavior and attitudes. Even if the whole family is not seen together in a session, the family therapist views each individual in a family context. Treatment considers the entire family as the instrument for change. For this reason, family therapists—especially those knowledgeable about the effects of alcoholism—seem particularly well-suited to treating adult children of alcoholics. Family therapy, in which members come together to work on the "family problem," is being utilized more and more as people come to accept the family-disease concept of alcoholism. Adult children don't have to be living at home to engage in family therapy. Coming to even one of several sessions can be extremely helpful—to you and to everyone else involved.

In addition to providing therapy, marriage and family therapists who specialize in working with alcoholic families can make assessments that will help you find other appropriate services for your specific needs. At different stages of recovery, one kind of therapy may be more advisable than another. If, for instance, you are just beginning to recover from an addiction of your own, a good family therapist would refer you to AA or another appropriate Twelve Step program: abstinence would be the immediate treatment goal. After you have a solid period of abstinence, individual or group psychotherapy might supplement

AA. At some point, even years later, marriage or group therapy might be indicated.

In addition to alcoholism and substance abuse, family therapists can help resolve relationship problems, sexual dysfunctions, premarital strife, pre- and post-divorce conflicts, parenting problems, school problems, teenage depression and threats of suicide, physical or sexual abuse, bereavement, and acute or chronic illnesses—each of which can be related to an alcoholic background.

Generally, the family-therapy process gives family members the opportunity to learn about themselves and each other; to communicate openly, and thus effectively; to discover origins of old dysfunctional family patterns; to perceive relationships more positively—and turn the family system into a healthier one, one that works better for everyone involved.

If you would like to find a qualified family counselor, the American Association for Marriage and Family Therapy, an organization of thirteen thousand professionals, can refer you to one. The address and telephone number of the national office follow: 1717 K Street NW, Suite 407, Washington, D.C. 20006; (202) 429-1825.

WORKSHOPS

Many alcoholism treatment centers now have family programs that will help you confront old but not forgotten issues. And more and more centers are designing workshops specifically for ACOAs. In addition, you may find workshops in your area on a variety of topics that, although not aimed specifically toward ACOAs, may help you in your personal growth and development. Some are much more effective than others, so it pays to ask around. Try to find ACOAs who have had good experiences at particular workshops.

Kay recently went to a workshop at an alcoholism rehabilitation center: "I decided to go to a Renewal Center for a week after a friend in my AA group told me how helpful it had been for her. I didn't realize until I got there that they were having a three-day intensive workshop for ACOAs. It was incredible. It was just what I needed, and I didn't even know it. All I knew was that I was feeling very ungrateful for my three years of sobriety and I was unhappy with myself. For months I'd been snapping at the people around me, especially my children. I felt empty inside. 'Renewal' sounded like a good idea.

"In my adult life I always seemed to be in depressing situations. Someone was always sick, and I was the classic caretaker and enabler. I married an alcoholic and lived with him for twenty-five years. He died three years ago of cirrhosis at age forty-seven.

"The ACOA workshop was the highlight of the week. It helped me see that I need to let go of the caretaking role I know so well. It gave me some inner strength, which I hope to build on now that I'm more aware of my ACOA characteristics. It's helped me to get over a plateau that I was experiencing in my recovery programs. Now I feel I'm at another place in my journey, and that I am going to move ahead and get to a place that is much more comfortable, much more positive."

Workshops, unlike Al-Anon/ACOA or therapy, bring people together for an intensive period of time (hours, days, weekends, and sometimes more lengthy retreats). Because the concentrated group experience usually breaks down defenses and makes people feel extremely close to one another, workshops can be cathartic. But they are not magic and some ACOAs complain that they feel the intimacy is forced. There are no instant cures; so don't make the mistake of thinking that your entire life will change forever as a result of one intensive workshop. This is highly unlikely. Many ACOAs, in fact, report a big letdown, a depressive reaction, once the workshop is over.

"With so much addiction in their backgrounds, ACOAs have to be careful of being workshop junkies," warned Fran, herself an ACOA. "Being obsessed with ACOA things isn't the answer. Recovery should be a bridge back to life—it shouldn't become someone's *sole* life. People who run to every conference and workshop on the subject can get too intellectual."

Workshops can be extremely helpful, but recovery almost always involves much more time and effort than a single workshop, for instance, may permit. As most ACOAs know by now, there are no quick fixes. Workshops can help you focus on a particular problem that troubles you, but because the effectiveness of particular workshop leaders varies widely, it pays to ask others who have attended workshops for their impressions—before you sign up.

■ ■ ■

It is clear from the disparity of viewpoints voiced in this chapter that different ACOAs prefer different paths of recovery. You too should choose the recovery route with which you feel most comfortable. ACOAs need to develop a healthy balance in all areas of their lives, and recovery is no exception. A balanced view should reflect the criticisms as well as the merits of the help available to ACOAs. One person's experience is likely to differ from another's; what works for one person isn't necessarily going to work for the next. But the educated and enlightened ACOA will have, one hopes, sufficient information on which to base a personal choice.

· 9 ·

MOURNING AND FORGIVENESS
―――
PUTTING GUILT, SHAME, AND BLAME BEHIND US

In order to move forward in our lives, we have to accept the past and put it behind us. Then we can get on with the task of making changes, the changes that will ultimately lead to a better future. Recovery begins today; we have to accept the challenges the present offers with the courage to risk disappointment and failure.

Living according to past patterns keeps many of us emotionally insecure in spite of material success and personal and professional achievements. Putting the past in a framework (as we did in Part I), in a realistic and understandable perspective, is essential to your recovery. The past is always part of the present; but while it may be part of today's truth, it is not the whole truth.

SEPARATING PAST AND PRESENT

"I have to keep reminding myself that Hank, my boyfriend, is not my father," confessed Beverly, a twenty-eight-year-old woman with an eating disorder. "The other day he brought a bottle of Scotch into the apartment and I flipped out. He's not a big drinker and I don't mind alcohol in my house, but I can't be around Scotch. That was my father's drink of choice, and I spent too many years of my life hunting out Scotch bottles with my mother and throwing them away.

"My father was a very nasty drunk. He would yell and throw things. He didn't beat me, but he did beat my brother, and every time he got drunk I was afraid my brother would get hurt.

"Hank's not at all like my father, but it's hard for me to look at a bottle of Scotch and *not* think something terrible is going to happen."

It's easy for ACOAs to get mixed up about what is fact and what is fiction, and when past dangers cease to be present ones. Our memories of the past are often so strong and painful that the slightest association can take us back to those troubled, unhappy times—and we think that a similar situation in the present is going to have the same old results.

In facing a new situation, we may be used to reacting immediately; in past crises we often had to. But we no longer need to react to the present according to the ways of the past. When a potentially dangerous situation presents itself, we need to step back, observe what's going on, and listen to what other people may be trying to tell us. We have to be careful not to overreact, not to make assumptions, and not to let past history become part of the present. We have to stay in the now and respond according to present circumstances rather than react to the old tapes we hear in our heads.

Like Beverly, we may need to remind ourselves that the present need not be ruled by the past. Allowing yesterday to stay in the past, as this chapter will show, will allow you to make today and tomorrow better. By letting our unrealized hopes and outmoded strategies go, by no longer allowing unresolved and interfering feelings from the past to rule our lives, we can free ourselves to concentrate our energies on new ventures of the present.

GUILT AND SHAME

Debbie, a grandmother and an ACOA, said of herself: "I'm an alcoholic and an adult child of two alcoholics. I have three children who are adult children of alcoholics and nine grandchildren who are children of alcoholics.

"Seeing the alcoholism repeat itself in each generation makes me feel guilty that I didn't do enough. I feel I didn't protect my children from the emotional and physical abuse they suffered. I'm ashamed because I feel I wasn't a good mother.

"I stayed in an abusive marriage for fifteen years and didn't do anything to stop my husband from beating my middle child. He was the only one that got picked on. My husband beat me also but he never touched the other two. I just stayed there and took it, and I didn't do anything to protect my child.

"Once, when my son was in kindergarten, he was almost strangled by my husband, who was in an alcoholic rage. There were choke marks on Jim's neck, and I tried to cover them up by making him wear a turtleneck sweater to school.

"Now that I'm sober and in a recovery program, I realize that alcoholism is a disease and I couldn't have done anything to prevent it. But sometimes I have a hard time convincing myself that I did the best I could. Unless I'm careful, I can beat myself up with guilt."

Like Debbie, ACOAs, particularly those who are also alcoholic themselves, are often stricken with guilt and shame. Shame is a fear of being exposed, the fear of being found out. It is a fear of appearing vulnerable, of being imperfect, of having our secrets and flaws revealed. When we feel ashamed, we feel intensely, painfully guilty about being ourselves. And feelings of not being good enough, of not doing enough, and of not being right or doing the right thing are common among adult children of alcoholics.

Guilt and shame are ultimately self-induced anxiety states that reinforce our old feelings of unworthiness. We blame ourselves for faults or sins that no one else may know about. And often, if someone else did know, he or she would see these flaws much less critically than we do.

UNDERSTANDING GUILT AND SHAME

No one else can make you feel guilty. Granted, many will try. Alcoholics, often excellent manipulators, have a particular talent for pushing buttons that can set off guilt feelings. Children are especially malleable, but once we are adults we can learn to act in accordance with our own needs and desires rather than reacting to the guilt we may feel for failing to live up to another person's—or our own—unrealistic expectations. We can learn that we don't need to feel guilty for doing what we want to do instead of what someone else wants us to do. We do not have to feel guilty.

In your current relationships, the persistent guilt and shame you may feel can make you quick to judge yourself, to accept blame, and assume responsibility when blame and responsibility lie elsewhere. We have to accept the fact that we aren't responsible for all the problems of the world. ACOAs like to feel we can fix anything; but we can't. (For more on "fix-ups," see pages 154–156.)

As children, we often got blamed for things that we shouldn't have been blamed for. Our parents may have pointed fingers at us rather than acknowledge their own irresponsibility. It's often easier to cast blame than to acknowledge fault, but as a young child, you may not have understood this. As an adult, however, you can begin to understand and accept that the blaming was, possibly, due to the irrational efforts of sick parents to avoid responsibility.

"As a child I was asthmatic and my health was blamed for all kinds of things," James, a fifty-year-old salesman, told me. "My father insisted that we move out west and my mother hated it in Nevada. She'd always say things like 'If it wasn't for your sickness, we'd still be living in Brooklyn.' I always felt I made her angry, that it was my fault she was so unhappy. Since I was an only child there wasn't anyone else to blame. My father was a salesman on the road, so he escaped her wrath. I got it all—all the time.

"Now that I'm older, I can see that she was depressed and dissatisfied and her moods were not my fault. My parents fought all the time and I was a good excuse to keep the arguments going. Now I can see that most of their fights were at dinnertime when they were drinking, but I never before realized the drinking had anything to do with it. Neither one of them was a falling-down drunk or got into much trouble because of the drinking. But the drinking led to more arguments and more drinking."

In examining their pasts, many ACOAs are surprised and grateful to find out it wasn't always their fault when anger or irrationality erupted in the family. Feelings of guilt and shame lock us in the past. But we can't change our pasts and we have to stop feeling guilty and ashamed about the many things over which we had no control. "If only" thinking ("If only I had been better . . . ," "If only (s)he hadn't drank so much . . . ," etc.) is nonproductive.

FORGIVING YOURSELF: THE END OF GUILT AND SHAME

To rid yourself of self-blame, you will have to realize that you didn't cause the unhappy environment; you were a product of it. After all, you were just a powerless child. It is not easy for adult children to stop having these feelings. But we have to accept our inculpability. We have to forgive ourselves, applying a "no-fault" policy rather than the "my-fault" policies we have subscribed to in the past.

CUTTING DOWN ON YOUR GUILT FEELINGS   Ann had really crippling trouble with guilt until I suggested that she literally make up "Permission Slips" allowing herself to feel guilty. She limited herself to five slips a month, to be redeemed whenever she felt guilty. This helped her cut down on the guilt she had so often felt.

When you start to feel ashamed or guilty in any of your present relationships, try to find out what the other person is thinking or feeling. You may want to ask him or her one of the following questions:

- Is there anything I'm doing that's making you feel uncomfortable?
- I sense some discomfort between us. Can you tell me how you're feeling?
- I'm feeling guilty (or ashamed). Do you have any idea where that feeling is coming from?

The discussion that these questions initiate can take one of the following three courses, each of which should release you from the grip of your unproductive guilt feelings:

- The other person may actually blame you for something you have done or are doing. If you disagree with the objection, you can try to help the other person see that his or her expectations of you are unrealistic or unreasonable.
- If, on the other hand, you agree with the other person that your behavior may have been objectionable, you can apologize and agree to try to change your behavior to be more considerate of his or her needs. A caution is in order, however: Do not assume this course automatically, out of force of habit. The tendency of adult children of alcoholics to assume blame for anything that goes wrong may make this seem like the easiest or most natural direction to take. But you can't please everyone at all times. It is therefore important for you to recognize that you don't need to apologize for being yourself.
- Finally, you may discover that the other person wasn't blaming you for anything. Finding this out should diminish or dispel any lingering guilt feelings.

HAPPINESS AND HUMILITY

Patsy, thirty years old and single, spoke to me about her guilt feelings: "Recently I went to visit an old friend from college who had just gotten out of the hospital. The man was very depressed and talked sadly about all the things he could no longer do. He was obviously in considerable physical pain also.

"Before we got there, I'd been in a good mood, feeling excited about a job offer I'd just received. Once we got there, I felt terribly guilty for feeling good. I didn't feel like I deserved to be happy when he was so miserable. I felt I couldn't say anything positive about myself. I had to act as if I had more trouble than he had so he wouldn't feel so badly. I felt I had to be worse off; I could never be better off."

Rather than sharing her good fortune with her friend, Patsy allowed her feelings of guilt and unworthiness to defeat her happiness. Although her friend probably would have welcomed good news and the opportunity to focus on something other than his own pain, Patsy felt that her own well-being might have upset him or made him unhappy, and she didn't want to risk his disapproval or rejection.

Our deep sense of shame prevents us from revealing ourselves, from revealing both pleasant and unpleasant feelings. And, by stifling our emotions, guilt and shame can prevent us from allowing ourselves to feel good. Like Patsy, we may feel unworthy of good feelings—especially when someone we care about is suffering or feeling poorly. By reinforcing our low self-esteem, guilt and shame encourage us to feel bad about ourselves. We think we're bad people. These feelings isolate us, making us feel we are not really human, are not like everyone else.

We think that if other people really knew us—if we revealed the terrible truth about ourselves—they would reject us, abandon us. In order to move beyond guilt and shame, once you have found what you feel is a safe place you have to take the risk of revealing yourself. You have to own up to your secrets, talk about them. In doing so, you may discover that other people have the very same secrets. That's the only way to overcome the isolation and the self-hate that guilt and shame produce.

When we admit we're afraid, ashamed, or guilty, we admit to the imperfect condition that is everybody's condition. And it's a paradox but it's true: strength comes from weakness. By admitting our humanness, by learning to forgive ourselves for our human imperfections, we become part of the human race, not someone apart from it. And we can thus draw comfort, strength, and forgiveness from other people. Although fear and perfectionism may discourage us from sharing our secrets, we must recognize that as long as we hold on to our secret shame, we will continue to feel alone—and miserable.

MOURNING LOSSES

No matter how deeply we bury our painful feelings about loss, or how much effort we make to cover them up, these feelings must emerge if we want to put the past behind us and recover.

DEFINING LOSSES

Loss is an unavoidable part of the human condition. Besides the death of a loved relative or friend, we experience many other losses throughout our lives. We experience as loss any event that takes away something we value. These losses can include:

- Loss of someone we love through divorce or distance
- Loss of one of our functions or abilities (hearing loss, blindness, loss of an organ, limb, or breast)
- Loss of material objects (home, savings)
- Loss of youth, freedom, or faith
- Loss through changes in our own lives (leaving home, retirement, etc.)

Although in growing up in an alcoholic household you might have run a higher risk of suffering some of these losses, many adult children of alcoholics also experience the following painful losses:

- Loss of childhood
- Loss of trust and confidence
- Loss of love and affection
- Loss of feelings
- Loss of dreams and hope

In addition, because ACOAs run a high risk of becoming addicted themselves (to relationships, food, drugs, alcohol), it is important to note that it's not unusual to feel a sense of loss after giving up an addiction—even when abstinence is desperately wanted. Even though alcohol, for instance, negatively influences an alcoholic's life, he or she still values it, because it has provided an escape from the real world. Giving up the alcohol means the alcoholic also has to give up a certain lifestyle that, though destructive, meets some of his or her needs. Similarly, co-dependents often experience a sense of loss when they give up their enabling behavior.

GRIEF: THE PAIN THAT HEALS

Grief is the normal reaction to any of these losses, whether we experience them in childhood or adulthood. Grief is a pain that heals. The mourning process allows us to come to terms with our losses, to recognize and accept them so that we can then move on with our lives.

People usually expect grief time to be shorter than it really is. It can take as long as three or four years and is rarely resolved in less than one year for most people. It is important for you to remember that grief is normal. It may cause physical illness, emotional pain, impaired judgment, and distortions of perception and thought. But all of these are normal reactions to loss.

As defined by Elisabeth Kübler-Ross in On Death and Dying, the stages of mourning are denial, anger, bargaining, depression, and acceptance. And these stages apply not only to the grief we feel when faced with the death of a loved one, but also to our mourning over any other painful loss. In order to move through these stages of resolving grief, we need to give voice to the fears and feelings that accompany loss. We need to allow ourselves to be vulnerable, to shed tears, to acknowledge our pain and ultimately to release it. Unless we admit the anger, bitterness, depression, self-pity, and loneliness that we feel when experiencing loss, we will never be able to let them go. And these buried feelings can consume us—making it impossible for us to move beyond these losses.

BURIED GRIEF

Most ACOAs have not yet given themselves the chance to work through their grief. Considering that denial rules the roost in most alcoholic homes, it's not surprising that children of alcoholics tend to stop at the first (denial) stage of mourning. Because we have a difficult time expressing any feelings, it takes a great deal of time and effort to enter the later stages—which require us to recognize and express our feelings.

Our individual reactions to buried losses may vary widely. You may hide your inner fragility, projecting a hollow image (to yourself and others) of strength and self-sufficiency. You may simply feel numb, or you might cry easily, or cry at "silly things"—an ad for an animal shelter or something seen on the evening news—or certain events may set you off into intense, unexplained periods of depression or agitation: a high school reunion or Christmas Eve.

Adults carrying unresolved grief about childhood disappointments tend to replace those losses within the context of their current relationships. Wanting too much from friendships, for example, or expecting unconditional love to grow from a new romance, or even getting too involved in a child's schoolwork may be signs of unfinished griefwork.

Adults who have not resolved childhood losses may react inappropriately to loss or death. They may brush over a loss, barely even acknowledging it, both to themselves and to others. A friend's sadness at a death in the family may be met with an ACOA's invitation to go to the movies. Or an ACOA whose girlfriend has left him may stoically insist that "it's no big deal."

Your own physical or emotional reactions can often provide the best clues to unresolved grief. Many ACOAs complain of depression, but their depression is only an outgrowth of their underlying grief. Many of the ACOAs I treat have described these common signs of depression and buried grief:

- Chronic fatigue
- Excessive eating or drinking
- Withdrawal from people
- Strong dependency feelings
- Unexplained anger
- Denial of feelings
- Anxiety
- Sleep disturbances
- Uncontrolled crying
- Loss of appetite and energy
- Guilt
- Shame
- Lack of motivation
- Hopelessness
- Helplessness
- Inability to cope with normal routines
- Feelings of emptiness
- Tension
- Numbness

Some people actively avoid grief. When a current loss is encountered, for instance, they may ignore it, gloss over it, or wonder why everyone else is so upset. Likewise, there are people who never seem to get angry; always pleasant, they work hard to make things nice for everyone in sight. Compliance and conviviality are often cover-ups for buried anger.

RESOLVING BURIED GRIEF

Grief that isn't resolved doesn't go away. Nothing can make grief disappear altogether, obviously, but it can be put to rest through a process of reexperiencing earlier losses so that they become real. As Patty McConnell noted in *A Workbook for Healing: Adult Children of Alcoholics*, "Like footsteps or shadows, losses do not go away. Recovery asks that they be acknowledged and assimilated." In order to resolve grief as an adult, you must first reexperience the feelings you had about your losses, so that they become real to you again. When long-repressed, long-denied feelings come into our adult consciousness, however, we often feel out of control. They may open up wells of hidden anger at the disappointments and deprivations of our childhood. Fear, vulnerability, guilt, and anxiety may also surface when we begin to talk about the facts of our pasts. But, however painful, we must take on this painful task, because mourning is necessary to our personal recovery.

Griefwork, the process of working through our painful and angry feelings about loss, has to be accomplished, but it should be achieved in supportive and safe places. For most of us, it's much too frightening to wrestle with these powerful feelings alone. We need emotional support as we try to integrate past traumas. It is possible to make sense out of unresolved sadness, the sadness we felt, for instance, when confronted with parents who were often emotionally absent or with dreams that never came true. You need to talk about how you really felt when faced with these losses. It is important that you give yourself plenty of time in which to incorporate and absorb all the old childhood pains. But we need to be with people who are very supportive, people who understand the process of mourning and can help us confront our pain. Finding a nurturing nest is essential.

In addition to the self-help groups and other safe places described in Chapters 7 and 8, many professional therapists specialize in the area of griefwork. If you find it especially difficult to work through your grief, you might want to look for a workshop or group that focuses on dealing with loss. The social-services departments of many hospitals conduct such workshops or groups. Or, if you prefer individual treatment, the same department can refer you to therapists who specialize in griefwork. These specialists can be extremely helpful. Whatever safe place you choose, don't forget to give yourself the permission and time to find and use it.

FUNERALS: GRIEF RITUALS

For adult children of alcoholics, griefwork—especially mourning over the death of a loved one—is often made more difficult by the absence of rituals that normally help resolve the mourning process. Rituals are often lacking in alcoholic homes. Like many other people, ACOAs may choose to avoid rituals like funerals as a means of avoiding pain. Many ACOAs stay away from family funerals, remaining physically or emotionally removed from the event, sometimes owing to their own addictions. They either don't show up at all or attempt to escape the pain by using chemicals like alcohol or drugs to numb themselves. Once in recovery, however, they deeply regret having missed this opportunity to say goodbye.

Les, a forty-eight-year-old alcoholic and ACOA, remembered: "When my father died, I was in the Navy, on a ship in the Mediterranean. I was the radio operator and I was on duty when the message of his death came over the wire. I heard the news, but I didn't have any reaction at all. I could have gotten leave to go home for the funeral, but I didn't even ask. A few months before, I'd been home and had tried to talk to him. I knew then he didn't have much time left, but it was very uncomfortable. It felt like we were acquaintances, not relatives. We just didn't have much to say to each other.

"I was a heavy drinker then too, but didn't think I was an alcoholic like my father. I thought I drank like all the other sailors. Now that I'm sober I can see how much I'm like him. He never expressed his feelings and neither do I.

"I still feel guilty that I never experienced any grief over my father's death twenty years ago. Maybe now that I'm finally sober, I'll start to get my feelings back. I don't think I'm ready yet, but someday I'd like to be able to feel something about his death."

Survivors often lose out on adequately dealing with the pain of loss when the rituals of death are circumvented. Traditional ritual ceremonies provide a structure for finalizing and formalizing significant events. Funerals, for instance, serve as very important rituals in every society. They provide a catharsis that helps people accept the unwanted reality of death and return to the everyday course of living with a symbolic closure. Funerals provide, in a sense, a chance to say goodbye to the deceased and a chance to bring other people closer together in a mutually supportive environment. And, in doing so, funerals offer people a bridge back to life.

"I didn't even go to my mother's funeral two Christmases ago," admitted Clara, a thirty-eight-year-old singer who has been sober for two years. "I used the holiday and the weather to excuse myself.

"For the past few months I've been discussing her death with my therapist, and I'm planning to visit her grave this year—on the fourth anniversary of her death. I am writing a poem that I want to read aloud to her. I also want to talk about the many things she gave me for which I now feel grateful. I'm actually looking forward to my planned ritual."

It is never too late to confront unresolved grief. If you refused to take part in a relative's funeral—because of an addiction of your own or because you shut down all emotions—you may want to take the time to restage the original ritual that you missed, or create your own special ritual. Rituals provide a valuable function: they say goodbye to the past, allowing us to focus our energies on the present.

WRITING LETTERS AS GRIEFWORK

Writing a letter or poem to someone who is dead, and then reading it aloud at the gravesite, may permit you to express immense sadness as well as anger. It can help you remember positive and loving things. It is a means of making peace—and of becoming more peaceful. It encourages you to come to terms with your past, and then to let the past go.

Writing a letter to someone you love can also allow you to air out buried feelings about losses of any kind: death, the loss of childhood, the loss you felt when you moved away from home. Sometimes, writing our feelings down can be much easier than saying them aloud. Writing a letter doesn't mean you have to mail it. Often just putting the feelings down on paper will help you feel better—about yourself and about the person you are writing to.

AIRING YOUR GRIEF AND ANGER   You may find it helpful to write a letter to either parent: the nonalcoholic or the alcoholic. Writing down angry feelings about being neglected, used, or unprotected can unleash some of the old rage that keeps us unnecessarily locked in the regrets of the past. It doesn't even matter if the parent is dead or living; what matters is opening up and ridding yourself of long-suppressed feelings of anger and sadness.

You may find it both enlightening and unburdening to write about some of the following:

- Feelings you had as a child
- Incidents that caused you pain
- Events that brought you pleasure
- Your feelings about yourself and your family today
- The kind of relationship you wish you had been able to have with your family
- The relationship you would like to build with your family today

"I'm really mad at my father for dying before I had a chance to discuss my childhood with him," admitted Barbara, a single parent. "I know I still have a lot of anger to work out and that it's very, very deep. I'm in the process now of trying to write a letter to my father, to say all the things I never had a chance to say to him. My ACOA group is very encouraging and pushing me to do this, but it's very hard. It doesn't come easily although I've finally started working on it. When I finish it, I will probably read it to my group and then burn it up. I want to get all of that hurt out of me and I know the writing will help."

Barbara is on her way to completing a very difficult task. She wants to regain the personal security she lost in childhood by being constantly afraid of her father. She felt totally powerless with men her whole life; she wants to get some power of her own. Writing the letter and sharing her feelings with people who care about her is one tool for working through her profound loss. She wants to make up for the years she guarded her family secret and her own fears and shame. She wants to regain the self-esteem she lost to guilt and self-hatred. She wants to have the emotional trust and safety she never had and was always suspicious of. She was totally isolated and unprotected by her family; her ACOA group is providing the socialization and safety she lost. Closed off from her rage for years, she is finally able to express it in her letter writing and in her group sessions.

EXPRESSING ANGER

Mourning our losses requires us to move through our anger. But like Barbara you may have difficulty expressing the anger you felt when suffering the loss of childhood or the death of someone you loved.

Our strong fear of confrontation, coupled with the childhood rules that made it difficult to express *any* emotion, makes anger seem especially threatening to us.

"When I was growing up, I was taught not to feel, so I've spent a great deal of my life avoiding painful feelings like grief," reported John, a single thirty-seven-year-old lawyer. "I always glossed over loss and was 'too busy' to attend family wakes and funerals. I never spent much time thinking about the loss I suffered by not having good parents either. But without knowing it I was really furious at them for being so remote. Al-Anon/ACOA helped me learn to accept these bad feelings without seeing myself as a bad person.

"I'm in group therapy now and when someone leaves the group my first reaction is to say, 'Who cares?' But I know that underneath my flip attitude is sadness and underneath that sadness is anger. But my group doesn't allow me to gloss over these feelings like I used to. It gives me the chance to feel real grief over a real loss."

Once we have reexperienced the once-buried pain of loss, we should put these feelings aside. But it isn't easy to express feelings of grief and then to let go of them. Anger is an especially difficult feeling for us to relinquish. We may have stored up anger for years—and once we start giving vent to it, we may find it hard to stop. Anger can be psychologically addictive: as one ACOA told me, "Anger became my narcotic." When there has been too much anger for too long, it may be defending us against other emotions, such as fear and tenderness.

FORGIVENESS: THE END OF GRIEF

Forgiveness, the letting go of blame and anger, plays a critical part in ACOA recovery. Forgiveness of ourselves puts an end to the guilt and shame that perpetuate outmoded attitudes, emotions, and behavior. And forgiveness of others signals the end of grief, our willingness to put our pasts behind us. Before we can accept the past and let it go, we have to be able to forgive all past offenses: our own and others'.

The tools described in Chapter 5—constructing genograms, recording family tapes, examining family photographs, and keeping a personal journal—in addition to shedding new light on our family histories, help encourage forgiveness of others. By exploring the ways the past has influenced our family patterns, we gain greater insight into the pressures felt by our parents and grandparents. We often find it easier to see how and why certain events took place. We may feel more sympathy for, and understanding of, the trials in our relatives' lives. This understanding and sympathy can lead to a greater sense of forgiveness regarding the resentments and sorrows experienced in our childhood.

FORGIVING OTHERS   You may find this exercise helpful in concretely demonstrating your own ability to forgive others. First, make a list of the people in your life you would like to forgive. Next to their names, write down all of the reasons that you have been unable to forgive them before now. When you have finished, read what you have written to a close friend. Make a commitment, telling your friend that you are now ready to accept these incidents as past and forgive the people you have listed. Finally, with your friend, cut these pages into as many pieces as you can and throw them away.

Acceptance and forgiveness of past offenses in the resolving of grief often helps us realize that there were warm and loving feelings present in our childhood homes too. Positive feelings, just as easily as negative feelings, can be forgotten. Many of us eventually come to realize that, although our parents didn't do the best jobs possible, they probably did the best they could in a family under the influence of alcohol. Alterations of the past are impossible, but perceptions can change. Survivors move out of anger and depression and into acceptance as they alter their views.

Grieving requires letting go of the lost person or object and allowing yourself to enjoy life again. Your griefwork will be resolved when you learn to live without the wished-for past, when you learn to forgive, and when you focus your newly released energies on the present. When you can do this, the work of mourning is completed. You won't have to be told when you have completed mourning your childhood losses; the best sign is when you can finally feel some pleasure in living.

· 10 ·

FREEING THE CHILD WITHIN
RESTORING SECURITY AND SERENITY

One of the deepest losses adult children of alcoholics need to mourn is the loss of childhood. Most of us are born into the world with a healthy amount of vitality. Like most babies, children of alcoholics are naturally exuberant, curious, and spontaneous. Then, in the stressful environment created by sickness in the family, children of alcoholics lose a great many strengths they are born with. It's therefore very important for adult children to reorder their present lives to regain some of that original openness and spontaneity of feeling, of acting, and of expressing themselves. Children of alcoholics need to develop trust in other people and confidence in themselves.

"For a long time," Sallie told me, "I felt my childhood had been so depressing and damaging that I just gave up trying to make things better. I was a very sad and lonely teenager. My father spent all his time drinking and my mother spent all her time proving to the world that she was the career woman of the seventies. In high school I tried to get rid of my bad feelings by stuffing myself with food, and I gained twenty pounds my sophomore year. Not making cheerleader sent me round the bend. I felt like a total failure and became obsessed with my weight. I was bulimic for three years and did a lot of damage to my body.

"I was very lucky to find Overeaters Anonymous when I was eighteen. After a few years in the program, I stopped binging and purging.

I went to OA to lose weight, but I got much more than weight loss from the program. For the first time in my life I experienced unconditional love. It was just the medicine I needed. The love I got from my OA friends helped me to start loving myself.

"In the six years that I've been in OA, I've learned to dig in my heels and fight for what I need. I feel like a woman who is fighting to emerge, not a little girl too frightened to move. I'm learning to ask for what I want. I've had enough of giving myself away, of not being there for me. Now I'm determined to grow into the woman I intended to be."

CARING FOR THE CHILD WITHIN

The adult child of an alcoholic, as discussed in Chapter 2, has a wounded child within, a child hurt but not irreparably damaged, by family alcoholism. We have to love and nurture and try to make whole the wounded child within.

CONNECTING WITH THE INNER CHILD Looking at pictures of yourself as a youngster can help you connect with that child within, that child who never allowed himself or herself to feel like a child. Find a snapshot of yourself taken in childhood, with or without other people—when you were at an age that now brings back tender memories. Just let your feelings be your guide. Choose the photo you feel most sympathetic toward. You might carry this picture with you for a while, to remind yourself as often as necessary that this is the child that still needs protection. This is the kid you have to handle with care.

Try to think, for instance, what that four-year-old was feeling and, perhaps, missing. Are there ways you could nurture that child, still within you, who has some of the same needs today? Feeling compassion for oneself is very important for an adult child of alcoholics, who might have grown up too soon and lost sight of that needy youngster. Your new perspective will help you maintain a sympathetic attitude toward yourself now and will help you forgive the child who couldn't make everything right.

If you can be as good to that wounded child as you would be to some other hurting youngster, the healing will transform you. The hurt child does not have to hurt forever; a lost childhood does not have to be lost forever. To recover from the past, you will have to foster a feeling of sympathy for the child you once were.

DEVELOPING SYMPATHY FOR THE CHILD WITHIN   Imagine yourself as you were at six or seven, say. Describing to a friend just what that child looked like and how that child felt on some particular day can be very helpful. Think about what *you*, as an adult, would have done to love and protect that helpless child from the buffets of the world; that's precisely what you need to do for yourself today. This exercise can help you become conscious of the emotional deprivation you experienced as a child. The feeling of sympathy for yourself as a child is born of your greater understanding of the family experience you grew up in. Cultivate an alliance with your inner child—the child who felt criticized, often abandoned, and never good enough.

It's never too late to start nurturing ourselves. Remembering that every journey begins with small steps, we can start to do this by taking good care of ourselves, by making sure we get enough food, rest, support, and recreation or play—those little "extras" that we didn't seem to get in the past.

NURTURING YOURSELF   It's never the wrong time to start fulfilling old needs. But to treat yourself better, you will have to act differently. Here are some suggestions for ways you can nurture yourself, making up for the losses you suffered in childhood.

- Make an "extras" list.
- Plan a long weekend away.
- Take your phone off the hook for forty-eight hours.
- Treat yourself to a cab instead of taking the bus three days in a row.
- Give yourself an allowance to spend on fun things at the dime store. Be generous!

WRITING THE CHILD WITHIN   You may find writing a letter to yourself, addressing that child within, very nurturing and validating. It can be a kind of nice gift to yourself. After all, letters do take time and effort; and directing that effort to that child inside you, who may never before have received much in the way of concrete support, can enhance your self-esteem while acknowledging previously unvoiced fears and needs.

Sandy, now in her thirties, wrote this letter to the thirteen-year-old girl she used to be.

Dear Sandy,

You really are doing beautifully in school. Don't be upset that you got a B+ average instead of an A−. You had to take care of your kid brother and didn't have as much time to spend on your homework as you would have liked. You are doing very well and your grades would be better if you didn't have so many of Mom's responsibilities to take care of. You love school and that's what is most important.

Be proud of all the good things you do for your friends and family. They really appreciate and admire you even if they can't tell you how proud they are.

I know you are afraid much of the time and don't have anyone to talk with. Maybe you can speak with your gym teacher, who thinks you are a great swimmer. She is really nice and seems eager to be your coach. Maybe she is a good person to talk to about your mom's drinking. Maybe she can help you understand what is going on at home.

There is a funny movie downtown. Why don't you take some of the money you've been saving for your brother's birthday and take him to the show? After all, you're giving him a tremendous amount of love and support and he needs that more than a fancy new toy.

Keep up the good work. You really are an excellent student and a very terrific kid.

Love,
Sandy

CHILD'S PLAY

Programs for families at many alcoholism rehabilitation centers provide exercises in game playing, which most ACOAs find rejuvenating. If you missed out on many fun times when you were a child, you don't have to keep missing those good times now.

A group of ACOAs in their thirties recently got together and decided to have a pajama party—something none of them had ever done as kids. They dressed up in the most outrageous p.j.'s they could find and stayed up all night playing games, watching horror movies, and eating all kinds of junk food. In pretending they were all thirteen years old and trying to do all the silly things they imagined teens do, they created their own wonderful time.

HAVING FUN   Giving yourself permission to play can be very healing; and it can act as a reminder that the child within is still there and still longing for love and play. Look through your snapshots again, to remind yourself of the child who always wanted to play but never allowed himself or herself to play. Could you take that four-year-old child to the zoo today and see the sights and smell the smells from that perspective? It might be fun. Or what about that twelve-year-old girl who was forbidden to wear makeup by a raging alcoholic parent? Could you take her to a fancy beauty salon and treat her to a makeup session? Maybe you have to consider that fourteen-year-old boy who never got taken to a football game because Dad said it was better on TV. Could you borrow a friend's kid, if you don't have one of your own, and take him to a pro game? It won't make up for the games you missed, but it could be exciting to witness the child's excitement. (Chapter 16 will suggest other ways that you can have fun with kids— your own or a friend's.) To heal, ACOAs need to learn how to be children again. We have to have playtime, and it's helpful to learn about play from kids. They know it best.

Children of alcoholics deserve a second chance. We can't be children again, but we certainly can be childlike—open, playful, frivolous. It's never too late to have fun. We need to *learn* to have fun, to play, and to enjoy. We don't have to be serious *all* the time, and we *can* have some of the things we never expected to have.

REALLY GROWING UP

Growing up too soon in an alcoholic family made many of us seem more mature than we really were. Because of all the turmoil in an alcoholic family, we often didn't—and still don't—get sufficient nurturing. We repressed our disappointment because we were afraid that we would be abandoned altogether. We learned to act as if the love and support we so desperately needed wasn't important. It is vital for us, as adults, to acknowledge our emotional deprivation.

Pamela, a thirty-three-year-old nurse recalled: "I have a vivid memory of coming home from school in tears when I was in the second grade. Another kid had pushed me. I wasn't hurt, but my feelings were. I cried and cried. My mother was sober enough to be sympathetic and comforting.

"The very next day the same thing happened again. And once more

I came home in tears. This time my mother was very annoyed and said, 'Pamela, you're going to have to stop crying, you can't be doing this.' I think that was the last time I shed a tear my entire childhood. From then on, I became very tough and independent. I wasn't supposed to have any needs of my own. I wasn't supposed to be a hurt little kid. I was expected to act more like a grown-up and take on grown-up responsibilities. She needed more taking care of than I did, it seemed.

"It's been hard for me to learn that I have a need to be nurtured, that it's normal to be needy, and it's okay to want to have your needs met. And now that I've asked for and gotten help, I can see that that's the truly adult thing to do. I don't have to pretend I'm independent like I used to, because I finally *am* mature."

Those ACOAs who don't grow up and constantly avoid responsibility are often pegged by others as immature. But those of us who took on adult responsibility when we weren't really ready for it may be no more mature; we only *seem* more mature. Because we haven't allowed ourselves some of the benefits of being a child, we often, as adults, reject offers of caretaking from others.

John, a group member, told me about one way he learned how to receive care from others: "When I fell on the ice and couldn't leave my apartment for two weeks last winter, my friends pushed me into allowing myself to be cared for. They brought me food, delivered the morning paper with juice and a bagel every day, and kept me supplied with silly old movies for my VCR. I watched things I'd never seen before and always considered too frivolous for me. But they were so funny, they turned my confinement into a mini-vacation."

Like John, we are often afraid to make demands on anyone. We have a difficult time knowing how to express our needs. As children, many of us stopped asking for what we needed. We stopped expecting that anything we hoped for would come our way. As adults, we have a hard time asking—and a hard time receiving.

We have to give ourselves permission to be the kids we never were, to let other people do some caretaking. We don't have to wait, as John did, for some accident of fate to show us that we *can* allow others to take care of us. It may not be easy for us to reclaim the normally irresponsible part of childhood that we lost when we took on adult responsibility prematurely. But we should try.

There is room in adulthood for us to be not so adult. To be truly mature, we have to let people know that we have needs, that we aren't strong all the time. You may want to practice saying, "I need . . . ." You don't always have to be the caregiver. You can be on the receiving end for a change.

ADMITTING FEELINGS

As children in alcoholic homes, we learned to deny our feelings in order to survive—to ease the pain of incredible disappointments. Downplaying the importance of earlier life events, and our past and present hurt, we continue to keep our feelings to ourselves long after we've grown up.

In all likelihood, you still deny and repress your feelings and needs today. And by not acknowledging both past and present feelings, especially those born of pain and suffering, you prevent yourself from asking for—and receiving—the help you really need.

"I have a very hard time revealing my feelings. No one really talked or listened in my household," recalled Sandy, a thirty-seven-year-old health worker.

"As a teenager, I was a rebel. I acted out all over the place. I used drugs, dressed weird, and got poor grades. But my parents never did anything. My father was a workaholic so he was never around. My mother was very depressed and I could never get her attention; you could tell her something and she would just look the other way. Eventually, I gave up acting out and became very, very quiet. I was really very depressed, but no one seemed to notice, not even my teachers. I still get depressed and people don't notice.

"I really never knew how to get attention. I don't know how to say what I'm feeling. Even when I feel terrible, I don't think I have a right to be sad. I act like everything is fine. Most people have no idea what is going on with me. I seem very together because I'm so competent at the work I do.

"Recently I stopped smoking grass and drinking coffee. I took those things to numb myself. I used them to cut off my feelings and I really don't want to do that anymore. I don't want to run away from my feelings.

"Going to ACOA meetings has been a revelation for me. People actually talk about their feelings. Even though I'm not an ACOA, I identify with all the feelings that are expressed. People know what I've been feeling all my life and never was able to share. It's a great relief. I think I'm finally discovering how to ask for attention."

MOVING TOWARD OTHERS

Many of us have difficulty expressing our feelings because we remember all the early messages that said, "Don't feel." To keep our feelings submerged, many of us turn to drugs, alcohol, and/or food as comfort.

"Food was a mood changer in our house," remembered Alice, the twenty-six-year-old daughter or an alcoholic gambler. "Everyone in the family but my father had a weight problem. We satisfied and rewarded ourselves with food. We used eating to avoid talking. Going out to breakfast, lunch, or dinner was our only recreation. Father's destruction was money and alcohol; mine was food. I overate to compensate for all the deprivation I felt. I couldn't talk about my anger at him for squandering most of his paycheck at the racetrack so I treated myself to junk food.

"Now that I'm in Overeaters Anonymous I don't have to do that anymore. It was such a relief to finally find a safe place to express all my rage. OA helped me with my food program, but ACOA helps me deal with my anger."

Dealing with our submerged feelings will have an enormous impact on our thinking and behavior. When we find a safe place to voice our feelings, we will no longer need to turn to food, alcohol, or other addictions as an outlet for our pain and anger. ACOAs who have overcome their addictions say that learning to share their feelings with others has given them new lives. Instead of withdrawing from people, we have to move *toward* them. Instead of keeping our secret feelings inside, we have to divulge them.

ASSERTING OURSELVES

Because the benefits of revealing our true feelings to another are so great, we *have* to take the risk. We have to learn that showing our feelings will not cause other people to push us away or abandon us. On the contrary, it will usually bring us closer to others. Our strong people-pleasing tendencies reinforce old patterns of not acknowledging our feelings and needs. The fear of abandonment—the fear that we keep strong by locking it up tightly with the child within—is a strong force in the lives of many ACOAs. It often compels us to try to be all things to all people, never taking the risk of refusing the request of a friend or relative for fear we will be rejected or abandoned.

"Even though I'm forty-five years old, I feel that my emotional life is at a grade-school level," Phyllis, an artist, admitted with difficulty. "I used to think I was the only one with fears, conflicting feelings, and doubts. Now I know that everyone has those insecurities.

"Today I want to act like an adult in all areas of my life. I've been much too guarded in my life, but I know that to be successful in my personal relationships I have to take more risks. Someone recently told me that the 'road to success is under construction.' That made me laugh and realize that I'm successful if I'm taking risks in spite of my many fears. I have to construct and reconstruct my life on a daily basis.

"I have a very big problem saying 'no' or even 'I don't know.' I always think I have to say 'yes' because that's what someone else wants me to say. There is no risk at all in being a 'people pleaser,' but I find it scary to say what I really think or feel.

"A few weeks ago my boyfriend called me in the afternoon to ask me to go to a play that night. I said 'yes' although I was exhausted and really wanted to go home right after work and go to bed. I had a miserable time because I really resented going when I didn't want to. I was very angry at myself and decided the next time something like that happened I was going to be more honest."

Like Phyllis, many adult children of alcoholics have difficulty asserting themselves. But our fearful compliance to any request often breeds resentment toward those who ask and anger toward ourselves. We might feel put upon or afraid to decline a request, even when we feel it is unreasonable. When we give in, we get angry for being "used" or being "forced" to take charge.

In order to rid ourselves of these feelings of resentment and self-hatred, we have to take the risk of being honest. We have to say what we need when we need it and learn to say "no" when we mean "no." By starting with small steps, we'll learn, little by little, that taking risks is not nearly as risky as we imagined it to be. With each new undertaking, we'll feel better about ourselves and the measure of our growth.

"Someone suggested that I could say 'let me think about it' in order to give myself time to decide what I wanted to do," Phyllis told me with surprise. "I had never even considered giving myself that option. For me it was 'yes' or 'no' and 'no' might make the other person angry and I'd be rejected forever.

"This week when my boyfriend suggested a concert, I said that it sounded like a good idea but I needed a little time to think about it and I'd call him back in an hour. He said 'Fine,' which wasn't the response I anticipated. I decided to go and it was fun; but what made me feel great was that I had given myself permission to take time to make a decision. I really think that next time it comes up, if it's something I really don't want to do, I'll be able to say, 'No, thank you.'

"I'm sure it will take some practice before I get totally comfortable saying what I really feel. My old pattern of saying what I think the other person wants to hear is a very old one. But now I'm willing to take a risk, no matter how difficult it might be."

To help you learn to take risks, you may need support from friends, therapy, and self-help groups. The love, support, and consistency you can get from a group, the sense of a safe family that you may never have had before, can help you overcome abandonment fears. This support can teach you to recapture the child's trust that other people will accept you, often long before you are able to accept yourself.

RECOGNIZING YOUR WORTH   To help you learn to assert yourself by becoming more self-accepting, try to do one of the following today:

- Acknowledge your own point of view. You have an opinion and your opinion is worthwhile.
- Allow other people to know what your opinions, thoughts, and feelings are. They're yours and they're valid.
- Make a list of your accomplishments for this day, this week, this year. Take pleasure (and pride) in the fact that you did the best you could.

By becoming more honest, open, and vulnerable, you will stop being a doormat and learn to put the focus back on yourself. You'll no longer feel the need to pretend you're happy when you feel sad. And, in standing up to the anger, criticism, or authority of others—in confronting conflict, rather than hiding from it—you will stop being a people pleaser and start pleasing yourself.

"I always felt responsible for my mother's misery," confessed Bettyann. "I was always trying to please her. I always had to be very careful what I said to her because I didn't want to upset her. I never knew what would send her back to the hospital.

"I also felt very guilty because the times she was hospitalized were the happiest times of my childhood. I got to stay with my grandmother and two aunts, who made a big fuss over me and were demonstrative.

I never had so much attention. I got the hugs and kisses I never got in my own house.

"The happiness didn't last long. My mother would get released from the mental hospital and things would be just as unhappy as before.

"It's been a very big thing for me to talk at ACOA meetings. I had no experience with being open and honest. I had become very guarded; everything I said was calculated not to distress or displease my mother.

"I also have trouble with my dependency. Because I don't want to disappoint anyone else, I cling to people, jobs, situations, long after they aren't good for me. My relationship with my mother was so precarious—I never knew when she'd go back to the hospital—that I don't know how to let go. I'm terrified of being abandoned.

"But today I know I can say what I feel and I have people in my life I can count on who aren't going to abandon me. Knowing that intellectually and accepting it emotionally are two different things, but I'm working on it."

RESPONDING RATHER THAN REACTING

Growing up in combat zones makes children very self-protective. Our survival depended upon our ability to react first and think later. We often had to remove ourselves quickly from dangerous situations. After we've grown up, we are likely to continue reacting quickly. Not being able to trust people puts us on the defensive. We feel we have to do something. Many of us haven't learned to reflect or to consult our feelings before we act.

Philip, a thirty-year-old actor, told me: "I used to react to everything. I experienced anything anyone said as an assault. I was defensive, on guard every minute. I never gave myself the choice of not reacting, of not doing anything.

"If someone paid me a compliment my reaction was immediate: there must be something wrong with them, they had poor taste, or they were manipulating me. My typical reaction was automatic anger or hurt.

"I can handle all kinds of criticism, but I have a much harder time with compliments. Saying 'thank you' rather than 'but' has been a major achievement."

As adults, we often react according to old, established patterns of thought and behavior instead of responding to present circumstances. We don't trust our instincts to respond appropriately to situations we find ourselves in.

THINK FIRST   The next time you are confronted with a conflict or a difficult choice, ask yourself:

- What was my very first thought about what to do in this situation?
- What could be the best possible result of going with my "gut" reaction?
- What could be the worst possible result?
- Am I willing to risk having the worst thing happen? (If you think the best possible result is worth the risk of the worst possible result, then go with your instincts.)

"I was over at Hank's place last week and his dog got into the garbage and made a huge mess," said Beverly, the woman who had overreacted when her boyfriend brought home a bottle of Scotch. "Naturally Hank got upset, but my first reaction was to want to pack my bags and leave immediately. I was so afraid Hank would go from being upset to becoming crazy with rage, like my father."

As you grow less frightened and more trusting, you'll begin to respond (doing what you *want* to do) rather than react (doing what you feel you *have* to do). You need to give yourself the time to think about what you are feeling and then decide how you wish to respond. Explore the available options first. Then you can make thoughtful choices about how you want to behave in any situation. You may want to try Beverly's method:

"Instead of leaving, I took a walk around the block and calmed myself down. Later we talked about my overreaction. I had to remind myself that Hank isn't my father. He's not really like him at all—he's the sweetest, most sensitive guy I've ever known. He doesn't even have a bad temper.

"Today I have options. When I get afraid, I don't have to either run away or clam up. I can let things settle down and then discuss whatever is upsetting me."

CALMNESS OUT OF CHAOS

Growing up in confusing, even chaotic, households, we learned to live with constant uncertainty. Frequently, adult children of alcoholics equate turmoil with caring, and think a lack of it signals a lack of love. In adult life, while some of us actively avoid chaos, removing ourselves from any situation that could possibly be perceived as a threat, many of us seek out high-drama situations because we're so familiar with them. To feel involved and loved, we try to recreate conflict. Stormy scenes are so familiar to us that when first out of alcoholic environments we don't know how to live calmly.

"My parents were both artists and alcoholics," said Benjamin, a thirty-one-year-old librarian. "They had a very intense love-hate relationship, and as an only child I was very involved with them. I always knew they loved each other and they loved me, but they would also have crazy fights when they were drinking. Once my mother locked my father and me out of the house and another time she took me to a hotel. I grew up very fearful, never knowing what was going to happen. I had emotional ups and downs all the time.

"Growing up with them was like living with four personalities. My mother, especially, would change when she drank. When she was sober she was meek and mild and when she was drunk she was loud and argumentative. Her whole appearance changed when she drank, not just her personality. She could be very scary-looking.

"As an adult, I found myself drawn toward chaotic relationships and situations. It became a terrible habit for me, but my recovery as an alcoholic and an adult child of alcoholics has been the calm after the storm of my very stormy childhood."

Fortunately, many of us who grew up in combat zones develop combat fatigue. We grow weary of feeling weary, and finally listen to the child within, the child who begs for comfort rather than conflict. We realize that living on the edge is not easy living and that "calm" is not the same as "boring." If you are a dramaholic, you too may grow tired of life on a roller coaster and begin to look for comfort in your life.

Mark, a thirty-two-year-old writer, remembered: "I grew up in a family where there was lots of abuse. My mother was an alcoholic who was never able to take care of us. My father left when I was eight years old. I was the oldest of four and my mother was terrible to me. I look just like my father and I guess that's why she hated me so much. The worst part of all was the neglect; we could never, ever count on her.

"For a long time everyone I knew was an alcoholic. They were charming on the surface, like my mother, but could clobber you in a second. It was all very familiar. Since I've been in AA and ACOA I've learned to stay away from those kinds of people—the kind who would use and abuse me.

"A few years ago I left my job in advertising because it was such an abusive environment. That industry was too much like my homelife. It was demanding and I had a lot of responsibility with no authority. It was a classic COA structure. It became too painful to play the game that everything was terrific. I got sick of feeling ripped off and dealing with compulsive liars. Fortunately I have friends in the program who are going through the same thing. It's good to know there are people I can share with—and get something valuable back."

Safe places—whether they're in the privacy of a therapist's office or in the more public setting of a self-help group—can encourage you to discuss the pain of your past, to express all of your feelings, without fear of punishment, ridicule, or rejection. Learning, in such a safe place, to view the world as less calamitous than you once thought can lead you to remove yourself from potentially explosive situations. You'll decide it's nicer—and safer—to be in the audience rather than center stage in one more alcoholic drama. You may even be surprised to find, as you get more centered and calm, that old excitements pall, and what used to seem dreary isn't so dull after all.

"I used to hang out at the discos till around four in the morning. I thought the people there were the most interesting, most glamorous people in the world," Barry admitted. "Most of them were really on the fringe of society. They were part-time workers with full-time fantasies. And I was just like them. I was going to set the world on fire— tomorrow! Meanwhile, I was barely holding down a waiter's job and waiting for my big break in the theatre. But going out to the discos, smoking pot and dancing, left me too tired to even get to my acting classes.

"Today I don't think those people are very bright at all. Who can possibly do a good job—or anything—on three hours' sleep? Now I can see that most of these people didn't have any real life—just the 'scene.' They didn't have anyplace else to go.

"After being away from that scene for three years, I went out to a disco recently. The same people were hanging out. They didn't look glamorous and trendy to me at all anymore. They looked raggedy and wornout."

By distancing ourselves from outer chaos, we can cultivate an inner calm—a calm that will encourage and maintain our contact with the child within. Listen to that child. The chaos of the alcoholic home is what caused him or her to withdraw from the world in the first place. In order to reconnect with your inner child, to stay in touch with your newly discovered feelings, you will have to maintain this calm, providing a safe, secure environment for the child within.

· 11 ·

LETTING GO
CONTROLLING OUR NEED TO CONTROL

Nothing disrupts the inner calm so necessary to our recovery as much as our insistent efforts to control everything outside of us. At one time, confronted with the chaos of the alcoholic home, control may have seemed like a good idea. But now we need to break away from these past patterns instead of replaying them in present situations that don't require insistent, inflexible behavior.

CONTROLLING RELATIONSHIPS

Generally, controlling people don't have good relationships with others; with the weight of control entirely in their hands, the relationship is one-sided at best. Fear of dependency makes it hard for us to relinquish caretaking and be care receiving. But, as we saw in the previous chapter, we can heal the wounded child: recognizing our own need to be needy (as well as to be needed) makes it easier for us to give up the need to control.

"I'm always attracted to helpless people, men especially," confessed Eileen. "Even today I cater to my father. When I'm around him I find myself being very solicitous and saying things like, 'What's wrong, can I get you something?' I do this with all men. When I hear myself, I hate myself but I can't seem to stop it. Men bring out the caretaker in me.

"I think my relationships with men are very similar to my relationship with my father. Once in a great while he would be there for me, between his binges, and it would feel so wonderful. I'd get my hopes up and forget that ninety-nine percent of the time he was unavailable. And that's just what happens with men. I get hooked by their rare displays of availability. So I end up giving a great deal and settling for very little."

Controlling ACOAs don't allow themselves to be wrong, vulnerable, or needy. We're ashamed of not being able to control. Trying to seem self-sufficient and self-satisfied, we are actually afraid and alone. Controlling behavior lets us cover up a multitude of insecurities. Being in control allows ACOAs to hide real emotions; it often makes us unapproachable. It distances us in all our personal relationships—romantic or otherwise.

Controlling ACOAs usually reveal themselves through their:

- Fierce determination to be right
- Adamant declarations that their way is the best way
- Stubborn maintenance of their view as the only view
- Total disregard for any other than their own agendas or opinions
- Subtle manipulations to get other people to act according to their wishes
- Chilling silences that speak disapproval

Controllers can be overreactive as well as overresponsible. ACOAs have told me of wanting to lash out at people who approach them with conflicts. Sometimes we may actually feel angry when a friend reveals his or her vulnerability or inability to solve a problem. ACOAs feel they have to supply the solutions.

"My friend James was really down and out a few months ago," said Lennie, a fifty-year-old ACOA. "He had lost his job as a copywriter and he was being evicted from his rent-controlled apartment. I felt blind rage, but I couldn't understand why I was so mad at him. It finally dawned on me that I was angry because I couldn't get him another job or talk him into suing his landlord. I hated the fact that he wasn't doing anything and, worse, he didn't seem to appreciate all the advice I was giving him."

When someone else shares a problem with us, we often feel we're expected to have the answer—that we should be able to control someone else's out-of-control feelings. We don't always understand that just being there is usually sufficient—we don't have to be there with all the solutions. Most people in crisis are simply asking for the kind of support that comes just from listening. As one of my patients recounted, "No one was asking me to do anything. I finally realized that all I had to say was, 'I'm sorry you're having such a terrible time.'"

The reason it's hard for controllers to deal with other people's problems is that it reminds them of their own vulnerabilities. It is very threatening for us to be faced with the possibility of someone else's lack of control when we're struggling so hard to be in control ourselves. Acting angered, offering advice in a "why can't you get your act together" manner, puts the focus back on someone else's vulnerabilities—and obviates the need for ACOAs to examine their own. Ironically, we depend on our ability to "fix" other people's problems to define our relationships to other people, yet we get angry at those who actually ask for that help.

RELINQUISHING CONTROL

If you find it really hard to give up control, you need to practice getting out of the driver's seat and allowing someone else to take over. This will perhaps make you feel uncomfortable or irresponsible the first time, but it will help you learn that you don't have to be all things to all people at all times. You just think you do.

Relinquishing control involves trust: trust of ourselves, trust of other people, and trust that the future will take care of itself. We need to stop feeling afraid that if we don't stay in control no one else will.

"Staying out of situations where I could be in control is not easy for me," said Jane, who had always tried to be the perfect daughter in an attempt to stop her father from drinking. "You'd think I'd have learned from my experience with my father that you simply can't control another human being. But I'm gradually learning about letting go, and that's a big help. I'm starting to get rid of some of the fear about what will happen if I'm not on top of everything and everybody. Actually, things seem to work much better when I'm not trying so hard to make them work."

BUILDING TRUST   It takes time, effort, structure, and commitment to build up trust in another person. But it can start with something as simple as setting up a weekly coffee date with someone. Ask your best friend to meet you at a specific time and place on a regular basis. When you get together, talk about three issues or problems that are important to you. Ask for feedback and give your friend time to respond to the subjects you've brought up. Don't press your friend to respond, though, if he or she has nothing to say on an issue. The object is to say how you feel about things that are important to you. Trust your friend to respond in kind.

MASTERS OF THE PLAN, SLAVES OF THE PLAN

Controlling behavior and perfectionism go hand in hand. We feel as if we not only have to do everything, but we have to do everything right. And, in our efforts to control, many of us try to be Grand Masters of Perfect Plans. What we don't always realize is that we become slaves to our own plans.

"I have a very hard time with my perfectionism on the job," said Joan, a forty-five-year-old ACOA. "I'm an administrator of a human-services program for disabled people, and it's part of my job to come up with plans and to implement them.

"I get some very good ideas and become very excited about what can be done. I try to make accommodations for any contingencies that could create problems. I try to anticipate all the bugs. I want it all to work without a flaw. Naturally, these plans involve people and what sounds good on paper isn't always possible in the real world. I get very, very upset when things don't go the way I planned. And, of course, they never do. I forget I'm dealing with the imperfections all of us human beings have.

"What happens when I hit my first snag is that I want to abandon the whole plan—I'm ready to chuck it right out the window. If there is something wrong with my wonderful plan then I think it's worthless. I give up. I feel that it's not worth my time and effort if I can't carry it out perfectly.

"The same thing happens in my home life. My husband and I bought some property recently and started building a house. I have very set ideas about everything. For instance, I had a garden plan all worked out, and then I learned that the plot of ground I wanted to use was not a good spot because of poor drainage. My immediate reaction was to give up my garden. If I couldn't have it exactly where I'd envisioned, I wasn't going to have it at all."

Many of us continue to cling to the totally unrealistic fantasy of perfection we created in our youth. Some of us have so much fear that life will become totally disordered that we try to manage every single aspect of it. To do this, we have to lay down very strict rules. We who tried to be perfect become judgmental, rigid, and inflexible. We become strict taskmasters and rule makers, law-and-order people. We make the laws, however impossible to uphold, and everybody (especially us) better keep order.

NOBODY'S PERFECT

"I've always thought of things in absolutes," Peggy admitted. "Things are all black or all white, no shades of gray. I feel I'm either right or wrong. I never allow myself to be just okay. If I'm not a success, I'm a failure.

"Something happened last year that made me reevaluate my old way of thinking. My old way almost killed me.

"I lost my job because of a merger; it had nothing to do with my work performance. You wouldn't think losing a job could throw someone into a suicidal depression, but it did me. I *was* my job. When I lost it I felt like I was nobody.

"I had worked my way up in the company from a file clerk to a supervisor. I started there at eighteen, right out of high school, and twenty years later I was in charge of thirty people. All the other department heads except me had college degrees. I worked hard and was very proud of my accomplishments. My husband had a good job too, but I was considered the real success in the family. I made lots of money and everyone at home looked up to me. I made all the major decisions both at work and at home. I was the boss.

"When I lost my job I felt like I was a total failure. I couldn't handle things at home, and I was sure that I'd never work again. I felt like my life was over. I developed ulcers, gained weight, and had such severe anxiety attacks that I was afraid to leave the house. I was like this for eight months until I finally went for some help.

"I can see now that there was nothing wrong with me except my thinking. I had become totally rigid. I had no compassion for myself. All of my self-esteem had come from what I did and not who I was."

What seemed like the worst thing in the world for Peggy, losing her job—and thereby being thrown into emotional and physical turmoil —led to some very positive changes. Peggy was surprised to find out that people still loved her even when she was not superboss, super-wife, and supermom. Her husband and children were extremely supportive, taking on the responsibilities that she had never let them assume. She started to see her family in a different light—they were not the helpless people she thought they were. She became grateful rather than resentful. Her husband got a better job and her kids took good care of the house. Thinking that she had to do everything, she had never before given them the opportunity to help out. Losing her job and letting her family start to do things for her gave Peggy the break she had never given herself.

ALLOWING OTHERS TO BE THEMSELVES Try letting other people do things their own way—especially if they've volunteered to do something to make life easier for you. If your roommate has agreed to share cleaning your apartment every other week, for example, recognize that you have relinquished a certain amount of control over the situation; you can't demand that he or she be as "good" or as thorough a cleaner as you are. You can't stand around and be the boss once you've delegated responsibility. You have to keep your part of the bargain.

Rigid adherence to a rigid plan does not allow for enjoyment. The end justifies the means. But, since the end of any project usually doesn't live up to controllers' unrealistically high expectations, they are often very unhappy with the results.

When a winning plan is the only one on the drawing board, you can be pretty certain of a no-win situation. There are no perfect plans because there are no perfect people. In our hot pursuit of excellence, we sometimes forget that. A perfect plan is a grand—and sorry—illusion. Grandiose plans ultimately result in magnificent failures.

Rick, a thirty-five-year-old ACOA, shared this story in one of my group-therapy sessions: "It's hard for me to talk about what happened this weekend. I'd really like to keep it a secret, but I know that's not a good idea.

"Jenny and I were house guests of my friends, Steve and Ellie, in the Hamptons. It was my idea that we go and, as usual, I felt I had to control the whole show. We were going to leave their house Sunday morning and go off to the beach by ourselves for the day but that never happened.

"After church Jenny and I came back to the house and waited for them to get back from breakfast in town. I wanted to say goodbye; I didn't think it would be polite or proper to just leave. We sat around for three hours and Jenny was getting angrier and angrier. She loves the beach and we spent the whole morning sitting in the house—which was very hot—with Ellie's parents.

"Steve and Ellie still hadn't come back by noon, and at that point, it didn't seem worth it to go to the beach, so I told Jenny we had to leave. She was furious—we were both furious—but we drove directly back to the city, a three-hour drive, in the hottest part of the day. It certainly wasn't pleasant. We fought or didn't speak the entire way.

"The funny thing is I knew I was wrong but I couldn't admit it. I still haven't apologized even though I know I should. But I can't bring myself to do it and it's been three days now.

"Why couldn't I leave earlier? It ruined the whole day for us but I just couldn't do anything different. That was my plan and I had to stick to it. I'd decided we should wait for Ellie and Steve, and I wouldn't look at any other alternatives."

"You could have left a note," suggested John, also an ACOA. "You could have called them the next day to say thank you. Why did you think you had to sit there and wait?"

"Once I have a master plan in my head, I can't do anything else," Rick replied. "I'm like that at work too. If I make plan A, I can't substitute plan B. Come hell or high water, I'm going to implement plan A and only plan A. I know it's crazy, but that's the way I always seem to see things."

Group members persuaded Rick that it's all right to let people close to him know that he doesn't always feel in control, that he doesn't have to have all the answers, and that the answers he does have don't need to be right all the time. Learning to live with his mistakes and accepting the fact that he is sometimes vulnerable is a very big step for him. After seeing how his inflexibility and his intense need to control resulted in self-sabotage, he was able to begin to let go of that smothering control.

Adopting a more affirming attitude—accepting your own imperfections and the imperfections of others—can help you see that the "only" way may not be the "right" way after all. By working on developing patience and tolerance, you can become more flexible. And this new-found flexibility will increase your chances of achieving your goals.

"I used to worry a lot when I asked friends over for dinner," Harry remembered. "I thought I had to do everything myself, from soup to nuts, and if the piecrust was burned the dinner was a failure. I learned after a lot of practice to just let things happen. Now when I invite some friends over, I try not to get too wrapped up in all the details. I try to have a casual gathering instead of the *perfect* party. People like to come to parties because they like being with others—not because you've served the soup at exactly the right temperature."

Ironically, with lowered expectations, you'll get better results. In any situation, the goal you are striving for may not be nearly as important as what you learn in your attempts to achieve it. When you are no longer addicted to the plan, you will finally begin to enjoy the process. After all, it's growth and not perfection that promotes well-being.

NO MORE FIX-UPS

In an unattainable quest to make everything just right, ACOAs tend to become obsessed with trying to control and take care of others. A sense of being able to fix almost any situation makes adult children choose careers based on who they feel they should have been in their families. As children, they were very aware of parental needs, but understandably unable to do anything about them. As adults, they may still be unconsciously trying to respond to old family problems. In fact, many who felt they couldn't help as children choose to get into one of the helping professions. By becoming doctors, nurses, therapists, or social workers, for example, many ACOAs can finally see some positive results from their helpful efforts—the same efforts that failed to help in their alcoholic homes. Others act like therapists even without degrees. Because they have gained a reputation as good listeners or advisors, neighbors, co-workers, and other family members seek them out for their help.

James, a therapist, analyzed his own choice of careers: "My alcoholic father was always depressed. He even had shock treatments when I was about thirteen, and I was always very concerned about his mental condition. I think I may have chosen my profession as a therapist as a way to rouse him out of his depression. I thought I should be able to make him better. And I think I handle my own depression by being a professional caretaker to prove that I'm worthwhile. Since I couldn't do much for my father, I try to fix other people's lives."

Commonly, adult children of alcoholics love to think they can fix anything. An early member of ACOA remarked, "If it works, ACOAs will fix it anyway." Feeling a need to control everything and everybody, they often take on work and responsibility whether it's needed or not.

Grace, another therapist, recalled: "In my family, my father was the alcoholic and my mother was the controller. She took care of everything. She had a very hard life. Her father was killed in a coal-mining accident when she was ten years old and her mother had to raise six children alone.

"My father was never 'there.' He was a shoemaker and had his own business in our home but he drank all the time. He put shots in his coffee mug and sipped his bourbon all day long. My mother ran a dressmaking business from home too. She had to keep a constant eye on him. He would go off fishing or down to the corner saloon and she would be in charge of his business as well as her own.

"My mother never sat down. She was constantly angry and she never felt well. I'm a lot like her. I can't relax. I have to make a conscious effort not to do things, not to fill up all my time with chores and caretaking. I'm anxious, as she was, and always doing the laundry if there's nothing else to do. I have a big need to have things together, just as she did. I think it was her defense against the reality of things falling apart. My life isn't chaotic at all, but I still act overresponsible.

"Being superresponsible isn't all bad. I do get a great deal accomplished. But obviously I can be so obsessed with taking care of my life that I don't actually have much of a life. I try to have a balance, but it doesn't always work. I seem to thrive on other people's crises. Something or someone always seems to need fixing up. And there I am."

ACOAs with a compulsion to control need lessons in occasional irresponsibility. They need to lighten up, to lessen their loads. We have to stop being our own worst enemies. We need to learn how to be bending and benevolent. The unceasing judgment and hatred of ourselves and others for not being perfect has to stop.

LETTING OTHERS TAKE CARE OF THEMSELVES Why should you always feel you have to be johnny-on-the-spot? Terry helped unburden herself in a way that might prove useful to you too. "In my office, which is large and rather loosely organized," she told me, "I was always the first to volunteer to take on extra typing or filing, always defending chronic latecomers to our supervisor. I just quit being so helpful. It didn't turn me into someone else overnight, but it did prove to me that the firm isn't going to fold if I hang back and let someone else go first."

In trying to solve other people's problems, we don't give them the chance to figure things out for themselves. Whenever we step in to fix things for others, we are depriving them of the opportunity to learn from their own experiences and from their own mistakes. And those we are trying to help may even resent our intrusion.

Fixing things up for others is also a way of people pleasing. We try to win someone else's approval by trying to solve his or her problems. If you undervalue yourself, you may be overly helpful as a way to get others to validate you. But all you will really gain is a false sense of self-worth, one based on other people's impressions of you.

In order to change your controlling behavior, you don't have to give up your admirably helpful instincts. But you do need to learn to moderate them. If you tend to step in at the first sign of trouble, try to step back. Sometimes the simple act of waiting, of not doing anything, will keep you from trying to fix everything up, while at the same time allowing others to solve their own problems. Helping others is fine, but not if it requires you to take over every aspect of their lives. By moderating your helpful instincts, you will be able to start doing things with other people, instead of just doing things for them.

When you begin to feel the immense relief of not being in control, you will let go. Controlling behavior tends to surface and resurface, rarely disappearing completely. However, as you recover, you'll begin to let go more and more often. You'll become less afraid of not being in control. A group experience can be very helpful; in this regard, members are quick to point to control when they see it, since it's so familiar to everyone.

Emotional tightness and anger can tip you off that you are fighting an urge to control. This need often makes us feel quite anxious or angry. If you feel angry that things aren't going your way, you are probably trying too hard to control. Instead of getting angry, you might be better off talking about the fears that are at the root of your need. Another ACOA may be able to help you figure it all out.

GIVING UP CONTROL OF THE FUTURE

To help ourselves today, we have to be willing to stop worrying about tomorrow. We have to reconsider the future. Having full and active fantasy lives may have been absolutely essential and helpful to us as youngsters—it may have provided an escape from grim reality. But the real world for us as adults exists only in the present. Agonizing about the future prevents us from truly living. The future may hold limitless possibilities, but constantly worrying about it is very limiting.

Rosalie, a twenty-nine-year-old divorcee, shared her new perspective with me: "I've had a gradual change in my view of life. I have an inner resource I never had before, a willingness to live each day without worrying about the future. When I can let go of my willfulness and worry, and trust that somehow I will still be all right, I will still be taken care of, I am in a much better emotional place. I need to stay in that place now. My history proves that my own will never got me very far. On a daily basis, I try to be the person I believe my higher power wants me to be; and that makes me the person I like being."

When we stop worrying about the future, that doesn't mean we don't expect to have one. It just means we have to let go of trying to program every feature of it. Living in the future isn't living at all, it's mere anticipation. Waiting for tomorrow makes people miss out on today.

"Recently I ended a very important relationship," Sara, a single woman in her thirties, explained. "It's easy for me to get caught up with worrying about whether or not I'll meet someone else. I sometimes wonder whether I'll be alone five years from now.

"I can't keep thinking like that, though. It cripples me from doing anything about where I am right now, today. I have to concentrate on making this day personally satisfying. I have no idea what tomorrow will bring."

Staying in the "now" does not mean that ACOAs can't have plans and goals. It means that we have to be careful not to allow ourselves to be consumed by obsessions about a projected life, rather than relish the life we have today.

We need to try not to let the future become the prime consideration of our lives. We can't control it; we can only prepare for it by making plans and taking steps that will further our goals. The way we choose to live today *may* have a great deal to do with what happens tomorrow —but the future doesn't come with any guarantees. Ultimately, it's out of our hands. There may be some comfort in believing that the future is in the hands of a benevolent supernatural power. Having faith, adopting a philosophical view that a power higher than ourselves is in charge of the future, can decrease our anxiety. Making today our first priority allows us to take good care of today. The future will take care of itself.

THE POWER OF POWERLESSNESS

For many ACOAs, after years of trying to stay in control, the power of powerlessness is not an easy concept to grasp. It doesn't fit in with long-standing assumptions that they can do everything alone, and do it just fine. It can often come as both a rude awakening and a relief to discover that a process greater than themselves determines how, why, what, and where things are in the universe.

"The emotion I've felt most of my life is fear. Now, for the first time, I am experiencing freedom from it," said Anne, a forty-six-year-old sales representative. "The support I get from other adult children of alcoholics has helped to dispel many of those fears. I now have two things in my life that I never had before, peace and a relationship with God. It was an enormous relief to realize that I'm powerless over all the things I had been trying to figure out all my life.

"Today I know that, whatever action I take in any situation, the results are out of my hands. I am powerless over the people in my life, but I'm not powerless over my own attitudes and behavior. I can control my own responses, no one else's. In ACOA, I've learned that my power is in my powerlessness."

Recognizing that we only have control over our own actions can liberate us from our need to control. We must accept the fact that we cannot fully control even the results of our own actions (for example, another person's reaction to them). Every action has its consequences, of course, but those consequences are beyond our control.

But, if you can't control the consequences of your actions, how do you know what action to choose, what the right action is, the one that will have the least harmful consequences for yourself and those you love? Trusting your own instincts to do what feels right is a good choice. As one ACOA recently told me, "Whenever I focus on doing the next right thing, it's always the best thing I can do." Most people, unless they have very serious psychological disturbances, really know the difference between right and wrong. Even though we may have come from chaotic, confusing, and crazy homelives, most of us have a healthy sense of what a bad idea is and what a good idea is. We have to trust that we are basically good, not evil.

Developing a sympathetic attitude toward ourselves will encourage us to trust our instincts. And allowing ourselves truly to feel our feelings will make it possible for us to respond to any situation from our emotional center. We *can* follow our best instincts.

ACCEPTANCE: THE ULTIMATE KEY

Acceptance may sound like a passive word; but in the context of ACOA recovery, it is not passive at all. It's a conscious and powerful decision to face reality squarely. It's a commitment to establish our personal truth without guilt, shame, or blame.

Acceptance doesn't mean giving up. It's an attitude, the realization that we cannot fully control our lives. But that fact is not tragic, it's liberating.

"I believe I have to confront myself on a daily basis. I have to face the realization that I am who I am. Just as I accept the fact of the alcoholism in my family, I have to accept myself as a product of that environment," said Martha, an ACOA and a recovering alcoholic.

"I used to want to get my mother sober and I had terrible guilt when my daughter committed suicide three years ago. I blamed myself and felt responsible until I accepted the fact that I did the best I could. I couldn't save my daughter's life and I can't save my mother's. No matter how hard I try, I can't control anyone else's life. All I can do is take care of my own alcohol problem, by not drinking. I go to meetings regularly and work on the program to the best of my ability."

Acceptance can help you recover from almost any kind of sickness. It's this important step that will move you out of denial and into a process that can bring you out of suffering. When you accept your powerlessness over other people and situations, you will see yourself taking a great leap toward health and happiness. Accepting yesterday's events and influences will give you the energy to recoup your losses and continue with the business of living. Accepting today's challenge ensures that you will get better.

"Today I have a pretty good sense of who I am and what I need," Martha added. "Accepting who I am on a daily basis gives me the serenity and courage to face the work of change. I think I have a healthy and positive perspective on my life. Each day is a new beginning. Whatever happens, I feel I'll learn from it."

Acceptance often gives ACOAs a new, positive vision of the world and ourselves. It allows us to focus on what we have rather than on what we don't have; to be grateful instead of envious. We always have a choice of how to view the world. And acceptance can help us see the world in a much more positive way. We can make today a good day or a bad day simply by the way we look at it. Acceptance can help us make up our minds, as Martha did, to learn something new, whatever happens.

Acceptance encourages us to believe that when one door closes another one opens. It encompasses a "live and let live" philosophy. Acceptance involves changing the things we can and not trying to change the things we cannot.

One person spoke of acceptance. "The combination of therapy and ACOA has helped me to grow both professionally and personally. At thirty-five, I think I'm finally growing up," admitted Betsy, a city planner. "I don't approach authority figures as a victim anymore. And I don't try to manipulate people to get my own way.

"I think acceptance is the key to my growth. Today I can accept my parents for who they are without trying to change them. I accept myself and no longer think that 'if only' I was brighter, or thinner, or more beautiful, then life would be better. My life is better.

"I feel that I deserve the health and happiness that I used to think were only for other people. The foundation of love and support I get from ACOA has made me see that my childhood experiences weren't imagined and that other people had similar experiences. This validates me and gives me hope."

SPIRITUALITY: BEYOND SURVIVAL

Controlling people often cannot find meaning in their own lives; and they try to fix people's lives through their controlling behavior. These efforts at control distance them, keeping controllers unconnected to other people and to the world. In this way, perfectionism and control —leading a completely ordered life—often mask an inner emptiness.

"I was always a survivor, but I don't think I really knew what living was like until a few years ago, when I began going to ACOA meetings," confessed Jonathan. "I became a social worker because I was always very good at listening and taking care of other people. But nothing I accomplished seemed to mean anything. I had a sense of emptiness. Other people looked at me and thought I was successful, but I knew somehow I was failing. I wasn't enjoying my life. From the outside I may have looked very good, but I had a big black hole inside of me.

"When I went to my first ACOA meeting, I took my professional attitude with me, distancing myself from the others at the meeting. But my professional distance didn't last long. I was quite amazed that a group of strangers could know me so well and so quickly. There was a feeling of welcome and relief immediately. It took me some time to open up and tell my secrets. But eventually I did. More and more I'm increasing my ability to share and I often feel very connected. I knew something was missing before, but I didn't know what. Now I do.

"What was missing was a sense of connectedness with the universe that I call spirituality. Many of my colleagues think that realm is kooky and sick. And for many years I did too—I thought spirituality was religion. Now I feel quite differently. For me, spirituality is a special need, a special gift.

"Today I don't merely exist—I live each day as fully as I can. My spiritual life gives me the inner comfort I always longed for. I saw the healing that took place in other ACOAs before I began to experience my own healing. I'm very aware of how significantly the program has changed my life."

Beyond survival is the realization that life is more than just going through the motions. We may be survivors, but we may not have learned to live. Until we begin to recover from the family disease, we are "dis-eased." We feel uncomfortable and don't know why.

Spirituality, a higher level of being—an awareness that goes beyond the ordinary state of consciousness—can take us beyond survival. Spirituality has helped many ACOAs in Twelve Step programs feel more comforted and comfortable. It's a special gift that one gets, not by looking for it but by being open. There is a Buddhist proverb, "When the pupil is ready, the teacher will appear." This could be said about spirituality. When we are open to it, a personal transformation can put us in touch with the spiritual nature of being.

Most ACOAs find that a belief in God makes it easier to attain this spiritual vision. However, this belief is not essential to sensing the connectedness of the universe. More than anything else, spirituality imparts a sense of belonging, the feeling that we are not, in fact, alone. And this sense can be very comforting to us.

ACOAs who embark on a spiritual journey often find a peace and serenity that promise a much deeper satisfaction than mere survival. The spiritual quest often affords us the opportunity to find wisdom and strength, to seek progress rather than perfection, and to embrace unexpected challenges for growth.

· 12 ·

RECOGNIZING OUR STRENGTHS

BUILDING SELF-ESTEEM

Accepting the past for what it was, giving up the idea that everything was normal in our childhood homes, mourning our losses, and letting the child within come to the surface are all essential aspects of ACOA recovery. But in relinquishing controlling behavior and other outmoded patterns of thought, action, and feeling, we should take care not to discard the good with the bad. As ACOAs, we have many inner strengths, born of our childhood experiences and our innate human qualities. Recognizing and accepting these strengths can give us hope and carry us past old pain and through new pain.

Our vision of the present and future need not derive from the hopelessness we felt in the past. Recognizing our own assets gives us not only an affirmation of our strengths, but also the confidence needed to overcome present difficulties and to meet future challenges. Building self-esteem by recognizing and accepting our good qualities can help us see that there is a light at the end of the tunnel and that we are finally on the right track, one taking us to a healthier and happier place.

In the past, many ACOAs have taken emotional beatings from alcoholic parents—we were often manipulated or abused—but as adults we can find the strength to give up the doormat syndrome and learn to love ourselves—a prime requirement of recovery. Using this chapter to recognize your own strengths and build your own self-esteem will show you that you are indeed worth loving.

DRAWING A COMPLETE PICTURE

Experts in the field of alcoholism—people concerned with emotional, physical, social, and behavioral problems—have drawn up dozens of lists of personality traits shared by adults who grew up in alcoholic households. Along with the ACOA laundry list, these definitions of character traits have had a powerful impact for the good: they have helped to make us introspective and have pushed us to seek help for what troubles us.

But these inventories, by focusing solely on our faults, have only been half-truths: they do not tell us how good we are. And we need to hear that message too.

For, despite our backgrounds, indeed often *because* of them, the truth is that we emerged from our childhoods with great strengths. Many of us have become quite remarkable people, but we don't always know it since, through force of habit, we dwell on our failures. This tends to convince us that we are never good enough.

Discovering our strengths is vital in building self-esteem, in diminishing old feelings of worthlessness.

GIVING YOURSELF CREDIT   If you have a hard time giving yourself credit for how nice you are and all the nice things you do, keep a daily log of things that you should give yourself a pat on the back for. Be sure to include the compliments that other people have given you, which you might otherwise overlook.

Your list might look something like this:

I deserve a pat on the back for:
  1. Getting to work on time.
  2. Watering my plants.
  3. Making a phone call to my friend.
  4. Paying my bills.
  5. Taking the dog for a long walk.

I received a pat on the back from:
  1. My boss, telling me "great job" on that memo I wrote.
  2. My friend Jane, telling me I helped her by phoning her last night and being supportive.
  3. My boyfriend, telling me I looked great in that blue dress.

A self-esteem trampled on by the pain and chaos of the alcoholic household may need a great deal of bolstering. Finally learning to recognize your strengths and believe in yourself will take practice. It takes time to defeat the habit of self-negation you may have learned in focusing on other members of your family rather than on yourself.

"When I was seven years old I won a personality contest for kids," Fran remembered with a sigh, "but I tore up the prize letter when I was ten. I felt that my mother had won the prize, not me.

"Throughout my life I've given other people credit for my achievements. I always felt undeserving of any praise. It is only recently that I can admit that my own talents have let me build and run a successful business. It still feels a little dishonest to say I have strengths, but I have to learn to accept the discomfort until I get used to the new idea that I am a winner. Forty years of labeling myself as a fraud is a tough habit to break. But at least now I can see that I really am a very accomplished human being."

Although you probably had talents and strengths all the time, you may have been unable to acknowledge them before now. It helps to take some time out from "assessing the damage," past and current, of your family background in order to take stock of the accomplishments and attributes of the person you are today.

TAKING STOCK OF YOUR TALENTS   Imagine someone else's dinner party. How might the host or hostess benefit from having invited you? Could you be a good listener, a witty, or charming, or informed guest? Do you tell a story well? Are you willing to lend a hand in the kitchen? Do you have a good sense of humor? Do you get along with people? Can you make a relative stranger feel comfortable? List all the reasons a friend would invite you, and read it aloud to yourself—to remind yourself of all your good qualities.

You also might want to try issuing yourself a report card of sorts. Grade yourself on what you've accomplished in your family life, office life, social life. At first you're likely to be much too hard on yourself, assigning yourself a D minus when you probably deserve a C plus, or even a B. With each new report card, try to be more generous. Adopt a more sympathetic attitude, giving yourself credit for progress, attitude, and effort even if you haven't achieved a desired goal. Doing this once a month can work wonders in helping you chart your rising self-worth.

Reading this chapter should also help you recognize some of your own strengths. Like any list of characteristics shared by a group of people, this list of positive traits is not meant to suggest that only ACOAs possess these qualities, or that all ACOAs share them. But you will probably see many of your own strengths described below.

SELF-MOTIVATION

"Once I knew what I wanted, I went for it."

. . .

When we were children, our parent's preoccupations—either with alcohol or with the alcoholic—may have forced us to become self-starters, to get our own shows on the road.

"Early on I got the notion that I had to learn something to get ahead in life, and that I wasn't going to get much help from my parents," said Cynthia. "They were just too unavailable. Books became my escape from the fighting at home and my hope for the future. I spent every minute I could at the library. I loved the quiet solitude."

While some alcoholic family systems are overprotective, many fail to provide the emotional boosts and buffers that children need to get off to good starts. If no one else in your family was capable of setting goals and carrying out plans, you learned to make adult decisions before you were an adult. You learned how to initiate actions.

"I had a teacher in junior high school who was very supportive and gave me the direction and encouragement I needed," recalled Cynthia. "I decided I was going to be a teacher. Studying was my salvation. It was one thing I could do by myself and didn't need help from my parents. I knew if I studied hard I could get a scholarship and go to college. Once I knew what I wanted to be, I went for it."

Many ACOAs have a talent for independent action. If you are a self-starter, this characteristic may serve you well in your personal life, your work life, and your love life. But you should be careful that your talent for independent action doesn't isolate you from other people. It's okay to get by without help, but it's also important to be able to ask for and receive help when you need it.

SELF-RELIANCE

"We even did the cooking, which was pretty awful."

■ ■ ■

As we were growing up, most of us learned to take care of our own business—and often the day-to-day business of coping and caring for the family as well. The skills we were forced to learn—taking charge, getting it done, and doing it well—often pay off in the adult world.

"My parents divorced when I was twelve and we didn't see much of my father after that. His drinking and gambling took up most of his time. My mother was frantically trying to support us and was so concerned with paying the rent and having food on the table that she left the running of the household up to my brother and me. We did all of the chores, even the cooking, which was pretty awful," recalled Mary, a nurse in her thirties.

"My brother was two years older and he's the only one I felt I could ever ask for advice. We just didn't get any direction at all from our parents."

In many alcoholic households, parents don't have the time, or don't take the time, to teach children very much. Left without direction, they often have no choice but to figure things out on their own.

"I guess we were supposed to learn from our mistakes and I certainly made plenty of them," Mary admitted. "But it forced me to take care of myself. I made the important decisions by myself: where to go to school, how to apply for tuition aid, where to get a job.

"Today I supervise five other people on the job and I think I'm pretty good at it. Having only myself to rely on made me independent, aggressive, and fairly competent. I just always knew that if I didn't do 'it' no one else would. So I learned."

And we *do* learn. Your self-reliance makes you hard-working, reliable, resourceful, capable, and successful as employers and employees, as friends and as parents (see Chapter 16). It also increases your autonomy, helping you maintain a healthy independence in your personal relationships. But beware of becoming *so* self-reliant that you isolate yourself from others. Don't forget to rely on your friends and family for the love and support they can offer you.

PERCEPTIVITY

"Always being on the alert has paid off."

■   ■   ■

While most of us observed a "don't talk" rule at home, it didn't keep us from wanting to know what was going on around us, and from using every tool at our disposal to find out.

"I always wanted to know what was going on at home and no one talked much," admitted Bernie, a forty-year-old bachelor. "I had to listen very carefully to catch what was happening since I lived in an atmosphere of silent rage. My parents didn't talk; they just fought about money. And the last year they lived together, when I was eleven, they didn't speak at all.

"Listening and always being on the alert has paid off. I'm naturally curious. Often I get to know things before anyone else does and can act on them. I'm perceptive, and pick up things very quickly. It has real advantages in my work as a negotiator in labor disputes."

Like Bernie, you probably developed a knack for interpreting overheard words and unspoken signals. Since messages in the alcoholic family are often unvoiced, many of us learned to pick up on unspoken clues—someone's stance, tone of voice, or look in the eyes—to see if we could make some sense out of the chaos. As adults, we can generally make acute and accurate assessments of the world around us.

Don't be content to rely solely on nonverbal clues though. Sometimes nonverbal clues can be read the wrong way. Your perceptions will not be 100 percent accurate, so when in doubt, check it out. Use these clues as a starting point for honest and open conversation.

LEADERSHIP

"My sisters went along with anything I said."

■   ■   ■

Although first-born children tend to become leaders rather than followers whether or not they grow up in an alcoholic family, first-born children of alcoholics have an unusually high degree of authority thrust on them at a very early age. When parents will not or cannot take charge, often older children take charge.

"My parents were never around the house much when I was growing up," Liz, a middle child, told me. "My father worked all the time at his garage and my mother was depressed. The usual dinnertime scene was my father passed out in front of the TV with a beer in his hand and my mother in her room nursing one of her many migraine headaches. My sisters and I would be eating TV dinners by ourselves at the kitchen table. I was older so I was the leader. My sisters went along with almost anything I suggested. They looked up to me since my parents were rarely and barely conscious.

"I've been a supervisor in an emergency room for ten years now, and people wonder why I'm not 'burned out.' But I love the excitement; I love being the boss. I don't mind the pressure and chaos. I seem to thrive on it."

A pattern of overseeing siblings, ingrained early, can encourage strong leadership qualities in many of us. Take care, however, not to seek out chaotic situations in which you can demonstrate your leadership ability. Just as you don't have to be perfect to be good, you don't have to be a leader to prove your worth. Let yourself follow someone else's lead too; you'll find it can be a lot of fun.

RESPONSIBILITY

*"We worked hard at being the adults
our parents never were."*

■ ■ ■

Until he was nineteen, John didn't realize that his mother was an alcoholic. Although she acted irresponsibly and was abusive toward him, singling him out from the other children to receive most of her beatings, John just thought she was "crazy."

"My stepfather had a bar and that's where they spent all their time," Frank, now the father of two preschoolers, remembered. "He had to be there, I guess; but she would go every day after she got through with her own job. They were never at home. We raised ourselves. The two oldest, my brother Tommy and sister Frances, were the authority figures. They ran the show. Even when my parents would tell us younger kids to do something, we'd check first with Tommy and Frances to see if we should. They had the last word, not my parents. I guess my parents were happy that the older kids were taking all the responsibility.

"We grew up in a very competitive atmosphere and still are competitive with each other. We've all managed to become successful in our careers. We're all superresponsible. People are always amazed at how much I can accomplish in a short period of time. I tell them I got my training at boot camp, but I don't tell them that the camp was run by my brother and sister, who would have put Marine drill sergeants to shame. I guess we all worked very hard at being the grown-ups our parents never were."

Often, as children, we shouldered many of the responsibilities in our homes. We continue to be responsible in aspects of our adult lives. Take care, however, not to take on *too much* responsibility—beyond the limits of whatever demanding situation arises. Guard against getting in over your head. It's possible to find a comfortable balance between doing too little and doing too much.

HARD WORK

"There's a new challenge every day."

■　■　■

"I was the oldest of five and the only boy, so I was very used to rounding up my sisters and getting them ready for school and church," remembered William, a plant manager in his mid-thirties. "My father was a big drinker and would go off on toots for days at a time. Our mother would be out looking for him in bars, hospitals, and jails. I was in charge of taking care of my sisters and had to keep the household running whenever my parents disappeared.

"My management skills at home also came in handy in my occupation as manager of a production plant. I have my hands full trying to get the work done and keep the workers happy. But I love my job. It's like having a few dozen kid brothers and sisters, even though many of them are older than me. There's a challenge every day, and I enjoy coping with new and difficult situations. Life is never boring."

Even though many ACOAs are workaholics, taking on many more responsibilities than they need to, a large number are simply very hard workers. Because we take our jobs seriously, our performances are usually above average. Although we need to make sure we don't over-extend ourselves, we take a no-nonsense approach to work and believe in doing a good job. In general, we are excellent workers. And good hard work can benefit us emotionally and physically as well as financially.

Alcoholic homes often produce children who have learned perseverance, endurance, and resiliency in coping with difficult home situations; children grow up to carry these traits into the workplace. We have such a tolerance for hard work that it's not uncommon for it to become part of our leisure activities as well. Volunteering to do the work nobody else particularly wants to do—but which we relish—is commonplace for adult children of alcoholics. ACOAs are great organizers; it's not at all surprising to find that the people running charity benefits, office parties, and Little League teams are adult children of alcoholics. Take-chargers, we have the emotional fortitude to see a project through to the finish.

SPOTTING TROUBLE

"I don't need to put myself on anybody's firing line."

■ ■ ■

An alcoholic environment breeds youngsters who are good at knowing when, where, and with whom they are likely to land in trouble. Being on the lookout can mean the difference between disaster and staying out of harm's way. "I've had to learn to stay away from high-stress situations and critical people," admitted Lisa, a single mother in her fifties. "I've turned down some very lucrative job offers because the workplaces were cut-throat and crazy. And I've learned it's not in my best interest to be around critical people. I criticize myself quite enough, and I don't need to put myself on anybody's firing line. There was a time when I almost sought out abusive situations; now I avoid them. Today I know what I'm about and what I can tolerate."

Many of us retain an ability to sniff out potentially harmful, stressful, or tension-ridden situations. Although some ACOAs may move toward trouble to perpetuate the chaos so familiar to them, most of us almost instinctively know to head off in a different direction to avoid it. Immediately recognizing the difference between beneficial and harmful situations can save us a lot of wasted time and energy in our adult lives.

CRISIS MANAGEMENT

"I wasn't afraid or embarrassed."

• • •

The often chaotic alcoholic household seems to produce more than its share of crises, emergencies, and disasters—sometimes a new one every day.

"The first time I handled an emergency really well was when I was about ten," recalled Ann. "I rowed to an island with a couple of girl-friends, and we were picnicking when one of the girls broke a Coke bottle on a rock. The glass flew all over and one piece badly cut her arm.

"I went into action immediately: I wrapped her arm in a T-shirt, rowed to the mainland, and ran into the first house we came to, drag-ging my friend, who was dripping blood all over these beautiful Ori-ental rugs. I didn't care. I wasn't either afraid or embarrassed. I just knew she had to get medical attention as soon as possible."

As a child, you may have grown accustomed to expecting the unex-pected. If you did, you developed a talent for quick thinking and for coping with emergency situations that you carried with you into adult-hood.

"Last week I handled a crisis at my parents' home," Ann continued. "My elderly mother is an alcoholic and was in the hospital for the twenty-third time: not for alcohol, but for 'depression.' My eighty-seven-year-old father was home alone. In one weekend there I mobi-lized the neighbors to do certain things for her, hired a housekeeper and night nurse, arranged for my mother to come home on pass, cleaned the house, and did the laundry. I'm always good in crisis situations; I've had lots of training."

Emergencies often call for crisis intervention of some sort, and ACOAs make good interveners. However stalwart you are in crisis, though, be careful not to court them or create your own.

COOPERATION

"We rallied round if any one of us was in trouble."

■ ■ ■

Within a disturbed family, brothers and sisters, unable to get sufficient nurturing from emotionally unavailable parents, care for one another in very special ways. Even if we didn't talk about family problems, we tended to look out for one another. We often behaved generously and protectively toward our siblings.

Jackie, who talked about her family's isolation in Chapter 3, related this experience: "The way my family always did things as a unit had its advantages and disadvantages. It did keep us pretty isolated, but we learned to get along well within the family. Our parents were quite removed from us: my father because of his traveling and my mother because of her drinking. We took care of each other and rallied round if any one of us was in trouble. We had our arguments certainly, but we were quite loyal. My mother's drinking was pretty advanced by the time my younger sister came along so I took care of her most of the time. I was twelve when she was born. We're extremely close today, despite the age difference."

The spirit of cooperation within the family circle widens to include helping others. Sam, the director of a very large and successful program for the homeless in New York City, reported that most of his volunteers are adult children of alcoholics. "About ninety percent of them attend meetings of AA, ACOA, or Al-Anon. I don't know what we'd do without them—they're extremely good at taking care of people."

ACOAs are certainly well-represented in the helping professions. Even if you aren't among them, you are probably a compassionate and caring person. But whether or not your caretaking is professional, you may have a hard time letting people take care of you—your practice has been on the giving end. And, although helpfulness is commendable, many of us are discovering that it is equally important to receive care. (If you have a hard time allowing others to take care of you, you might find it valuable to reread Chapters 10 and 11.)

EMPATHY WITH OTHERS

"Our home environments were very different, yet we feel exactly the same."

■ ■ ■

It's not surprising that many ACOAs choose professions that require understanding and sensitive natures. Our childhood experiences made us highly attuned to other people. Often, we developed an empathy for others with problems, an empathy that contributes to our skill in helping people—whether professionally or on a neighborly basis. It can also make us more sensitive to friends and family members.

"Being in a therapy group with other people who both are and aren't children of alcoholics has given me hope," said Susan, a social worker in her early thirties. "I grew up feeling 'different' and don't want to feel that way now. I identify most with a woman in my group who came from a home that sounds fairly normal—no alcohol or drug abuse.

"I was really surprised to learn that she has her insecurities also. In fact, hers and mine are almost exactly the same, although they apparently come from very different experiences. Her parents were wealthy, generous, and very loving; they've always been there to put out a helping hand. But the fact that they are always offering help has made her feel she isn't capable of handling anything in her life herself. She is forty, married, and has three children, yet they still treat her as a kid who can't quite get her act together. Even with all that attention compared to the zero amount I got from my alcoholic parents, we both suffer from low self-esteem and self-doubt. We both think we're going to end up 'bag ladies.' Our home environments were very different, yet we feel exactly the same."

When we empathize with others, we realize that although we may have particular problems directly related to family alcoholism, all of our symptoms, feelings, and behaviors fall within the mainstream of human responses. And in this way empathy can help us as much as it helps those with whom we empathize. It can be comforting to know others share our fears and insecurities.

COURAGE

"I push myself even though I'm terrified."

■ ■ ■

Many of us have seen what it's like for our parents to be locked into their fears, and a healthy sense of rebellion can make us determined not to lead such narrow and isolated lives. Because we ourselves are fearful, though, it takes a great deal of courage to make a commitment to change. Nevertheless, every day more and more of us are doing just that.

Twenty-two and unemployed, Carol has slowly begun to face her fears: "It's been very hard for me to get out of the house and find a job and make friends. When I graduated from high school, I stayed home for two years, too afraid to look for a job. My mother is overprotective —when she's not being verbally abusive. She didn't encourage me to leave the house; she wanted to keep me around. It was my aunt who kept after me and went with me to a few employment agencies and waited outside for me when I went in. I guess she wanted to make sure I wouldn't run right out the door.

"A month ago I saw an ad in the paper about an ACOA therapy group that was starting and I called up the therapist. It took a lot for me to do that and follow through with an appointment. I've been to the group three times and I think I'll stay. There are about eight other ACOAs and they seem very nice. I could never go to a big ACOA meeting.

"I know I have to try and get over my fears about people and I'm hoping this group experience is my first big step in that direction. I want to be normal, to have friends, a job, and not be afraid of everything and everybody. My mother is paranoid, and I don't want to end up like her. I have to push myself even though I'm terrified."

Carol, like all ACOAs involved in recovery programs, is showing her courage in the face of her fears. To find courage, we often have to act "as if"—as if we're not afraid when we're actually frightened out of our wits. The desire to grow makes us want to stop running from fear. And, when we stop running, we have no choice but to turn around and face our fears.

There is nothing wrong, though, in admitting that in certain situations we do not feel courageous. Some fears have a very powerful hold on us, while others serve a healthy purpose by protecting us from danger. Just as we no longer need to be fearful all the time, we cannot expect ourselves to act courageously in every situation. Yet the simple, albeit scary, act of sharing your fear with another person can often give you the courage you want and need.

HOPE

"I want to be free at last."

■ ■ ■

The strength it takes to grow up with an alcoholic parent gives birth to our hope that things can change for the better. Because we survived an unhappy past and have moved into a happier present, we believe in the promise of the future. We can't always see the light at the end of the tunnel, but most of us believe it's there. People in recovery often adopt attitudes of gratitude and hope. Most of us strongly believe that we haven't been "taken this far just to be dropped." We feel that someone or something outside of ourselves will take care of us. We have faith that we will find a way to a better life, because we have already found a way to survive.

"I'm fifty-two, and I'm still trying to find out who I really am," confessed Harry, a divorced television producer. "I spent years and years running away from my feelings by distracting myself with alcohol, drugs, sex, money, and food. They were all mood changers for me. Now I can't stuff my feelings any longer.

"ACOA meetings have been the safest place I've found to be honest. It's the one place where I can sit down and really tell people how I feel. I don't want to avoid my feelings anymore. I know the process is going to be painful, and I also know it will free me. And I want to be free at last."

Those of us who are new to a recovery program may begin with self-pity for our suffering, but because it may be a necessary first step taken toward loving oneself, self-pity may be better than no pity at all. And in recovery we tend to give up self-pity as soon as we see how profitless it is, how much it hurts us. Knowing that revenge and retaliation do not work, we learn forgiveness—we let go of bitterness.

Too often, children who grow up in unhappy homes fall into the habit of viewing the world today in the same bleak way it looked yesterday. When we become adults, many of us need to be reminded that we do have choices. It may not be easy, but it is certainly possible to diminish feelings of despair and increase feelings of hope. We can see the challenges of life as opportunities for growth. We do not have to be afraid of adversity. It can even make us stronger because we can learn from it. More than anything else, hope can change our views. Hope can help us believe that whatever happens will ultimately be in our own best interest.

COUNTING YOUR BLESSINGS   Many people in Twelve Step programs have found that *gratitude lists* can help make them feel more hopeful. By spelling out the things in your life that you feel grateful for today, you can diminish the clouds that may hang over your tomorrow. To positively acknowledge the good things in your life helps push out negative and self-pitying thinking.

Roberta, who wrote this gratitude list, writes a new one whenever she feels down and needs to give herself a boost. She said it really helps to see the pluses in her life rather than the minuses.

Gratitude List

Herb baths
My apartment
My job
The clothes in my closet
The things in my house
The people at work
The ability to communicate with friends
My upcoming vacation
My therapy
My ACOA group
My willingness to recover
Good health
My relationship with my parents
My feelings

At the end of any given day, what can *you* be grateful for? Write down any small happiness that came your way. What happened that made you feel comfortable? What needs of yours were met by someone else?

■   ■   ■

Now that you have an awareness of just how strong you might be, having looked at just a few of the many inner strengths you probably have, you are ready to take full stock of your character. You need to do some work on your personal ledger, accounting for both your assets and your liabilities.

FOCUSING ON YOURSELF   Taking your own personal inventory can help you look at yourself more objectively, recognizing both strengths and flaws. You may want to try listing the characteristics that you like about yourself and making another list of things that you don't particularly like but would like to work on. Barbara, one of my patients, made this assessment of herself:

My Personal Assets

A willingness to work on improving myself
Courage and strength
Positive attitude
Self-confidence in my work
Independent nature

My Personal Liabilities

Impatience
Misdirected anger
Lack of commitment
Inhibiting fear
Not being able to say "no" to people
Giving in to what I know is wrong
Cutting down other people to build myself up
Selfishness
Resentments
Procrastination

Like many ACOAs, Barbara finds it easier to list liabilities than assets. Keep in mind the importance of balance in your self-assessment: try to make sure your inventory has as many assets as liabilities. With a little encouragement, Barbara was later able to add:

Sense of humor
Kindness
Intelligence
Sensitivity
Humility

You too may have to dig a little deeper to come up with your good points, but you *will* find them. You just may not be used to validating yourself and giving yourself credit for all your strengths.

In your effort to build self-esteem, joining an ACOA group or finding professional help can be especially enlightening. A more objective observer—a trusted friend, for instance, with whom you share your inventory—can often spot your strengths more easily than you can yourself. Accept from outsiders the compliments and recognition of your accomplishments.

· 13 ·

MOVING TOWARD INTIMACY
—
REALIZING TRUST

"One of the reasons I married my wife was that I fell in love with her family," confessed Henry, a fifty-one-year-old truck driver. "She came from a warm, loving Italian family that was very demonstrative. It was the family I never had and I loved it. Her family was intimate; mine was estranged. She had real family structure; there was never any in mine. I thought I would learn to be intimate and become like them. But instead I used alcohol to create distance rather than learn how to get close. I wanted intimacy, but I was afraid of it.

"In my marriage I had a very hard time with closeness. I think I desperately wanted love and affection from my wife but I couldn't accept it.

"I grew up the third of four in a middle-class Irish family in Brooklyn. But it never felt like a family—I don't remember my mother ever putting her arms around me or kissing me. She was very cold and distant.

"Now that I've been sober in AA for eight years, my understanding of my disease has made me recognize that she was always stoned and had no idea how to be affectionate or giving in any way. She didn't know anything about intimacy, so how could I?"

The Big Quest of our age seems to be for intimacy, that is, emotional —not sexual—closeness. And the lack of intimacy in relationships comes up constantly in day-to-day conversation. But what exactly do people mean by it? Is intimacy a goal or a feeling? Are emotional people more intimate? Is there such a thing as too much intimacy as well as too little? Is intimacy just another word for commitment?

Like "love," "intimacy" means different things to different people. What might feel like the right degree of intimacy for one person may feel like intolerable closeness for someone else. When it comes to what we expect of the people we love, each of us has his or her own needs and values. Sex, age, family patterns, culture, and social milieu strongly influence individual needs and preferences for intimacy. At different life stages, our needs for intimacy are also different. Major life events such as births, death, separations, illness, new jobs, and moves can act as catalysts, changing our needs for intimacy. As an individual changes, or the people close to him or her change, their intimacy needs become different too.

And often your changing needs may have nothing to do with your partner. One person can never satisfy all of your intimacy needs. It is important to allow other people to satisfy your need for closeness too, and not to rely solely on the most significant individual in your life. As Judith told me: "I have to guard against putting all my needs for companionship onto my husband. I know I have to do more to find friendships outside our marriage. It's very comfortable to feel he's enough. But I know that's not a good idea." Friends, in-laws, and siblings can also provide the crucial emotional support we need to protect us from loneliness and isolation.

Some people feel that other aspects of a relationship are more important than intimacy. The need for intimacy, like that of all other needs, has individual levels of importance. It is highly likely that you and your partner differ on what intimacy should be. Most likely, this difference comes from your previous individual experiences. You may run into problems if, for example, your need for closeness conflicts with your partner's need for distance in the relationship. For some people, a "good enough" relationship is good enough. But most people want to have the Ideal Intimate Relationship.

NOVICES AT INTIMACY

The work of developing intimacy involves bonding, talking about feelings, trusting, and problem solving. Both partners need to be heard and understood, and get feedback. The basic ingredients for intimate relationships are trust, love, sharing of vulnerabilities, other-awareness, ability to solve problems together, and a commitment to each other and the relationship, all of which will be explored in this chapter.

Families in which everyone pays attention to the drinking and the drinker are unable to pay much attention to developing intimacy. Families that rigidly center themselves around chronic illness don't promote enduring relationships that are loving, supportive, and adaptable. ACOAs learn to cope and usually cope very well, but the kind of coping we become expert at makes us novices in situations that call for more intimate roles. The roles and behavior patterns necessary in our childhoods become unnecessary and unsatisfying when we try to develop intimacy as adults. For instance, the child who took on the parenting role in the family keeps finding people to parent. That behavior may seem to work for a time, but adult "child-parents" usually get very angry about doing all the parenting all the time.

MINDS DO MATTER

Intimacy has intellectual, emotional, and physical components. People rank these three components differently. Intellectual and emotional intimacy can exist without physical, or sexual, intimacy. But a relationship that is only sexual is not really intimate. Minds do matter for true intimacy to occur.

However, the body can often warn that you and your partner are having difficulty with intimacy. In my practice, I've observed that sexual problems are usually a sign of deeper intimacy problems. You cannot expect your sex life to be fully satisfying if the rest of your relationship is falling apart. Although there are those few exceptions who report great sex at terrible times—during a divorce or after learning of a partner's infidelity—our sex lives almost always reflect our level of closeness.

Trying to have a caring, affectionate, openly communicative relationship is probably the best guarantee against sexual problems. Some of the most common causes of sexual problems are that people don't make time for sex, they wait for their partner to initiate it, or they avoid talking about something else that is really bothering them. In other words, they're not practicing intimacy. They're not being totally open and giving.

REPEATING OLD PATTERNS

Alcoholic family members, as we know, find it difficult to construct appropriate boundaries. Being close doesn't mean being intimate—in fact, the rules that keep an alcoholic family together directly oppose what's needed for intimacy: being able to trust, talk, and feel. Our own family history often provides the clearest picture of how we will regard intimacy. Whether we like it or not, we follow the examples set by our parents. Your perceptions of intimacy were learned at your mother's and father's knees. It is not surprising that many of us are concerned and confused about intimacy. Our experiences have not been much help in teaching us about it.

Arriving at intimacy in adult relationships always requires work. But, if you grew up in an alcoholic family, you probably have to work harder.

All children begin life with a wish for a loving, satisfying emotional attachment to a nurturing parent. We never give up this wish for intimacy. But at the same time we are looking for it, we may unconsciously play out unfulfilling roles retained from childhood. What happened in family relationships tends to happen again and again in later relationships.

But we can break out of the outdated patterns of our early lives. One way to do it is to stop playing intimacy hide-and-seek. We don't have to hide from it the whole time we are seeking it. We can find what we deserve to have.

Many of us talk about wanting love and never really feeling that we received it. We grew up feeling uncared for, and so we unconsciously seek out relationships in which we are once again emotionally deprived because we choose unloving people.

THE STRONG, SILENT TYPE

"For a very long time, I chose men who were really unavailable," said Cathleen, a thirty-nine-year-old copywriter. "If someone held my hand and said I was attractive, I was automatically in love. I was so starved for attention that I didn't question whether the person was good for me or not. And then, once in a relationship, I'd never want to get out.

I was so convinced that no one else would ever like me. And, of course, the more insecure I became in a relationship, the more the man would want to withdraw.

"I used to choose men who were the strong, silent type, thinking that 'still waters run deep.' My experience has taught me that's nutty. It usually means unavailability. The strong, silent type usually turns out to be withdrawn and quite angry under all that passivity.

"I used to try to get approval from men just like I tried to get it from my father. I'd be so careful. I just knew that if things didn't work out, it was all my fault. But I'm sick of taking all the blame for relationships that don't work.

"I think I'm finally beginning to make better choices in my relationships though. I hope that I'm more aware today and can learn to spot unavailable men before I fall head over heels. I'm tired of going through those familiar and painful old scenarios. I'm tired of thinking I can change the person who says he isn't interested in a committed relationship. When I hear that kind of talk now, I tell myself I had better believe it. I had better give up those stupid notions that I am going to make a difference."

Sometimes we connect with a loving person and then proceed to behave so badly that we elicit the emotional deprivation we expected all along. We recreate our family histories in the present. In order to avoid repeating history, we have to let go of the roles that are a carry-over from the defensive behavior we learned in our families, those roles that rule out intimacy.

FEAR OF INTIMACY

Fear of intimacy is not an uncommon fear among both ACOAs and non-ACOAs. Unfinished family business is counterproductive to adult intimacy; it breeds fear instead of openness. Growing up in an alcoholic home may have made you a runaway child, running away from any kind of close relationship with your friends.

Fear of intimacy is often intensified by the choice of inappropriate and unrealistic partners. These choices can be made over and over again until they start to be very unsatisfying. They start to hurt. Tolerating pain isn't difficult for us, though. We've tolerated a great deal in the past, and this habit often works to delay our willingness to change. Only when painful life circumstances become extremely uncomfortable do we decide to do something about the discomfort.

Intimacy, like spirituality, is not achieved by willful pursuit. You can be open to it, but you can't make it happen. It's not an answer or a solution that one gets from books or other people. It's a life process of living a day at a time in the most open, honest, and loving way possible. Intimacy is not a static condition; it's a human condition that is forever changing. It comes and goes and is, periodically, both available and unavailable. Intimacy is a choice to be a part of, rather than apart from, personal relationships.

For many of us, reaching for intimacy means choosing to forgo old survival skills that keep us isolated from other people. These skills impede rather than enhance intimacy: controlling, manipulating, denying, distancing, withdrawing, smothering, enabling, distrusting, withholding, and lying.

By letting go of old behaviors built on past fears, you can become open to finding new feelings and experiences in the present. The process of awareness, insight, and acceptance provides a way of letting go of the anti-intimacy roles we no longer need.

ANTI-INTIMACY ROLES

The environment of the alcoholic home seldom allows children to grow up sharing, trusting, expressing their feelings, and working out problems in a mutually rewarding manner. Although we often band together in order to survive, children in alcoholic homes often view affection as the object of a competition rather than something to be shared. In homes consumed by a family disease, there is usually a great deal of rivalry for very slight expressions of love. When emotional support is involved, siblings may not learn as much about cooperation as they do about competition. We don't learn how to come together, move apart, and come back together again, the normal course of an ongoing relationship. In too many cases, we are never given the tools we need for consistent, reliable, and mutual care-receiving and care-giving. We may not have learned about flexibility, compromise, and joint problem solving.

In working with adult children of alcoholics, I have observed seven common roles that many ACOAs tend to adopt that directly conflict with intimacy:

The Rejector/Rejectee
The Ultimate Victim

The Clinging Vine
The Interminably Insecure
The Loner
The Rescuer
The Manager

These adult roles are based on childhood ones—and on fears that you might not have acknowledged. Indentifying the role(s) you play in intimate relationships and recognizing the changes that need to be made comprise the first step in your journey toward more satisfying intimate relationships. Like the childhood roles discussed in Chapter 3, these roles are not necessarily constant or mutually exclusive. At various times in your adult life, you may have shifted roles or adopted elements of two or more of these roles simultaneously, depending on changing needs, situations, and relationships.

THE REJECTOR/REJECTEE

"I'm thirty-two years old and for the first time in my life I'm in a relationship with someone who is nice to me," reported Kara. "My ex-husband was a philanderer. He wasn't even discreet about running around with other women. I was always humiliated by him. He was constantly rejecting me and running off with someone he thought—and I knew—was brighter, prettier, and more fun than I was.

"But I was always attracted to rejecting men like that. Even in junior high I was goofy over the boys who frightened all the girls. In high school I had a crush on the captain of the football team; he didn't even know I was alive.

"Now I'm living with someone who is wonderful. He loves me and is always there. When I come home from work I'm greeted with a smile, a hug, and dinner on the table. I finally found someone who loves to take care of me, and I can't quite believe it. It's very hard for me to let him do these things for me. I'm so used to gravitating toward rejecting people. I rejected men who were nice to me. Sooner or later, I found them very boring and I'd become supercritical. Not surprisingly, they'd get tired of my abuse and take off.

"I'm in a support group for women ACOAs and they have a lot to do with my staying in this relationship with Jim. My tendency is to run. They remind me that it's my low self-esteem that tries to convince me that I'm not good enough for him, or that he's too good for me. The truth of the matter is we seem to be very good for each other, and it has the potential of being a close, positive relationship.

"My group has to remind me that I keep saying I want an intimate relationship so I have to work at it. They tell me it's okay to be uncomfortable with being loved and cared for and that I have to practice getting used to it. Of course, I keep thinking he's going to get sick of putting up with me, that he'll find out what a terrible person I am and leave.

"Meanwhile, he's there and doesn't seem to be going anyplace. Believe it or not, it is getting easier. The more I can validate myself, the better I am at accepting the relationship. I'm beginning to believe it's very good, and that I deserve it."

A rejector/rejectee often has one foot out the door. If you have adopted the rejector/rejectee role, you either push your partner out the door or push him or her into rejecting you. You avoid intimacy by leaving or being left. The childhood fear of being left, of not getting your emotional needs met, has led you to expect inconsistency and abuse. You are so afraid of being abandoned that you often jump ship first. Or you put yourself into situations in which someone else will abandon you. If you never let on that you needed affection as a child, the rejector/rejectee role may let you continue this unhealthy "I don't really need anyone" routine.

If you are a rejector/rejectee, you have to work on trusting other people. You may also be afraid of commitment. By rejecting, and being rejected, you avoid emotional connections that could lead to commitment. You don't know how to accept unconditional love, and you may not think you're worth it. Building up your self-esteem (see Chapter 12) can pave the way for trusting others to love you too.

You can reverse the old patterns and struggle to get out of bad relationships and try for good ones, but this new assertiveness will feel strange and uncomfortable for some time. Normal anxiety is part of emotional growth. When you confront your ambivalence—the normal conflict between wanting to get close to another person and wanting to maintain some distance at the same time—you can make much healthier choices. Ask yourself what you *really* want in your intimate relationships. The answer will help you see that "one foot out the door" leaves you neither here nor there. Until you grow more comfortable with your own ambivalent feelings, you will keep playing the rejector/rejectee—and feeling alone.

THE ULTIMATE VICTIM

"I never trusted my own judgment," recalled Fran, a thirty-seven-year-old woman fighting to save her marriage. "I was the middle child of ten and always compared myself to the older ones. I never measured up. I felt I was never as good as they were and that I was always wrong.

"My father was an alcoholic, and he loved to make fun of me when he was drunk. I was very shy and he called me 'Mouse.' He criticized all of us, but my brothers and sisters didn't seem to let the criticism bother them as much as it bothered me. I felt totally self-conscious, terribly inadequate.

"Ten years ago I married an alcoholic—a very critical man, a very flamboyant person. He wants to be the center of attention and I'm just what I was in my own family, the little mouse in the corner. Len always accuses me of not having anything to say, but he never stops talking long enough for me to say anything.

"I started going to Al-Anon a few months ago and am finally learning to take responsibility for myself. I've been telling him very calmly and straightforwardly that I won't accept being criticized like that. I'm amazed that it works. He actually stops the verbal abuse. When I used to carry on or cry about it, it just made him more abusive. Now I say what I feel; and if he keeps it up, I leave the room. I'm tired of being a victim."

As children in troubled homes, we believed that the trouble was all our fault, that things surely wouldn't have been so terrible if it hadn't been for us. We thought we must have been doing something wrong, but we had no idea what. This self-blame often continues into adulthood, making us feel we deserve any abuse or hardship heaped upon us. If you are a willing victim, you still shoulder all the blame for anything that goes wrong. Whatever happens in your life, you almost always end up saying, "I'm sorry." You apologize for everything—the old shame and disapproval you felt in your childhood has carried over into your adult life. You choose unloving, disapproving partners who are incapable of intimacy—bullies who are only too happy to victimize you.

Villains seldom admit to being vulnerable; victims are *terminally* vulnerable. The victim role assures an ACOA that he or she can stay in the one-down position and never have to deal with the normal conflict associated with an equal relationship. If you take all the blame, all the time, you make it impossible to grow closer to anyone else. Until you give up the role of willing victim, you don't stand a chance of becoming intimate. By setting yourself below and apart from the villain, you create an adversarial, rather than a companionable, relationship.

Since villains cannot be trusted, victims don't have to deal with their fears of trusting. If you keep yourself so emotionally distanced from a villain, there is never the opportunity for dialogue. Feelings stay frozen for victims, who hang on to the disapproval so familiar to them.

Actually villains and victims need each other to survive in their respective roles. The victim is actually in a very controlling position: what would the villain do without a victim? Find another victim, of course. If you play the victim, you need to see how powerful you are before you can hope to give up the victim role. You have to recognize that you are not nearly as helpless as you feel.

When you decide you no longer want to isolate yourself as a victim, recovery programs and therapy can help you get out of your hopeless situation. "Therapy has helped give me a better understanding of my mother and her attempts to control everyone in our house," said John, a professor. "That understanding has paved the way for me to be less afraid of controlling women in general. I used to pick very dominant women who I thought could run my life. Maybe I still choose strong women, but I no longer let myself be manipulated. Group therapy has taught me how to assert myself and finally say, 'No way' when I feel someone is asking too much of me."

As you begin to lose some of your shame (see Chapter 9) and get closer to supportive people, you'll begin to feel better about finally asserting yourself. The more you refuse to allow yourself to be victimized, the better you will feel. Some of the strongest, most assured people I know are ex-victims. They've come a very long way, and they don't forget it.

THE CLINGING VINE

Someone once said that people from addictive family systems don't have relationships—they take hostages. Addicts need their drugs, whether their addictions are people or chemical substances. If everyone in the family is addicted to something or someone, it's easy to see that dependency could become a crucial issue, and autonomy a frightening prospect.

"Today I can look back and see that my father's alcoholism had a lot to do with the men I was interested in," admitted Regina. "I chose very dependent men who were quite immature. I never treated a boyfriend like a friend. I was very dependent and possessive. I would hang on to very destructive relationships for long periods of time. I didn't feel right if I wasn't connected to a man.

"I was very very close to my mother when I was growing up. We shared the same bedroom. My father slept on the sofa in the living room. My parents never married. That was very hard on me, growing up an only child in a small New England village. I was very shy and embarrassed all the time. I couldn't have people over to my house. My father drank all the time; and although he wasn't violent, he was very loud and used bad language. My mother would try to ignore him but would usually end up fighting with him. It would become a loud shouting match.

"I was very dependent on my mother, but I hated to be at home because of my father. I left when I graduated from high school and moved around quite a bit. I lived in Europe for several years, but I moved back home after my father died. I now live with my mother, who is eighty.

"I used to have a tremendous fear about being abandoned. I never felt okay on my own. But if someone else told me I was okay, I felt so grateful that I would devote myself totally to him. I had no identity of my own. I needed someone else to tell me who I was.

"I've been looking closely at my dependency, and I feel that I'm finally beginning to shed my old self. I made a list of all my character defects in terms of my personal relationships recently; and sharing it with my sponsor was like being at the funeral of a sick twin sister. I felt very sad, but also relieved, that this 'twin sister' was no longer diseased and suffering. The experience really opened me up. I feel now that I can take the risk of staying open, being alone, and being there for whatever happens in my life. I feel much more whole and less needy than I've ever felt before. For the first time in my thirty-six years, I feel I'm okay all by myself."

The message of the clinging vine is "Don't leave me, I can't survive on my own." And "I'm no one without someone." Survival in an alcoholic family often depends on dependency. As we have seen (in Chapter 3), alcoholic family members have difficulty creating appropriate boundaries, and fears of separation and individuation keep members unhealthily connected. Staying tied to someone in the family isolates you, prohibiting you from making ties outside of it. If you've never had a chance to observe adults behaving in independent ways, you will find it difficult to imagine life alone, outside the family. As sick as family members may be, they seem to need each other to stay alive. Even when the parents' relationship is ugly and stormy, children still see them being very connected.

Children in alcoholic families, especially younger children, often become clinging vines in adult life. But older children can also become clinging vines—especially if the nonalcoholic parent reacted to the chaos by becoming obsessed with control. If you had older siblings, you may have gotten used to the way they looked after you, and they may not have known when to let go. You may have been deprived of independence because of the neurotic needs of other family members to keep you in your dependent place.

Often the younger children in an alcoholic family can become the focus of attention to take the focus off the disease in the family. As a result, you may have become a clinging vine, who gets attention by demanding attention. Clinging vines are the waifs of the world, children who never grew up. If you didn't grow up, you probably still avoid relationships in which there is mutual give and take. You take and expect other people to give. You are probably terrified of anger, abandonment, and disapproval—so you try to get by on childlike behavior long after you have become an adult. You try to get all your needs met by acting helpless.

If you are a clinging vine, you may have difficulty becoming truly intimate because you probably already feel close to your partner. But the blurred boundaries between you and your partner mean that though you may be close, you're definitely not intimate. After a while, extreme dependency becomes a problem for both the tree and the vine. Breathing space becomes less available. Your smothering attempts at intimacy will succeed only in getting people to want to shake you off. You won't be able to get *really* close to anyone until you grow up. You have to work on developing a trust in yourself before you can begin to trust anyone else.

Being intimately connected requires a good amount of autonomy. Being your own person, making your own decisions, and not becoming emotionally overdependent on another person are the best ways to build the appropriate boundaries that will permit you to become connected in a mature and healthy way. Recognizing your own strengths, as you did in the previous chapter, can help build the self-esteem necessary for this independence. Once you become your own autonomous self, you can become a partner in the true sense of the word.

THE INTERMINABLY INSECURE

"I worry about everything. What-should-I-wear-today requires a momentous decision. And I always feel I should have worn something different. I just can't seem to give myself a break," admitted Phyllis, a thirty-three-year-old bookkeeper.

"The story of my life is 'tell me I'm okay.' The problem is, even when that happens, I don't really believe it. I'm married to a man who is very supportive of me. He's always telling me how great I am. But, since I don't really believe it, all his compliments aren't going to convince me of my worthiness. I don't trust anyone. I always feel they're not being honest. I know that's something I have to get from myself. My group is a big help. I'm finding out that other ACOAs have the same insecurities I was always so ashamed of.

"My parents divorced when I was fifteen but it was never explained or discussed. One day my father was there; the next day he wasn't. My father was a gambler and a drinker, but I didn't know that or know it had anything to do with his leaving. There were no arguments or drinking scenes at home; there was mostly silence. My parents barely spoke to each other. One day my mother said, 'We're going to move; this time it's just going to be us girls in the new apartment.'

"My father telephoned every day and asked how I was but I couldn't tell him how horrible I felt. I wanted to ask if he was coming back, but I didn't dare. In our house you weren't supposed to cry or complain or ask questions. You weren't supposed to have problems—my parents would always point to someone who was worse off. When I cried my mother stood me in front of a full-length mirror and said, 'See how ugly you are when you cry?'

"My husband is in graduate school and I always think he's going to find someone younger, prettier, or smarter than me. And, of course, she'll have a better head of hair.

"Recently Jeff went away for the weekend to visit his mother, who's in a nursing home in another state. I knew it was crazy, but I couldn't help thinking things like maybe he really wanted to get away from me and be alone, maybe he was really going to visit someone else, maybe he was getting ready to leave me."

You too may be riddled with self-doubt in your intimate relationships. If you constantly feel insecure, your low self-esteem is probably reinforced by negative feelings that convince you that you are undeserving of love and affection. You can't accept love because you probably didn't get it while you were growing up, and you haven't learned to love yourself. You cannot trust because you still have all the mistrust you picked up in unreliable home situations. Your fears of abandonment are so great that you may imagine you are being abandoned even when you are actually being loved. You worry more about fantasies of what might happen than the reality of what is happening. And your own insecurities may be so powerful that it's very hard for you to imagine that other people are vulnerable too.

By allowing your insecurities to overwhelm you, you keep other people at a distance. After all, it's not easy to be around someone who is interminably insecure. Everyone has insecurities, but most healthy people can tolerate only so many in others.

The "I'm not alone" messages that you'll receive in groups like ACOA can help you get rid of "I'm not enough" thinking. Other ACOAs can reassure you that you are liked and accepted just for being the way you are. By finding out that other people have similar insecurities, you'll stop feeling so different and "less than" other people. When you finally believe that you're "enough," you will be able to be receptive to another person and make a commitment. Otherwise, like the rejector/rejectee, you have one foot out the door.

If you are interminably insecure, you may even put yourself down for having normal insecurities. Phyllis's husband was recently away on a two-week business trip to Europe. An indication of her increasing self-acceptance and decreasing insecurity is revealed in her comment, "I was blaming myself for being depressed and dependent when I suddenly realized that I was missing him, and that it's quite normal to feel sad when someone you love is away."

Your insecurities may even tell you that you shouldn't have any insecurities. Like Phyllis, you may need to realize that feeling insecure in certain situations is perfectly normal. Be careful not to beat yourself up for feeling insecure—or for any other reason. Don't forget that two steps forward and one step backward still means you're moving ahead. You are making progress, but you probably demand much more of yourself than anyone else does. Allow yourself some of the same slack you would give to anyone else.

THE LONER

"I come from a big family and I'm married, but I still feel alone. My wife is always complaining that I don't talk to her. And I know she's right. But it's very hard for me to talk," confessed Albert, a thirty-two-year-old teacher.

"When we were growing up, my father tried to convince us we were normal. But there were many family secrets. My grandfather committed suicide, but my father didn't tell me that until just before he died of alcoholism, three years ago.

"I don't like it that I'm so cut off from people. I can see how I use my distrust of people and of my own emotions to keep myself isolated. I'm now working on trying to be more open and honest with my wife and friends.

"My family used not-talking to keep us distant from each other. The family style was to be close only indirectly. For instance, when I see my brother he might wrestle with me playfully, pin me to the wall, and then say, 'It's good to see you.' But he would never come out and talk about anything serious, especially his feelings. When we get together we still play like kids. We never have an adult conversation.

"I also see that I still use not expressing anger to keep myself distant from my wife. I can't get angry about anything. Just last week she confronted me with the fact that I hadn't spoken to her in three hours. She asked me if I was angry, and I consciously made myself trace my silence back to see what it was I was angry about. Of course, once I had figured it out, the next step should have been to let her know why I was angry. But it took me a couple of days to finally tell her why I had been so upset. In my family, if someone was angry, you heard about it through the grapevine, not directly from the person who was angry.

"I'm getting tired of my image as the strong, silent type. I know I have a lot of work to do to become intimate. I have to trust my feelings, trust my wife and share my feelings, especially anger, with her. Fortunately she is in therapy, and she's helped me to become more open. We've been talking about going into couples therapy, and I think we'll do that soon."

"Being fiercely independent has made me fiercely miserable and alone," complained Sara, a twenty-seven-year-old secretary. "The 'golden rule' in my household was the 'silent rule.' I don't remember one conversation about my mother's drinking. And we certainly didn't tell anyone outside the house either. My sisters and I were physically close all the time but we weren't, and still aren't, emotionally close. We're all loners. It's a terrible thing to grow up never really being alone yet always *feeling* totally alone.

"Today I put myself into situations in which I'll have to share my feelings if I'm going to get anything out of the experience. ACOA meetings and therapy are helping me to open up a little and admit I need people in my life. I have to make a real effort to be open and talk with people. I know that not talking is not the answer to anything."

Sara and Albert, like many of us, know what it's like to feel lonely in a crowd. They have tremendous fears about trusting or getting close to anyone. These fears keep them in the unenviable position of trying to control themselves and other people by staying emotionally removed. Avoiding closeness becomes their way of avoiding disappointment. If they don't get involved, they feel, they won't have to depend on anyone else. Maintaining a distance keeps feelings in and people out. Intimacy is impossible in this kind of situation.

Being alone may feel safer to you than being with other people. If so, you probably don't trust yourself or anyone else. You may be afraid that the only way you can control your own life is to shut yourself off from everyone else. And control is very important to loners.

But even loners get lonely. Like most co-dependents—and like alcoholics too—loners frequently have to hit an emotional bottom before they will start to sort out their emotions and begin recovery. We often have to play ourselves out before we are ready to begin a new game. When you bottom out and have your fill of loneliness, when your isolation no longer satisfies any of your needs, you will see that you may have to force yourself to take a risk in order to get some kind of closeness. You need to take an action that invites emotional contact with others, and in doing so, you will discover that each risk will make the next one that much easier.

The single most powerful revelation to most ACOAs is that we are not, after all, alone. Becoming part of an ACOA group is often a big step toward giving up the loner image. It comes as a tremendous relief for us to know that other people have had similar feelings and experiences, and to begin taking actions that allow us to discover how good it can feel to be one of the crowd.

THE RESCUER

Ellen, a thirty-year-old teacher, told me about her rescuer role: "I started ACOA group therapy fifteen months ago and it has made me see that I'm still trying to play the savior. I had an alcoholic father who died when I was thirteen, and a mother who had to work full-time. As the oldest of four children, I was well prepared to save people.

"My brothers were always in scrapes and I had to run to their schools to deal with the authorities since my mother could not afford to take time off from her job. They're in their twenties now and still very immature. One was recently arrested on a drunk-driving charge and asked me for the money to pay his fine. I know I probably shouldn't have given it to him, but I did. They've always been in trouble and I've always been there to bail them out.

"When I was younger, I felt very proud of the responsibility I took on. We had a neighbor who was a housewife and supermom, and I thought her kids were such babies. Compared to them, I felt very

grown-up, taking care of all the household duties and my three brothers while my mother worked.

"Today I have to make a conscious choice not to jump right in and
take care of every friend and family member who is in trouble. I have
to remind myself not to do too much, not to overcommit.

"Recently I was dating a man who I didn't think had a drinking
problem. But then one night he telephoned me and told me he had
been mugged. The more I got out of him, the more I realized I had
been wrong. He said he'd been in a bar and got into an argument. The
next thing he remembered he was out on the street with his wallet
gone. He didn't know exactly what happened. It brought back all the
old memories of my parents' fights, the hostility and violence. I remember the irrationality and self-destructiveness of alcoholism and I
don't want it in my life. I stopped seeing that man after the phone call.
I knew he had a problem with alcohol. And I've had to drop other
friends who drink too much. It's too uncomfortable for me to be
around people who drink and drug like that, because I always end up
thinking I can rescue them.

"It's much harder, of course, to drop my own family. I still want to
save them. I am pretty certain that two of my brothers are well on the
road to alcoholism. But I hate to admit that. It makes me feel disloyal.
I think it would break my mother's heart if any of her children became
alcoholics. I still want to protect her. And I guess I try to protect my
brothers by not telling them what our father was really like. I don't
want them to know how it was. They were too young to remember
much of the drinking, and my mom and I have never discussed it with
them. In fact, we don't discuss it with each other either. I doubt if they
even know he had a problem. I'm starting to see that I'm maintaining
the family secret, and that isn't going to save anyone. The secret keeps
all of us distant from each other."

Ellen provides a good example of an ACOA aware of her rescuer
role but nonetheless having a hard time not falling back into it. She
may not yet understand that by trying to rescue people she puts herself
in a one-up position—establishing an unequal relationship that can
never become intimate. To say "I'll save you" is not saying "I'll meet
you halfway"—which is necessary in an intimate relationship. The
scale is always unbalanced when the rescuer is rescuing. Saving someone may be an attempt to keep people attached, but it results in keeping us sufficiently unattached. It puts the rescuer on the scene only in
crisis. The rest of the time the rescuer can isolate and observe from
afar, getting ready for the next person who needs to be rescued.

If you are a rescuer, you haven't given yourself a chance to learn about mutual problem solving, since you take on the whole problem. There is no negotiation or compromise, no real one-to-one interaction in a rescue operation. That's just it, it's an operation—a time-limited situation in which you respond to the crisis and not to the individual. This is the opposite of intimacy, which is a committed mutual relationship. Rescuing is an attach-detach operation that doesn't allow intimacy to develop. It's one person acting for, rather than with, another.

As children who always tried to protect our families, it's easy for us to adapt quickly to adult rescuer roles. It maintains our investment in being the parent, being the responsible one who never gets into the unfamiliar position of being cared for. We do all the caretaking to prevent looking at our own dependency needs and fears. (See Chapter 11.) By trying to rescue another person, we avoid putting ourselves in the vulnerable position of relying on someone else.

THE MANAGER

"I've been involved in three relationships that haven't worked," said Marcia. "I keep marrying the same kind of man and leaving for the same reasons. My first husband turned out to be an alcoholic and my second was addicted to coke.

"I always end up being the super caretaker. As long as I can stay in charge, I pretend things are okay, but actually everything in my life falls apart.

"When I was about fourteen or fifteen I knew our family had a problem. My father was a traveling salesman, so he was on the road most of the time, and my mother stayed at home, getting drunk and taking pills. I was very resentful and embarrassed most of the time. She'd get me to telephone my father so he would come home. She was very manipulative, but I always thought she was just weak. I never wanted to be like her, to be that out of control. I ended up managing everyone else's life but I guess I haven't done so well with my own.

"My brother and sister still expect me to be there for them the way I always was, but I'm trying to break that pattern. My caretaking role was beginning to become too big of a burden. I was exhausted all the time and growing very resentful. I finally went for help. I began to see how much it was hurting me, always to be in a position of solving other people's problems. I managed everyone's life for so many years that they still expect me to be in charge. My sister recently complained that I didn't visit her very much and I told her she liked it the old way, when I used to run in to fix everything. She misses my omnipotent-mommy figure—the one that made everything work. I'm not doing that anymore, and they're just going to have to get used to it."

Like rescuers, managers like to stay in control of their relationships, maintaining a safe emotional distance by putting themselves in a one-up position. But, while rescuers save, managers boss. Unlike rescuers, who martyr themselves to save the "helpless," managers don't feel they have to save anyone. Managers simply feel they know what's best for everyone else around them.

If you still love to be a manager and hate being managed, you may not feel any more competent or capable than most people, but you are skillful at covering up your insecurities by projecting a larger-than-life image. Your way is the only way you can be sure of. You probably became so good at caretaking when you were a child that you still feel you have to be in charge.

If you are a manager, you may not see that the only reason you're not physically alone is that there are always people around who love to be taken care of. But you *do* stay isolated: you keep yourself far above all those people who can't get their acts together without your assistance. You really keep yourself very separate.

Managing other people's lives every minute of every hour of the day may allow you to avoid looking at the unmanageability of your own life. ACOAs with an obsession for control permit no negotiation or compromise. The only way is management's way. If you manage other people's lives, you can't possibly get involved in intimate relationships, since you won't allow yourself to show your own vulnerabilities. And you certainly can't count on anyone else to help you solve any problems that come up. At least that's what you may think.

It's perfectly understandable if, having grown up in a family in which one person was usually much less functional than the others, you find it difficult to trade the tried-and-true management style for the more unpredictable partnership arrangement. But, if you do have a compulsion to manage, you will find it worthwhile to review Chapter 11 carefully, practicing the exercises designed to help you relinquish control.

BECOMING INTIMATE

BASIC TRUST

Truly believing that another person is going to be physically and emotionally dependable isn't easy for adults who have grown up in very insecure home environments. In families that are chronically ill, child care is often insufficient and inconsistent. Parental stress is stressful for children too. Parents in alcoholic homes almost always do love their children, but are seldom able to show it because they have such severe problems of their own.

Children in alcoholic homes grow up feeling constantly on edge, never knowing what will happen next. And in a confused or chaotic home it's often hard for a child to find safety and security. Alcoholism prevents children from getting the kind of love and nurturing that all children need.

When these children grow up, they often find that they can't trust others. Since their level of distrust is much higher than their level of trust, they may still feel that they can't really count on *anyone*.

Parents are the people children most want to count on. When a child is disappointed, it can be devastating. Some kids develop tough exteriors to cover up the deep hurt; and many of us still wear masks. We acted as if it really didn't matter that our parents were constantly letting us down, that our needs didn't seem as important as parental ones. But it mattered very much indeed. Broken promises break hearts. What may seem like "no big thing" to an ill or overwhelmed parent is often a "very big thing" to a child.

When ACOAs tell their stories, that old pain is still there. The stories of emotional and/or physical parental neglect and abuse, intentional or unintentional, are filled with pain. To be deceived by the people you most want to trust is very cruel. To be harmed by the parents you depend on to care for you damages the heart as well as the body.

Lack of trust is evident in the anti-intimacy roles previously described. Rescuers, loners, and managers can only trust themselves; rejectors/rejectees and victims can't trust anyone; and the clinging vines and interminably insecure ACOAs can't trust themselves *or* anyone else.

Whatever role or roles you may have adopted that stands in the way of intimacy, you have to work on trusting other people. Building trust starts with a small but firm foundation. You may only need to find one "solid citizen," someone consistently caring and conscientious, to convince you that some people *can* be trustworthy. Or you may need therapy to help you establish this trust. A support group like Al-Anon/ ACOA or AA—anonymous and confidential organizations—can often nurture the basic trust you may need to develop. Start small, though. Don't expect a friend to jump off a bridge for you. Ask a friend to pick you up from work when your car is in the shop. Or ask a fellow ACOA group member to give you a lift to the next meeting. Establishing even a little bit of trust with another will immediately loosen the hold of rigid and unfulfilling roles, while creating a safe place from which to build more satisfying and intimate relationships.

TOXINS AND TONICS

Many of us still don't trust others because we find it difficult to distinguish the safe people from the dangerous people in our lives. Finding a loving and supportive partner for our intimate relationships is like taking a tonic; it makes us feel better, about ourselves and the rest of the world. But entering into yet another relationship with someone withdrawn, abusive, overwhelming, or hot-and-cold can be toxic; it poisons our view of ourselves and the world.

"It's taken quite a while for me to learn about people: which ones are good for me and which ones I should avoid," confessed Elizabeth, a forty-one-year-old social worker. "For a long time, I was attracted to people who were emotionally closed down and depressed, like my family.

"My father was an alcoholic who blamed all of his many physical ailments on other things. He was an immigrant who felt discriminated against in this country. He probably was; but it made all of his children paranoid. I still tend to see most people as The Enemy—especially if I feel I'm not being heard and understood. It's easy for me to feel people are out to get me.

"Years after my divorce, I ran into my ex-husband on the street. I was struck by how he had that same frozen look my father always had. I had never realized it before. He was an alcoholic also, and was emotionally stuck, just like my father.

"I have to try and stay away from people like that today. I have enough history to know they're not good for me."

Toxic people have an investment in negativity and illness. They can be poisonous for us. Being around depressed people is familiar enough to us, but we must realize that it's also dangerous. We usually feel hopeless enough on our own. People who are addicted to misery are not good choices for those of us who are trying to get out of our own miseries.

"My main addiction has been to critical men," said Lucinda, a twenty-seven-year-old bank officer. "My father, who was an alcoholic, was very critical of people. He always put my mother down in front of others, correcting her grammar, telling her she wasn't able to do anything right. He was critical of me too; I never felt he approved of me—

he was always blaming me for something. In my relationships with men, I was always looking for approval and usually looking in the wrong place.

"I try now not to be scapegoated like I felt scapegoated in my family. I can usually see who's poison, and when I find myself attracted to someone like that I walk away fast."

Recovery programs and peer groups in which people want to get better are often the best tonics for adult children of alcoholics. We need to get messages of hope and health, not doom and gloom. To feel uplifted, we need to have uplifting people around us. Most of us have missed out on reliable, supportive people in our lives; we have to find people we can trust and be intimate with.

ARE YOUR NEEDS BEING MET?   Consider your present relationship and make a list: Write "I need . . ." at the top of the paper. Take the time to fill in the list completely. Now go over the list and score your needs in terms of priorities—from most to least important. Divide the list into a top half and a bottom half, putting the most important needs first. Are most of your top-of-the-list needs being met most of the time, some of the time, or none of the time? Can you satisfy your bottom-of-the-list needs outside this relationship? Remember, of course, that no partner can meet all of your needs. But this list may give you some idea of how reasonable your expectations are and what the likelihood is of getting those expectations, or many of them, met in this particular relationship.

Family members who haven't yet begun their own recovery programs may still be toxic for us. But relatives can also often be tonic. Reestablishing ties—through letter writing or a family taping, for instance—with the people you may have once written off can often make us feel better about ourselves and the world, as you will see in the next chapter. Like rekindled friendships, revitalized relationships with siblings, cousins, and parents can often provide considerable love and support.

By identifying and reexperiencing anger, hurt, sadness, and shame in a safe setting, we learn that tonic people can get angry at us without staying angry with us; they don't reject us and aren't destroyed by us. They allow us to be whoever we are. Tonic people provide the reality that permits us to be real. People who are safe, people who are tonic, provide the kind of softness we need to feel liberated from the past and loved in the present.

SELF-ACCEPTANCE

Over and over again we hear, "You can't love anyone until you love yourself." But we hear it so often because it's true. Adult children of alcoholics, like other people, need a strong sense of self-identity before they can become emotionally connected in a healthy way to anyone else. The anti-intimacy roles are all characterized by low self-esteem. Even the managers, rescuers, and loners—who give an outward appearance of being self-contained and self-sufficient—are covering up the vulnerability they share with everyone else.

In order to achieve self-acceptance we have to change our self-images. We need to stop playing these old tapes:

"I'm not enough."
"It's my fault."
"I don't need anyone."
"I'm sorry."
"I'll take care of you, don't worry about me."
"I'm no one without someone."
"I'll do it alone."

We have to get rid of the self-doubt, self-blame, and self-hate that prevent us from becoming self-accepting. Trying to live up to our own conception of what other people's standards are often keeps us from self-acceptance. We spend a great deal of our time and energy being the person we think someone else wants us to be, but we can stop people pleasing now. Instead of becoming preoccupied with trying to figure out what other people want and expect of us, we need to focus on what *we* want in our lives.

Self-acceptance comes when you are able to feel, genuinely, "I am who I am." That happens when you stop trying to be someone else, instead of yourself. Excellence must be judged from a personal standard, not a societal one. The only real barometer of success is how you feel about yourself.

When your relationship with yourself is satisfying, you will be better able to have a relationship with someone else that is mutually satisfying. Self-love alone is limiting; but self-love and love of someone else provide limitless opportunities.

VULNERABILITY

Making ourselves vulnerable—sharing our innermost feelings—is what brings us closest to other people. If we don't allow ourselves to be vulnerable—to show another person our own neediness—we're not being totally open and honest. Letting others see the aspects of our character that we don't like—as well as the traits we do like—is the only kind of self-revelation that can encourage others to match our vulnerability. This mutual exchange is what marks the beginning of true intimacy.

Once we can admit our fears and show another person our whole selves, we can start to move toward intimacy. Obviously, we need to allow ourselves the time to build up a certain amount of trust before we can admit how vulnerable we are. Some ACOAs, in a desperate attempt at intimacy, reveal all of their secrets and feelings in a mad rush after building only a small amount of trust in another person— without first assuring themselves that the other person is tonic rather than toxic.

This kind of outpouring gives the other person too much power, and may set up the overly vulnerable ACOA for disappointment, hurt, and victimization. Making yourself vulnerable requires you to reveal yourself in small steps, allowing the other person to respond in kind. Only in this way can you both grow together. Revealing yourself too fast—especially if you have made an unwise choice of partner, someone who will take advantage of your vulnerability—may make the possibility of your own vulnerability seem even more threatening the next time.

When we refuse to allow ourselves to be vulnerable, though, we are still denying that we have emotional needs like everyone else. By now, you know enough about denial to know it usually outlives its usefulness. In most cases, it harms much more than it protects. People stay in denial when they feel threatened. Allowing ourselves to be vulnerable, revealing our darkest secrets and true selves, means taking a risk. But the rewards are well worth the risk.

Intimacy shouldn't be threatening—it should bring people great comfort. Without vulnerability, we deprive ourselves of the deep satisfaction that comes from loving and being loved. When we are accepted after making ourselves vulnerable, we are accepted for our whole selves, not just the parts we may think are attractive to others.

The anti-intimacy roles are defenses against vulnerability. Because they reveal only parts of our true selves, they are one-sided characterizations of two-sided characters. Rescuers may be strong, but they are also frightened. Victims may be frightened, but they are also strong. Rejector/rejectees may be distancing, but they also want closeness. Clinging vines may be dependent, but only because they are afraid to show their independence. Managers may be in charge, but only because they're so afraid of losing control. The interminably insecure may have low self-esteem, but they are also grandiose. Loners may be independent, but they're also afraid to lean on someone else. In order to be truly intimate, we—and our partners—need to reveal and make understood both sides of our characters. Intimacy will develop as our communication becomes more honest, open, and empathetic.

Humility, which permits us to give up our guilt and shame (see pages 118–122), paves the way for allowing ourselves to be vulnerable. Only by recognizing and accepting our own human imperfections and limitations can we prepare ourselves for acknowledging them to another person. Humility, by bonding us with the rest of the human race, permits us to make ourselves available to other persons without trying to exercise control through either manipulation or force. It encourages us to make allowances for ourselves and for the people we love; and this opens us to and readies us for intimacy.

RESOLVING AMBIVALENCE

The many uncertainties of the alcoholic homes in which we grew up made many of us unclear about what we really want and need in terms of personal relationships. For instance, an ACOA may *say* she wants to get involved with a warm, giving man, yet always finds herself attracted to cold, distant men. She feels ambivalent: she says she wants one thing but rejects it and goes for something quite different. Her internal conflict leaves her feeling confused, dissatisfied, and frustrated.

Ambivalence is a very human and common experience. Almost everyone in the world feels ambivalent about someone or something. But ACOAs tend to deny or repress our ambivalent feelings. Our conflicting feelings about the shifting personalities of our parents and the pressure we felt as children to choose one parent as all good and the other as all bad made ambivalent feelings seem threatening to us. And by repressing ambivalent feelings we prohibit any possibility of resolving them.

Those of us raised in alcoholic families, where conflicts were never negotiated or resolved, often have difficulty resolving individual ambivalence about significant relationships. If you find yourself wanting one thing but consistently pursuing its opposite, you need to sort out your mixed feelings. By staying trapped in unresolved ambivalence, you will probably continue to choose unavailable partners, partners who can't meet your intimacy needs.

SORTING OUT AMBIVALENCE   Make a "pain and pleasure" list. What gives you pleasure and what causes you pain? Make an effort to move toward the things that make you feel good and try to avoid the things that make you feel bad. This will help you move in the direction of less ambivalence.

Ambivalence is a normal condition that often serves as a prelude to resolution. Recognizing ambivalence presents you with a choice: You can move in either direction. Staying ambivalent means staying stuck and not getting real gratification. Making a choice, taking a stand, is the only way to get that gratification you want and need.

Ambivalence is seldom fully resolved. No relationship is totally without conflict, and no partner will ever be able to be all things all the time—lover, therapist, friend, parent, child, rescuer, victim, and on and on. But we can grow more comfortable with our unresolved feelings.

If these feelings are causing anxiety, you may have to take whatever actions you can to resolve your own ambivalence. Concentrating on what you can do to improve the relationship, what changes you can make in yourself, how clearly you express yourself and how willing you are to compromise and listen will help determine the ways in which your relationship will change. Waiting and wanting the other person to change will only keep the relationship exactly where it is. You have to be honest and clear with your partner, with the full knowledge that you may always be somewhat unclear or mixed up. No one ever gets rid of all ambivalent feelings, but you can try to make them work for you rather than against you.

ELIMINATING BARRIERS TO RESOLVING AMBIVALENCE   You might find this exercise helpful in sorting out your mixed feelings about intimate relationships. Make two columns, with the headings "I should. . . ." and "my partner should. . . ." In the first column, list all of the things you think you should or ought to do in terms of the particular relationship you feel ambivalent about. In the second column, list the things you think your partner should or ought to do.

Examine each item in these lists carefully. Then write "unacceptable behavior" next to each one. You are acting out your people pleasing in the first list and your need to control in the second. Neither will help you deal with your ambivalence.

TAKING CHARGE WITHOUT TAKING CONTROL

The factor of control, which disrupts so many aspects of our lives, plays an important part in our intimate relationships with others. All of the anti-intimacy roles are attempts at passive or aggressive control. Rejectors control by pushing people out of their lives. Rejectees control by manipulating their own exits. Rescuers control by "saving the lives" of people they perceive to be out of control. Victims are in control because they recruit and train their victimizers. Managers have to be in control because, obviously, no one else can do the job. Clinging vines control by hanging on so tightly that the people they are attached to can't move about freely. And the insecure don't let anyone forget their insecurities for a moment.

A controlled relationship can't be intimate because only one person can be in control at any one time. The features of cooperation, of mutual sharing and problem solving, are never evident when one person controls another. Control in a relationship is one-sided; it prohibits the mutuality essential to intimacy. The person who is in control doesn't have much sympathy for another point of view. Judgmental attitudes intensify the control: the controller insists that his or her way is the only way. Control is a one-way street—and it leads in the opposite direction from intimacy.

If controlling behavior gets in the way of your intimate relationships, you would be well-advised to reread Chapter 11 carefully. It will help point out ways in which you try to control others and suggest strategies for changing this behavior to allow for more-intimate relationships.

UNDERSTANDING AND BEING UNDERSTOOD

In intimate relationships, people are both understanding and understood. The give-and-take process of listening and talking brings people closer together.

"My mother would never actually fight with my father, so it took me some time to realize that my husband and I could have an argument and resolve a conflict," said Sally. "I'm just learning to express my emotions; the fact that he is open and emotional is very helpful. I was considered weak and oversensitive when I expressed my feelings as a kid. I wasn't supposed to be emotional.

"I'm beginning to learn how to be open, and to know that it's safe to say basically what I feel when I feel it. I always knew my husband could deal with problems, but I wasn't sure I could. Today I reassure myself that I can too."

Naturally, it is important to keep some things to yourself in a personal relationship. If your honesty will bring unnecessary harm to someone else, it is probably wiser to keep it to yourself. Being blatantly honest is not always the best policy. (For example, your partner may not want to hear about your sexual fantasies that involve another person.) In the main, though, honest and open communication benefits both partners. It reveals our true selves, with all our vulnerabilities, and usually spurs the other person to do the same.

Patterns of not being listened to, or understood, often stand in the way of our being heard. Coming from families with blurred boundaries, we sometimes think people should be able to read our minds, and we are very hurt when they don't. We often know what we need, but we don't always know how to ask for it. We have to learn to speak up.

But be careful not to forget the importance of listening. Finally breaking the silence after so many years, some of us become so concerned with being heard that we have a hard time listening. We may be so intent on forming our rebuttals that we never hear the argument.

PRACTICING COMMUNICATION You may want to practice good communication skills with your partner or a friend by:

- Setting talk time: "Let's spend this Sunday morning talking about whatever is on our minds."
- Giving equal time: "I'll talk for ten minutes about my feelings and then you can take ten."
- Refraining from interruptions: "I promise not to interrupt until you're done speaking."
- Agreeing to limit defensiveness: "I won't feel attacked; I'll just listen to what you have to say."
- Telling your partner what you heard. It may not have been what he or she said: "If I heard you correctly, you said . . ."

Setting ourselves up in either/or positions of either only listening or only talking prevents us from other-awareness. We either never get to learn what other people are feeling, or we never let them know what we are feeling. Obviously we can't experience someone else's pleasure or pain, but there is a great deal to be learned and understood by trying to put ourselves in someone else's shoes.

COMMITMENT

Adult children of alcoholics are not the only people who have fears about commitment. It is a word that has an unfortunately stifling connotation, when in fact commitment can be quite liberating. To make a commitment to oneself, to commit oneself to having a fuller, happier life, is a very important and exciting experience. Making a commitment is making a statement of intent. If the intention is to more fully develop personal relationships, why should it be so dreaded?

Commitment in an intimate relationship means the people involved no longer choose to be alone. It is a way for two people to live in consort, not in opposition. Granting that the living is not always easy, most people seem to find it a better way of life. People need people. Without meaningful relationships with family, friends, and lovers, life is very empty.

We are probably much more committed than we give ourselves credit for being. The very word can sound more ominous than the practice: to many ears, "commitment" suggests setting a relationship in cement. Promise yourself to turn a deaf ear to any such notion. Just as there are degrees of any kind of emotional investment, there are degrees of commitment. Different relationships have different levels. Commitment is a process of growing together to prevent growing apart. It's not the end of anything; it's the beginning of an intimate journey.

REAFFIRMING
THE FUTURE

· 14 ·

NEW BALANCE,
NEW PERSPECTIVES

REBUILDING RELATIONSHIPS
WITH PARENTS AND SIBLINGS

As you have seen throughout this book, today's demons tend to be the ghosts of yesterday. While you make progress toward recovery, you may want to reestablish and repair damaged relationships with some of those ghosts of the past: your parents and siblings. Perhaps you are not ready to take this step now. But, at some point along the way, the task of reconnecting with your family of origin will probably become important to you—indeed, it may be critical to your continued well-being. Restoring old relationships from a new perspective of recovery can often help further our own growth, and most ACOAs wisely want to avoid throwing the baby out with the bathwater.

WHY YOU CAN'T DIVORCE YOUR FAMILY

Most of us, understandably, have considerable anxiety when it comes to dealing with parents, siblings, and other relatives. But, no matter what our age, no matter how terrible our rage, we never really leave home. And, as many adult children of alcoholics know only too well, we cannot escape our families simply by creating physical or emotional distance. Our continued affection for family members and the blurred boundaries of alcoholic homes in general have resulted in our families'

211

being as much inside us as outside us. We never quite succeed in cutting ourselves off from them, no matter how hard we may try. Yet reconnecting in healthier ways with families of origin is a major task of adulthood. Because our families are so much a part of us, most of us want and need to make some effort to reconcile with them after we have recovered enough to make it possible.

To move toward a better relationship with our families of origin, we need to find a healthy balance between staying too close and being too distant. Constructing appropriate boundaries is the major task of reintegrating. If you have been habitually overinvolved—even as an adult—in your family, you need to create appropriate boundaries; you need to maintain a comfortable distance and develop your own autonomy. If, however, you have tried to cut yourself off completely—either physically or emotionally—you need to tear down the false boundary of physical or emotional distance and build new, appropriate boundaries that will allow you to establish healthier, more sustaining ties with your family.

GROWING UP BY GROWING AWAY

Establishing healthy boundaries may be particularly troublesome for those whose families didn't permit or accept separation. If you attempt to separate from the family that raised you, you may feel as if you are betraying or abandoning those you love. You may feel disloyal when you begin to have relationships outside the family. But, in order to grow as an individual and enter into new relationships, you will have to move out of the family, emotionally, and into the world. And paradoxically, in order to build new, mutually supportive relationships with your family of origin, you must first move away from the family.

You need to establish a healthy separateness and achieve some individual autonomy before you can safely attempt to improve these relationships. This isn't abandoning the family, but we often think it is. We simply have to accept ourselves before we can fully accept our parents and siblings. We need to get our adult lives together first. Your own recovery is therefore essential before you can begin to reestablish family ties on a new basis.

Before you can balance family relationships, you may have to clarify for yourself what is important to you and what is important to your family, where you are in terms of your well-being and where they are. You'll want to ask yourself:

- How do my values compare with those of my family?
- What rules do I now observe in my current life? How are they different (or like) my family's rules? How do they compare with the childhood rules I followed? (See pages 46–47.)
- How am I feeling about myself and the people in my family?
- How responsible do I want to be to my family, without being either overresponsible or underresponsible? Am I being responsible *to* and not *for* people close to me?
- What support can I expect to get, and can I ask for, from my family of origin?
- What support do I need to give myself? How responsible am I to me?

When we are adults, finding ourselves and establishing new relationships or new families should, generally, take precedence over attempts to redefine relationships in our families of origin. Creating new, healthy, and intimate personal relationships will give us the sense of being and belonging that we want and need more quickly than restoring old relationships. As Lillian B. Rubin noted in *Just Friends*, "We need our friends—not just for fun, not just as a replacement for a distant or difficult family or failed marriage, not just because they can provide the human framework within which we can make good the deficits of the past. All are crucial to our well-being. But we need our friends also . . . because the turning points and transitions that are inevitable accompaniments of living would be infinitely harder to negotiate without them." We need to grow up by growing away from our families in order to gain the autonomy that will eventually allow us to grow back in a healthy, adult way, maintaining a separate self without rejecting the familial associations that mean so much to us.

A FALSE SENSE OF DISTANCE

Those who think they have cut themselves off from their families are actually much more connected than they would like to think. Cutting yourself off is really very similar to staying too close: both require you to expend an inordinate amount of energy to maintain this distance or proximity. If you have completely cut yourself off from your family of origin, then you—like the "loner" in intimate relationships—have created inflexible, concrete boundaries. And, like the loner's position, this type of relationship is far too extreme to be healthy.

Cutting ourselves off from other family members also adds pressure to our current relationships. We cannot get very close to others when we devote so much of our energies to maintaining a distance from our families. Nonetheless, we desperately look to these others to fill the void left by the lack of emotional bonding with our own families.

Finding a healthy balance between our needs for autonomy and our needs for affiliation is a task that usually lasts a lifetime and repeatedly presents itself in all of our close relationships, inside and outside our families of origin.

"My recovery has involved a great deal of work on my relationships with people. I can see where the way I was treated in my family has a lot to do with the way I expect to be treated in other relationships.

"The relationship that I have to work on the most is the one with my mother. She is still very overprotective of me and sees me as fragile and unable to handle anything. I'm twenty-eight years old and married, but she still treats me like a child," said Sally, a young artist.

"My mother did all the bossing and made all the demands on us. My three sisters and I weren't allowed to make any decisions or confront her in any way. My father never argued with my mother. We all got the message that we weren't supposed to make waves; we were supposed to act like everything was fine. And she always expected each person in the family to feel closest to her; we weren't supposed to relate to anyone else. We didn't learn how to support each other, and consequently I have a difficult time with friends or groups of people.

"In the past few years I've gradually learned how to distance myself from my mother so I could begin to form relationships with other people. Now I know that it's okay to have relationships and it's normal to share with someone else besides her. My husband is now my best friend, not my mother.

"I don't want to sound like I'm blaming my mother. I'm not. But I've had to get some distance from her to disprove her belief that I'm a fragile little girl who needs her protection. I'm trying to reestablish my relationship with her and hope she'll be able to see me as an adult."

Both old and new relationships take constant work. As you get healthier, you will begin to put your parents in perspective: you'll no longer feel the need to see them as either saints or devils. You'll see them as real people, with both strengths and weaknesses.

"Group therapy has helped me reconcile with my mother," John, a divorced father in his forties, told me. "I can now see her for who she really is. For years, I blamed her for my problems, and I broke off relations with her for fifteen years. But now that I have a better understanding of myself and of her, I've been able to reconnect in a healthy way. I'm no longer afraid that she's going to control me, and I actually enjoy being with her."

One has to feel fairly grown-up in order to have grown-up relationships with one's parents and siblings. And you may be well into your thirties or older before you will feel free enough within yourself to be generous and understanding to your relatives. You need to heal your inner child before you can deal with your family. Because we still tend to hold on to yesterday's images, reconnecting with families of origin today can be problematic. But, by creating a little distance, you can break away from old childhood roles.

Consider the following situation, which one of my patients shared with me. Claire had always found herself in the middle of conflicts between her parents. Whenever there was any family tension, she was put in the position of having to choose between protecting her alcoholic mother or pleasing her father. This is very common in relationships, whether alcohol plays a part or not. Two people in conflict often call upon a third person to shift the tension within the relationship. Claire had always been triangled into her parents' partnership and was forced to choose between them.

Recently, while visiting her mother in the hospital after an operation, Claire was taken aside by a nurse, who told her the nursing staff was sure her mother was drinking in her hospital room. Should Claire say something directly to her mother? To her father? What would you have done? Her AA sponsor advised her to tell her father, which she promptly did. She realized that this problem fell within the boundary of her father's relationship with his wife. She appropriately removed herself from their conflicts by placing the responsibility where it belonged, with her father.

Like Claire, we need to see our relatives as they are today, instead of viewing them as we did when we were children. We have to clear out the old, false perspectives before we can gain new, truer ones.

Forgiveness is essential to recovery. Appropriate distance can often give us the perspective we need to see that our alcoholic parents were not necessarily worse or better than any other parents. They too are imperfect; but they probably did the best they could under the circumstances. Forgiving our parents allows us to put elsewhere the energy we once put into recrimination—and then it can work for us.

Charlotte recently learned that her mother was dying of cancer. She told me that, after getting over her initial shock, "I decided that I wanted to have some quality time with her. I don't want to be the angry child anymore. I want to be her daughter and my own person. The truth is we are both women and we are both recovering alcoholics.

"I've been going to ACOA meetings for two years, talking to other ACOAs *about* my mother. But now I have to talk *to* my mother. I've never given her much credit for her recovery from the disease. I've blamed my alcoholism on her even though I know she didn't cause it. I resented the fact I had the same disease as her. But she's been sober now for eight years and it's that sober alcoholic I need to talk with.

"I'm beginning to see how I isolated myself from my mother just as her disease isolated her from me. All of us kids, my three brothers and me, would rush to my father when he came home from work and tell him about all the things we had been involved in all day. We never let my mother know anything we were doing; we would come home from school and pretty much ignore her. Even after she got sober, we still didn't confide in her the way we did with my father.

"My mother started her own business a few years ago and she has been extremely successful. She has a lot of information she could probably pass on to me if I asked her for it. Before now, I had never seen her as a successful woman, someone who might have wisdom that I might be able to use. Dad was the successful corporate executive and we thought *he* had all the answers.

"Visiting my mother in the hospital has made me appreciate how strong and sensitive she is. I've also gotten a new perspective on my father. He's full of denial about the cancer and he's been saying some pretty insensitive things to her. The other day, he mimicked her when she started to cry, trying to joke her out of feeling so sad. I used to think he could do no wrong, but now I see he has his flaws too."

The forgiveness and appropriate distance Charlotte gained through her own recovery has allowed her to form closer, more realistic relationships with both her mother and her father. She no longer sees her mother as all bad and her father as all good; she sees them both as people. Changing herself made it easier for her to recreate new, healthier ties with her family.

After you have been able to forgive your parents, you will be able to take steps to bring you closer to them if you want to. Try to imagine, for instance, that years from now, after your parents have died, you are visiting their gravesides and thinking about the things you regret not having told them. You can make a list of these things. Breathe a sigh of relief and realize that you now have the chance, because they're still alive.

By sharing your feelings now, you may be able to prevent some of the "if only" recriminations characteristic of real loss. Unfortunately, most of us wait until death or tragedy to think about all the unspoken feelings we wish we could have expressed. Of course, it does take a great deal of courage to communicate with the people closest to us. But if we take the time, being grateful we have the time, it is amazing how much courage we really have.

CHANGE OFTEN BEGETS CHANGE

Once you begin to change, your relationships also start to change. In changing yourself, you force others to react, or change, in response to your new behavior.

Being in reality rather than in denial about family alcoholism identifies both problems and solutions. But you need to accept the fact that you cannot find solutions for anyone but yourself. You can, however, open the door to more healthy relationships with your family by sharing the courage, strength, and hope you have gotten through recovery. By communicating honestly with family members from your new perspective of recovery, you can draw closer to them and learn more about one another.

In approaching family members you run the risk that they may not respond to your changed behavior the way you would like them to. Most of us, however, feel that the possibility of a closer relationship with a family member is worth this risk.

SEEING THE EFFECTS OF CHANGE   To see what impact your own change might have on other family members, you might want to:

- *Behave differently with family members.* For instance, if you have a reputation in your family for always being the problem solver, discuss your own problem and ask for advice. Reversing your typical role will promote atypical responses.

- *Plan a meeting* with one or more of your siblings and parents. Sometimes an informal situation, like sitting in the backyard on a cool summer evening, can facilitate open family discussions. It is truly astonishing how little most people know and how much they can learn about their families of origin.

  In one of my groups, a woman commented that she "knew nothing" about her mother's past. Asked by another group member whether she had ever bothered to inquire about her mother's earlier life, she answered that she had always felt that if her mother had wanted her to know she would have told her. Other group members quickly pointed out that her mother might have felt that if her daughter was interested *she* would have asked.

  If you take the initiative by talking to your brothers, sisters, and parents, you may learn surprising facts and perhaps some family secrets as well. But, if you don't ask, you may never find out about them at all.

  You might want to consider making a family tape or mapping out your family's genogram (see Chapter 5), not only to gain a fresh perspective on your family history, but to begin forming new ties within your family.

- *Write a letter* expressing your true feelings and ask specific questions of the person you are writing.

  Writing and sending a loving letter to a sibling, parent, or friend, in addition to providing much-needed practice for those of us who have difficulty expressing intimate feelings, can help us restore damaged relationships. A giving gesture like this can help us regain some of the losses of our childhood—especially the loss of a relationship, however strained, with a sibling or parent.

Joanna had always had a difficult relationship with her older brother, Stephen. She felt he was the star of the family and she never seemed able to measure up. For years she resented the fact that her parents had paid for his college education, while she had to work her way through. But recently she decided to try and mend some fences and reestablish a loving relationship with him. Even though her brother now lives in Europe and she hadn't seen him in several years, she wrote him this letter:

Dear Stephen,

I've been wanting to write you for a long time. I wanted to send you a Christmas present and a birthday present but I couldn't think of anything to send you because I really don't know what you like, what you want, what you need. I worry that you might think that because I haven't kept in touch or acknowledged your birthday I don't care about you. Please know that I do. It's just that sometimes I don't feel I know you very well, you know, I don't know your interests or tastes. We haven't been in touch for so long! But I'm always so happy to hear from you.

Like when you left a message on my machine for New Year's. I missed you so much! I hope you aren't angry with me. Please understand that I've been going through a lot the last few years and I had to focus all my attention on myself for a while.

I don't know if Mommy told you, but almost two years ago I finally admitted to being bulimic and finally decided to get help. After a year and a half of therapy and going to Overeaters Anonymous and ACOA, I feel much better and happier than I've ever felt in my life.

The most dangerous, devastating part of my bulimia wasn't the binging and exercising or the starving and laxatives (don't get me wrong, I was very sick from that). But even more dangerous was the self-hatred I felt. I really had to be shown that I was an okay person and that nothing I say or do is wrong or bad. I guess growing up with all that fighting and Daddy's drinking and his accusations, I just started believing everything was my fault. I realize now that I was just frightened and gullible.

Stephen, please don't let my bulimia upset you. Please don't think I'm cuckoo—I was crazy then, but I'm sane now. I had to learn how to do the most simple things for myself all over again in a healthy way. I had to learn how to eat, how to exercise, and especially how to talk to people differently. I had to learn how to express my feelings instead of keeping them to myself. I had to learn how to like myself and how to protect and cherish myself instead of waiting around for someone to do it for me or save me from all my misery.

Stephen, please know that I am all right. I'm happy and fulfilled in a way that I never thought I could be. I live a clean and simple life now and I couldn't be happier. I just want you to know how much I miss hearing from you.

Please let me know what you would like me to send you. Is there anything you miss that you can't get in Spain?

I hope to hear from you soon.

Love and kisses,

Joanna

Joanna took a big risk in sending such an emotional, personal letter to her brother. She wasn't sure how he would respond, but she felt that the chance of forming a better relationship with him was definitely worth the risk.

Although Stephen did not respond warmly to her letter, Joanna is still glad she sent it. He still had many angry feelings toward her, and listed all his grievances in his reply. He was not ready to forgive and forget as his sister was.

Joanna's group helped her see that in writing the letter she had taken the action she felt was necessary; she could not control the outcome. Joanna took comfort in the fact that, even though she did not get the wished-for response, she did get a response. The lines of communication, although still conflicted, were finally open. Both were expressing their true feelings, and that meant there was a possibility that their relationship could still improve.

All of us want to be able to express our feelings to our families. We want to relate to our parents and siblings as fellow adults, telling them our angry and negative feelings as well as our warm and positive ones. But expressing feelings does not mean rushing home to tell and yell. It is inadvisable to "let it all hang out." Just because you have gained great new insights and understanding doesn't necessarily mean others want to share them. Although your recovery may serve as a healthy example for family members, and your changed behavior, attitudes, and emotions may spark changes in your relatives, it is important not to flaunt your recovery to those in your family who haven't recovered themselves and show no interest in your change.

DEALING WITH A SICK FAMILY

Most of us are naturally concerned, not only about our own well-being, but also about the well-being of our parents, siblings, and other loved ones. Once you know how deadly and destructive the disease is, you may not find it easy to sit by quietly while someone important to you is destroying himself or herself through either alcoholic or co-dependent behavior.

"My family is really messed up and it makes me feel very discouraged at times," Bill explained to me. "I think they need help with their addictions, but I can't seem to help them even see that they have problems. If I don't make sure that I talk about my feelings with my AA and ACOA friends, I can get quite down about it. They keep reminding me that my family may have to identify their own problems and come up with their own solutions.

"On the positive side I can see that my two years of sobriety and my wife's involvement in Al-Anon have made us very different people, with much more optimism about our lives. We're well aware of how messed up we were for a very long time, but we've made a decision not to live like that anymore. I only wish my brothers and sister would come to the same decision, but I also know it's none of my business whether they do or not.

"To maintain my own sanity I have to monitor how much time I spend with my family. It's very hard not to get angry and upset when I see them in such bad shape. It reminds me too much of what I used to be like, how crazy and irresponsible I was.

"My youngest brother, who is only twenty-six, could use every single Twelve Step program: he's an alcoholic, a junkie, a gambler, and he's about fifty pounds overweight. He lives at home with my parents, doesn't pay rent or work steadily, and he thinks he doesn't have a problem!

"I have to keep reminding myself that just because my whole family is sick that doesn't mean I'm sick. I'm the oldest and always had to take care of them, so it's hard not to feel I should be able to fix things for them, but I can't. Maybe they'll eventually see that I'm different and my life is better since I stopped drinking and drugging. But even that might not be enough to make them face their own problems. I feel very good and positive about my own life; I just have to remember that I can only change myself. I have to leave their changes up to them."

SPECIAL OCCASIONS   Family birthdays, anniversaries, holidays, and the like can be particularly tense for adult children of alcoholics—especially when other family members have not yet begun their own recovery. If you dread going to a special family occasion, you will have to accept the possibility that everything might not be the way you would like it to be. But your acceptance need not be passive. Yield control over the situation. Accept the possibility that the alcoholic (if still drinking) may get drunk or that an unpleasant argument may break out—but give yourself a contingency plan for escape. Drive there in your own car, or have the telephone number of a taxi company, or have a friend pick you up at a certain time and whisk you away.

Adult children of alcoholics are understandably anxious about who will show up in what condition at a family affair. A live-and-let-live attitude and contingency plans to handle extreme situations are just about the only avenues open to us.

Jack's daughter is getting married in a few months. "I've already instructed the band not to hand over the microphone to any guests. My mother loves to belt out her bawdy ballads when she's drunk," he explained. "My best friend has promised that, if my folks get totally crazy, he'll see that they leave the reception and he'll drive them home. I can't keep my parents from the wedding, but I will do the best I can to prevent a bad scene."

As adult children of alcoholics, we can hope our parents, siblings, or friends will one day get sober, but we need to accept the fact that we cannot control either the drinking or the recovery process for anyone else. Our relatives and friends may need help desperately, but until they themselves believe they need help, we cannot give it to them. Other than participating in a well-planned and well-supervised family intervention, a process discussed in the next chapter, there is very little we can do to get an alcoholic into treatment. And, although we may be able to exercise more influence with nonalcoholic members of our families, we can't force co-dependents to give up their enabling behavior either. The most important thing for us to do is to educate ourselves further about this family disease, get into a recovery program of our own, and stop our own enabling behavior. Help is available for those who want it.

ORGANIZING AROUND RECOVERY

"My father did go to a few AA meetings on his own after he hit bottom," admitted Denise, a young bookkeeper. "He stopped drinking, but he also stopped going to meetings. And my mother, who went to just one Al-Anon meeting, acts like she knows all there is to know about it. It's sad, because their relationship hasn't gotten any better now that he's not drinking. Without any kind of recovery program, their relationship just hasn't changed that much.

"I know that I've changed since I've been going regularly to ACOA meetings. I can talk to both my parents better, and I'm not nearly so angry at them. My mother and I actually have a relationship now. She says she feels I'm a good friend to her. I used to just listen to her, but now she listens to me too. The Al-Anon literature has helped my mother a great deal even though she doesn't go to meetings. She understands the basic principles and is much less controlling than she used to be. I feel very positive about this. Even if they don't get help and change, I know I have help and I'm changing."

As Denise's experience clearly shows, families don't miraculously transform overnight simply because the alcoholic(s) stops drinking. If the whole family is organized around the alcoholism and the alcohol is removed (the alcoholic gets sober, leaves, or dies), the family will find something else around which to organize. It is not at all unusual for a new problem to pop up once an old one is no longer there. But families can organize around health as well as around sickness.

In a new, sober family reorganization, you will need to experiment with new modes of behavior and learn to feel comfortable in them. For instance, a co-dependent daughter whose mother is a recovering alcoholic may have difficulty relinquishing some of her executive powers in the family. Newly sober, the recovering alcoholic may want to act as an involved mother for the first time in years. Her daughter may need time before she can trust her mother's ability to assume these roles. If the alcoholic in your family achieves sobriety, it's important to realize that it will take time to adjust to the changes in your family relationships.

HEALING OLD WOUNDS

One of my recent family sessions clearly revealed how different perceptions, and an unwillingness to talk, can create unnecessary wounds. But it also showed how talking about them can heal old wounds. Two sisters, both in their thirties, were talking about how it felt to grow up in their alcoholic home. Cathy, the older sister, remembered that she often felt misunderstood; she would run away from the dinner table crying, race up to her bedroom, and slam the door, feeling totally alone. Her younger sister Julie then admitted to Cathy that she used to follow her upstairs and sit outside the door, silently hoping that Cathy would open it up and let her in. She too felt totally alone and sad. This scene was repeated dozens of times during their childhood, but neither sister ever knew that the other really wanted to be close too. Since no one knocked and no one opened, the door had been shut for many years. Until this family session, that invisible door had stayed shut, preventing any kind of close communication between the sisters. But, by honestly sharing these early events, Julie and Cathy have finally opened that door.

· 15 ·

INTERVENTIONS

A RECOVERY STRATEGY FOR THE ALCOHOLIC *AND* THE FAMILY

Adult children are often instrumental in getting their alcoholic parents into treatment. The old theory that the alcoholic has to "hit bottom" and ask for help is no longer the only accepted avenue to sobriety. Families can precipitate a crisis that can induce an alcoholic to accept help even if he or she hasn't hit bottom—that is, lost a job or a family and friends. In a sense, the family "raises" the bottom through the process known as "intervention."

Interventions are designed to convince an alcoholic that he or she needs help to get sober; the subsequent treatment process, then, might convince the alcoholic of the need to stay sober. Interventions usually not only convince alcoholics that they need treatment, but let other family members see that they too can benefit from a recovery program.

Intervention cuts through denial; it's a loving yet firm confrontation between the alcoholic and those who care about him or her: family members or friends with influence. This concerted effort often gets alcoholics to accept the fact that alcoholism is a grave family problem and that treatment is necessary. Over the past fifteen years, interventions have come to be widely accepted in the field of chemical dependency. Some experts claim 80 to 100 percent success rates.

Often the person who initiates the intervention is someone in the family who has learned enough about the process and the disease to be convinced that something dramatic has to be tried. The conse-

224

quences of continued drinking are too hazardous for both the alcoholic and his or her family. An adult child, casting about for a way to bring the drinking to a stop, may decide to risk the anger and rejection of the alcoholic parent by planning such a confrontation.

PLANNING WITH CARE

Interventions, which are delicate operations, should not be conducted without expert supervision. The lives of everyone close to the alcoholic are going to be affected by the intervention process. Most of them are highly successful, but they can be harmful if not carefully planned and executed.

Once an ACOA has decided to explore the possibility of an intervention, a well-trained and experienced specialist must be found to facilitate the process. The Recommended Reading on pages 277–282 lists several sources on intervention, and the National Council on Alcoholism can provide you with additional information over the telephone. Most alcoholic clinics, hospitals, and rehabilitation centers will provide names of qualified counselors, therapists, or facilitators who can be interviewed. It's important that everyone involved in the process have confidence in the person conducting the intervention.

The facilitator will first do a careful assessment to determine if an intervention is appropriate for this particular family. The facilitator needs to make sure that everyone understands that his or her goal is not to get the alcoholic sober, but rather to initiate a recovery program that can yield benefits for the whole family.

One of the first questions to be addressed is who should be on the intervention team. These are usually the people, however many, most intimately involved in all phases of the alcoholic's life. Close family members, friends, employers, colleagues, clergy, and family physicians may be considered. The motivation and denial of each participant needs to be carefully determined so that the facilitator can decide if he or she would make a valuable contribution to the intervention team. Key people unable to attend the meeting may be asked to supply letters or tape recordings.

The intervention specialist explains the intervention process in detail and outlines basic concepts about the disease of alcoholism. He or she then takes a careful family history and work history, as well as a history of the drinking behavior.

It usually takes several sessions to prepare and rehearse the intervention. The people on the team are counseled and prepared in advance about the best way to state or read their specific concerns. The topics usually covered include the lack of power the alcoholic has over alcohol, the specific effects the drinking has on each person, and, at the prescribed time, the ultimatums should the alcoholic refuse treatment.

The statements are made as factually and unemotionally as possible. Blame, anger, and strong emotions are inappropriate to the intervention, since calm reason should prevail throughout the session. The alcoholic is much more likely to respond to concerned straightforward information than emotional criticism. The objective of interventions is not to make alcoholics feel defensive, but to make them see through their denial. They need to get help, not get angry. The focus is on facts stated within a framework of love and concern. The atmosphere should be nonjudgmental, but consistent and firm.

The team then presents the treatment plan as something that has been agreed on by all. The message needs to be stated clearly: the alcoholic needs treatment now. By grabbing the attention of the alcoholic and breaking through the denial, the group simultaneously communicates a sense of hope for the future.

Interventions are not the time for any more excuses; messages of concern have to be followed by well-orchestrated action. The goal for the alcoholic is to begin the treatment program planned by the intervention team; the goal for the children and spouse is to engage in their own recovery programs as well. They may commit themselves, for instance, to attending the required family week at a treatment center, and going to ACOA or Al-Anon meetings.

Family members have to be prepared to follow through on the ultimatums issued during the intervention process. A daughter might tell her mother, "If you don't go into the hospital today, you won't be able to babysit for your grandchildren anymore." Or a wife might warn her husband, "I will have to move out, and I have an apartment lease with me which I am ready to sign." These are examples of ultimatums that have to be followed if the alcoholic refuses treatment.

The plan has to be worked out down to the last detail prior to the intervention: medical insurance checked out, financial arrangements cleared up, a space reserved at the treatment center, and transportation arranged. Evasions and excuses on the part of the alcoholic won't hold up if the intervention team members have done their homework. It's "the car is waiting" approach, and everyone has to believe that the car is going to take off with the alcoholic in it that day.

Careful planning by the family includes getting the alcoholic to the designated intervention site. Once the stage is set, the alcoholic is brought to the session by one or more of the people on the team or is confronted at home. Sometimes he or she isn't given a clue as to the exact nature of the meeting and it comes as a total surprise. Family members may say they are seeking help for themselves—and they really are. Or the alcoholic might be told, "I've been talking to my therapist and he would like to speak with you in order to help me with some of my family problems." The surprise element may be eliminated if the intervention facilitator feels it is important to reduce the alcoholic's anger and resentment and prevent any obstacle that might interfere with the alcoholic's adjustment to the rehabilitation center.

The alcoholic may seem to be the principal player in this scenario, but in fact when ACOAs initiate interventions they have leading roles. Not only are they doing something worthwhile for the suffering alcoholic—they are doing something worthwhile for themselves as well. They are asserting themselves in a healthy and direct way to bring about change in the family and are finally taking constructive action after so many years of being made to feel out of control by the alcoholism. They are taking charge of their own lives by becoming informed and being direct. They are expressing their feelings honestly. They are opening the door to their own recovery.

Even when interventions do not conclude with the alcoholic's accepting treatment, ACOAs usually feel satisfied. They realize they did the best they possibly could. This genuine effort enhances self-esteem and gives participants the confidence to explore further the effects of the disease on their own lives. They may, for instance, begin to look at how their workaholism relates to their perfectionist behavior as children—trying to get parental approval by doing everything "right." Or someone with his or her own drinking problem may realize that he or she needs help too. Seeing the suffering alcoholic in a very vulnerable position may help other people to acknowledge their own vulnerabilities or addictions.

Throughout the intervention process, the facilitator expresses care and concern for the alcoholic and makes sure that individual team members feel supported as well. But the facilitator's active participation is really kept to a minimum. A post-session meeting is arranged, so that everyone is given an opportunity to discuss how they felt during the intervention.

THE INTERVENTION EXPERIENCE

What is the intervention really like, and what happens if the alcoholic doesn't accept the treatment plan? The two interviews that follow address both of these questions.

ACCORDING TO PLAN

Two years after the event, I interviewed the participants of a successful intervention.

Liz, twenty-eight years old, the middle child of the family, was the one who had come up with the idea of intervention. Her mother, Mary, is a fifty-year-old alcoholic. At the time of my interview with the family, Mary had been sober and active in AA for two years. Liz's husband, Tom, and her sister Jan, ten years her junior, were also present.

Joseph, the eldest at age thirty, couldn't come to this post-intervention interview, but he later told me on the phone that he felt the experience had been extremely worthwhile. Out of the family home for ten years, he had not been aware of the severity of his mother's drinking problem until his sister contacted him about the intervention.

We met for the interview at Mary's apartment.

Liz: Jan was living with our mother, and I was away at school when my parents got divorced. Mother's drinking was getting worse and worse. I first took real notice when I was in the ninth grade and I could see her personality change when she drank a lot. She would get incoherent, bitter, impatient, rejecting—not at all like her usual self. More and more she seemed to want to be alone. I remember talking to my father about it. I'd say, "Why does she have to drink?" Once I asked him if she was an alcoholic and he said she was. But he didn't seem to know what to do about it. He'd hide the bottles and just not talk about her drinking.

Jan and I were very close, and we talked about Mother's drinking. We were supportive of each other, but my father was pretty removed after the divorce, and my brother, Joseph, had been living out of the house for a long time and he didn't even seem to know there was a problem. Once in a while we would confront my mother about her drinking, but it was usually when we were very angry and she was very drunk. We'd explode and say terrible things, and then she'd cry and say she was sorry. We would all shed tears and that would be that.

The last year of her drinking was really terrible. Every time I came home, I could see her deteriorate physically and mentally; and I just didn't know what to do. We learned not to depend on her at all. If we made plans, we'd have to wait until she sobered up enough to do whatever we were doing. The sober times got shorter and shorter. Once she really upset us in a department store because she was staggering around and being nasty to us. When we got out to the car we really let her have it. I said, "We're not going anyplace until we talk about this," and we had a three-hour talk, during which she would go from denying the way she was to admitting it and then crumbling, saying she was glad we were talking about this. But she still wouldn't say she was going to do anything about it. We were frustrated and angry.

We had the names of a few good rehabilitation places that I had gotten from someone at college, and I asked if we could take her to one of them right then and there, but she refused. She wanted to wait until after my wedding, which was two months away. We said we'd go along with that, but that we were definitely going to bring it up again. I knew she needed help, but I didn't know what else to do.

Mary: My biggest fear then was, how could I survive without drinking? I couldn't conceive of living without liquor. I didn't know about convulsions or what can happen if you stop drinking cold turkey. But I was just afraid I could not live without drinking.

Liz: I found some toll-free phone numbers of treatment centers and called a few of them. All of them told me my mother would have to call herself and ask for help. I didn't know the word "intervention." This was 1984, before the media had really discovered it, so I just kept explaining the situation and that was the only answer they would give me.

Finally, I talked to a social worker at the hospital where I was doing volunteer work. She was a recovering alcoholic and was the first person who was truly helpful. She explained about the disease and that my mother couldn't do anything at this point. She said that I had to do it. I was in a real panic. I could see how sick my mother was physically. After reading some articles, I decided she must be in the last stage of alcoholism and was going to die.

Then I called another rehab center and was told the same old story: I was to explain to my mother what her drinking was doing to me and then give her the telephone number so she could call them herself. Well, we tried. My sister even threatened to move out if she wouldn't go for help. My mother's response was to say, "What do you want me to do, jump out of the window?" We lived on the twenty-eighth floor, so that ended that discussion.

I read a book called *Under the Influence* and was so impressed that I tracked down the author, and tried to call him. Someone in his office mentioned the word "intervention" and explained it to me in a way that I could really understand. I immediately called the same hospital I'd called before and said, "I think my mother needs an intervention." That was the magic word. I didn't get the usual run-around. A social worker got on the line and made an appointment for me, my brother, and sister the next week. I didn't know if Joe could come, but the worker advised me to tell him how important it was that he be there, too. We were not to tell Mother about this appointment. If she asked at any point, we were to say simply that we were getting help for ourselves.

Jan had dinner with Joe and explained the whole thing. He said he trusted us and would come, although he never realized her drinking problem was as bad as it was. My husband, Tom, came to the second meeting and to the intervention as well.

At the first meeting, our facilitator, a social worker, explained that alcoholism was a disease. She told us we would have to plan the intervention very carefully. We were impatient and wanted to do it immediately. Each of us was to describe three specific incidents of my mother's drinking and tell how we felt about each one in a clear, straightforward, detached way, just giving the facts.

We also had to have an ultimatum prepared—a statement about what we would do if she refused to go for treatment.

In the second appointment we rehearsed and had answers for any questions or comments Mother might come up with, like who would stay with Jan, who would pay the bills, etc., while she was in the hospital.

The biggest problem we saw was getting her to the facilitator's office. We set the date and agreed that Joe would take her shopping and then bring her there. We were afraid if she found out ahead of time she wouldn't go. My brother was upset about lying to her. Just when they got in front of the hospital, he told her that he was sorry but he had to tell her that we were all waiting inside and wanted her to talk to someone.

Mary: I was in a state of shock, but I also felt, "Someone is finally doing something," and had a pang of relief. They were all sitting there opposite me and I couldn't help feeling that they were ganging up against me. Besides, what they said was not news. I had so much remorse about my drinking. I half remembered all the incidents they mentioned. I was always concerned about my drinking and its effect on my kids. I knew the terrible things I'd done, the old stories. But what had the greatest impact on me and made me the angriest was my new son-in-law's comments. I resented his being there at all.

Tom: I explained that I was newly married and wanted a normal life with my wife and couldn't get on with my marriage because Liz was so torn up about her mother's drinking.

Mary: It was a new thing for me to worry about. I thought, who is this kid to tell me about my drinking? Yet I knew he was right. I couldn't stay angry at him. I was also very embarrassed at having my dirty laundry aired in front of this outsider. I didn't want Tom to hear all this.

I was ready to go for treatment before they even finished with their lists. It was very painful to hear these things; the social worker, who was extremely sensitive, had to stop them. She knew I had heard enough.

At the beginning of the session she had told me that she was a recovering alcoholic herself. Her comments gave me my first feeling of any hope for my future. She was an older woman, very together and very tough, but kind, and I trusted her and felt, finally, maybe someone could understand me. I never knew anyone who drank like I did. Certainly no one had ever given me any help, so I didn't think any help was possible. I liked the fact that the social worker didn't have a "poor dear" attitude—she was very matter of fact about what had to be done. I trusted her.

I agreed that I would go for treatment but I didn't want to go right away. I had to wash my hair, change clothes, pay my bills, and so on, but they had answers for all of these. Then I asked for some time to myself to think about it, but they wouldn't give it to me. They said, "No, you have to go right away." I thought, if they had planned all this then I'd have to go and do it their way. I guess I was glad I didn't have to figure out what to do for myself.

Liz: The first time we met the social worker, I knew she was the perfect person—I knew my mother could relate to this woman. She was on our side and also on Mother's. She was going to help us do it together. And she did stop us when it got to be too much—she was a really fine mediator.

Jan: I wasn't so sure it would work. I thought I was the only one who really understood what Mom was like and how manipulative she could be since I lived with her. I was really shocked when she didn't even put up a fight. I wondered, what if this doesn't work, what next? I kept thinking of the threat she had made—to jump out the window. What if I had to follow through on my ultimatum and move out to live with my father? How could I leave her there alone drinking?

I knew what Mom was like when she was drinking; I didn't know what she would be like not drinking. Also, it was so hard to be that tough in the session. Mom was down and we were hurting her. But I trusted the social worker and I knew we had to do it this way. It was very, very hard. I felt guilty. After all, I hadn't been the perfect daughter either, and here I was pointing out all her imperfections. I felt very sorry for her.

Tom: It was a very powerful experience for me, and afterward I felt a little jealous. I have a grandmother who is an alcoholic, and no one in my family has ever tried to get her help. I could see my mother-in-law getting all this help, and I felt very sad about my grandmother. I was angry at my own family, especially an uncle who is a doctor, for not doing anything. But the intervention also made me feel very close to my new family.

We all went over to the admitting room together and by then we could even laugh and make jokes. It was such a relief to know she was finally going to get the help she needed, and that we could finally be more open and helpful to each other in this family crisis. We all felt much closer to each other. It felt like, at last, we were acting as a family unit, rather than a split-up family.

Mary: The worst thing that I could imagine happening to me was losing my kids. At the time, I didn't know their ultimatums were to leave me alone—but I must have sensed that if I didn't get better my family would abandon me. I was very touched that they could care that much, that they could find help when I couldn't help myself.

Liz: The ultimatums weren't what we wanted at all—to cut ourselves off from Mother unless she accepted treatment. But maybe the fear of possibly having to go through with that made us even stronger in terms of insisting she get treatment. I wanted my mother back. I didn't want to abandon her.

All of us still have things to work out. I know I feel resentment now that my role is changing. I no longer have to be in charge. My mother is. My sister and I were totally dependent on each other because we didn't have Mother there for us. Now that she is there for each of us, our sibling relationship is a bit strained. The focus of our old relationship was always what to do about Mother. Now we have to develop a new basis for a relationship, and we're not quite sure how to do that.

It's scary to have a normal person back in the family. I'm still learning how to trust her, to know that she really is dependable after all, and that she'll continue to be there for us when we need her.

Jan: For so long, the topic of all our conversations had been Mother's problem. Toward the end of her drinking my sister was involved with her wedding plans and I didn't feel right talking about my own problems then. I was feeling very isolated and alone for a very long time and I had gotten used to not telling anyone what was going on with me. Now when Liz or Mother asks me how I am, I still have a tendency to say, "Fine." I have to push myself to reveal myself. The intervention was the first big push in that direction.

I'm so used to thinking that everyone's so caught up in their own lives that they aren't interested in mine. Even though I know this isn't true, it was my way of thinking for so long. Now that my mother and sister are emotionally available to me, I'm not always able to tell them how I really feel. I was my mother's caretaker for so long that I felt useless after she got sober and was doing fine on her own. I had been so stuck in that one role that I didn't see how I could have any other roles. I know my family is interested in me, but I have to stop acting like I don't need them. This is very hard for me. It really is like being in a new family and we're sometimes still very tentative with each other. But it is also wonderful to have a family again. We really look forward to our get-togethers now. We used to dread holidays and family functions. Now they're fun.

WHAT WENT RIGHT

There are several reasons why the intervention on Mary turned out as well as it did. Mary had been very beaten down by her disease and knew that she needed help; she just didn't know how to get it. Her children had talked to her about the drinking on several previous occasions; she knew they also knew it was a problem. As unhappy and as ill as she was, Mary loved her family deeply and knew they loved her in return.

The facilitator was respected and liked by the whole family. She knew exactly when to stop the intervention; she knew when enough was enough. There is usually one voice in the intervention that is heard above all others and, in this family, it was the least likely voice: Tom's. Initially Mary resented the fact that her new son-in-law was at the session; but it was his remarks, finally, that convinced her she had to do something about her drinking right then and there.

Mary got into a twenty-eight-day rehabilitation center that day and started going to AA meetings as soon as she was discharged. She got a sponsor and she also started individual psychotherapy. A year after she got sober, she started graduate school and embarked on a new career.

Mary was not the only one to benefit from the intervention, though. Her daughters felt that, after all the years of talking about the problem, they had finally done something about it. Liz realized that trying to deal with her mother's drinking was causing problems in her new marriage. She felt that she had to make this last try to get her mother some help so that she could focus her energy where it really belonged: in her own life.

Before the intervention, Tom had felt somewhat outside the family. He was fond of his mother-in-law but resented all the attention she was getting. In the intervention session, he was able to be more honest than he had ever been in his own family. This brought him closer to everyone else. Mary was able to tell him later, with real appreciation, how significant his contributions had been to her recovery. The intervention also drew him closer to Liz, since they had dealt with this family crisis together. He learned a great deal about alcoholism from the facilitator, and it opened his eyes to the dysfunction in his own family: the denial of an alcoholic grandmother.

Although her children initially resisted going to self-help meetings, Mary called, several months after my interview with the family, to tell me that Jan had started going to Al-Anon/ACOA meetings. It is not at all unusual for family members to resist going to their own recovery programs. They have often been very hurt and are angry. They want to know that the alcoholic means business before they start dealing with their own business.

Just as alcoholics have to get down to their own level of powerlessness before they ask for or accept help, nonalcoholic relatives often have to hit their own emotional bottoms before they start to take the first steps toward recovery. Alcoholics who finally sober up are usually insistent about having family members get treatment, too. They are often surprised and angry with nonalcoholics who refuse to go to Al-Anon. But alcoholics are just as powerless to compel members of their family into treatment as those same family members were to stop the alcoholics from drinking. Nonalcoholic family members will look for help when they decide they need it, not when anyone else decides. Usually, adult children find their way to Al-Anon, ACOA, or psychotherapy, but the alcoholic's beating of the drum does not get them there any faster. Mary didn't know help was available; her children now do know and, when ready, they can take advantage of it.

In a subsequent conversation with Mary's son, Joseph, he had this to say: "I'm the oldest and I always thought of Liz as my little sister and Jan as my baby sister. Since the intervention, I just think of them as my sisters, period. The intervention changed my perceptions of them. I had never thought of Liz as a confronting or assertive person, but I was so impressed with how she researched and organized the intervention and how she handled herself in the process that I saw her in a different light. I was surprised by Jan, too. They were both very nervous but went through it really well. Liz did an unbelievable job, handling the whole thing. As soon as she told me about it, I felt certain it was the right thing to do. It became clear from the way Liz presented it that my mother had been getting progressively worse over the past fifteen years. From what Liz told me, I knew our mother was unable to help herself.

"The only thing that bothered me was that, for the first time in my life, I lied to my mother. I invited her to go shopping with me, knowing I was taking her to the intervention. That was very difficult for me.

"The intervention changed not only my perceptions of my sisters but my relationship with them, too. The open communication that started that day has continued and that's been a great bonus. Naturally, I'm very glad my mother went into treatment, has made so many changes in her life, and is a much happier person. But I'm also much closer now to my sisters.

"Recently I broke up with my girlfriend and had a very rough time. For once I was able to really tell my sisters what was going on in my life and they were extremely supportive. They were just great."

First tries don't always succeed. Sometimes another intervention is necessary. Even if the intervention does not work in terms of getting the alcoholic to enter treatment, he or she may later seek out help on his or her own. Interventions are seldom total failures. Enough may have been heard to begin to erode the denial of the alcoholic. Interventions can be extremely powerful declarations of love and concern, which the alcoholic cannot totally ignore. Even if anger and feelings of betrayal are initial reactions, alcoholics may realize at a later time that the family was rightfully concerned after all.

AN INTERVENTION THAT WASN'T

The best-laid plans are sometimes foiled by the best intentions. In this case, a friend thought she was doing the right thing: she "spilled the beans." This kind of "good-will" sabotage is a big risk in any intervention.

The intervention idea was not a complete failure. It did bring the subject of the mother's alcoholism out into the open and she did agree to go into family therapy to discuss the explosive situation with her daughters. Grace is sixty-two, divorced, and has two daughters: Lisa is thirty-two, and Lynn, thirty, is married to Hugh, thirty-five. Lisa, a photographer who is in psychotherapy treatment with me for relationship problems and also goes to Al-Anon and ACOA meetings, gave me the following account three months after the fact.

"The intervention was actually Helen's idea. She's my mother's best friend, and she'd become alarmed because my mother often didn't get to her job and was drinking more and more heavily in social situations. Helen spoke with Lynn and me separately and recommended that we try an intervention.

"Initially, I was very skeptical and asked some of my Al-Anon friends about it. They reassured me that the method and the institution Helen was recommending were excellent. They said that interventions were a way to convince alcoholics that treatment was necessary.

"I was also reluctant because I wondered about Helen's motivation to 'fix' our family. I suggested she go to an Al-Anon meeting with me, but she declined. It seemed to me she wasn't interested in working on herself.

"My sister liked the idea that Helen was interested. She and her husband didn't know that much about alcoholism or the AA program. They seemed relieved that someone else was coming up with an idea to cope with my mother's drinking problem.

"We went to see the counselor at the alcoholism center. We were shown a film on intervention, and she recommended a rehabilitation center in the Midwest. But we didn't have the money to go out there for the family week, and my mother's insurance wouldn't have covered that particular place. The counselor didn't think we should waste any more time. We were directed to check out other facilities and start calling people in my mother's life who would come to the next meeting prior to the actual intervention. We were not supposed to tell our mother anything other than that we had decided to go for help ourselves.

"There was a big question about whether we should tell my mother's boss and we decided against it because we were afraid she might lose her job. The women that she worked closely with were very upset that we were doing something behind our mother's back. They questioned the ethics of the whole thing and clearly didn't want to be involved.

"I called my mother's best friend on the job, who was horrified by the plan. She was very critical, and she asked me if I had ever discussed the drinking with my mother. I said that I had, many times. She was quite nasty and said, 'I've been there for your mother, *you* haven't.' She acknowledged finally that what I was suggesting was coming from a loving place, but she thought we were being very disloyal.

"I think I now have a much better perspective on the loyalty issue. I believe you can never be loyal to someone's addiction. I separate my mother's addiction from my mother. I don't think it's disloyal to confront the addiction. You can still be loyal and loving to the person who has the addiction.

"As you may have already guessed, this woman told my mother that we had contacted her co-workers about her drinking problem. My mother was devastated. She thought I was totally off the wall to be calling her friends. I told her I could understand why she was so upset. I listened to her and tried to be calm and centered. I told her what I felt her problem was and that I felt she needed help. I told her we were trying to help her, not harm her. But she was very upset—she was drinking—and kept saying, 'Why do you hate me, how could you *do* this to me?' I kept calm and explained, over and over again, that we were all concerned about her and loved her and we wanted her to get help. She finally admitted that her drinking was a problem, but she assured me she could control and handle it herself. I offered to take my mother to an AA meeting and she agreed to go if there were no 'bums' there. I found what I thought was the right meeting for her, but, of course, she still had complaints and said the room was too cold. She felt it wasn't the right meeting for her but promised to find another one. She hasn't yet."

WHAT WENT WRONG—AND RIGHT

"My sister's mother-in-law started calling it the 'inquisition,' so my sister and brother-in-law started to have doubts about the whole process," Lisa continued. "We decided to give up on the idea of the intervention. My sister and I did, however, convince my mother to go with us to a family therapist.

"Actually the intervention wasn't a total failure because my mother's cover was blown and some of her denial started breaking down. We were told that interventions should be last resorts, and I guess we weren't convinced that it was time for a last-ditch effort.

"We are talking about the drinking in the family therapy sessions and we are now feeling much closer. My mother realizes that if she can't control her drinking more drastic measures will have to be taken. She agreed that if she cannot stop on her own, she will go to a treatment center. I don't think she can stop on her own, of course, but she will have to find that out for herself. The best thing is that we are finally talking about the drinking out in the open.

"Meanwhile, I'm still going to my Al-Anon and ACOA meetings and taking care of myself. I have to accept the fact that my mother may never stop drinking or get into the Alcoholics Anonymous program. But I'm more hopeful than I've ever been before and I don't have any regrets about what we tried to do."

Grace, the alcoholic mother, was in considerably more denial than Mary had been. She had a full-time professional job and offered this as proof that her drinking was under control. Her daughters were very caring, but Grace's self-pity, her constant criticism, and her behavior when drinking had always made them keep their distance from her. Consequently, Grace felt a great deal of rejection even before she learned of the intervention attempt. She thought the fact that her daughters had discussed her with co-workers was the ultimate rejection and betrayal.

Hugh, Lynn's husband, had a great deal of denial, partially because his own mother drank rather heavily—although he did not identify it as a "problem." Grace saw him as an ally who would help take some of the heat off her if her daughters were putting the heat on. Given this implicit alliance, Hugh would not have been a good candidate for the intervention team without more preparation by the facilitator. A person with this degree of uncertainty about the severity of the alcoholism can be detrimental in an actual intervention.

This aborted intervention was successful insofar as it ultimately led Grace, Lisa, and Lynn to agree to work on their problems together in family therapy. They were able to begin a constructive, concerted effort to improve their relationships. The daughters respected their mother's decision to try it her way. They all concurred that, if she was unable to control the drinking herself, professional alcoholism treatment would be necessary. They indicated that another intervention at a later date might be in order if Grace didn't stop drinking on her own.

Despite the fact that Grace was not yet ready to deal with her disease, Lisa, Lynn, and Hugh took positive actions to deal with the effects it had on them. Lynn and Hugh decided to find out more about alcoholism and Lynn stepped up her commitment to Al-Anon and ACOA meetings. The adult children had done the best they could to get their mother into treatment; now they had to focus on improving their own lives.

· 16 ·

POSITIVE PARENTING

RAISING CHILDREN WITHOUT RAISING FEAR

"I never thought too much about having children, but I decided very early that I wasn't going to get married. My parents fought all the time about my father's drinking, and none of their friends had good marriages either. My parents weren't responsible or dependable, so I didn't think I had learned anything from them about how to be a good partner or a good parent. I decided to avoid the whole thing.

"Now that I've had my thirtieth birthday," admitted Sandra, "I'm starting to reconsider. I think I'd really like to get married and have children. But the idea scares me. How could I be a good parent? How could I prevent a child of mine from becoming an alcoholic?"

PREPARING FOR PARENTHOOD

After surviving the chaos of disrupted and disorganized homes, adult children of alcoholics are often very hesitant about embarking on the journey of parenthood. Some are aware of the roots of this hesitancy; others just instinctively stay away from the experience. Like Sandra, you may wonder what kind of parent you will be, or you may be understandably concerned about the genetic predisposition to alco-

240

holism. But becoming a parent, if that's what you decide you want, doesn't have to be as overwhelming as you may anticipate.

"My father was forty when I was born and very domineering. I was never allowed to be a kid around him," remembered Albert. "My parents never got angry or argued. We just all lived according to my father's rules. He never treated any of us like children. I feel uncomfortable around little kids myself and I think my ambivalence about having a family of my own is that I'm afraid I'll be the cold, rejecting parent my father was."

Regardless of their backgrounds, most people worry about whether or not they will be good parents. Adult children of alcoholics just worry a good deal more. We worry about whether we can be *model* parents, and have *model* children. Being "good enough" usually doesn't measure up to our unrealistic, perfectionist standards. The tendency to be an overresponsible child often carries over to being an overresponsible adult—and an overresponsible parent.

"I definitely suffered from acute perfectionism when my three children were young," said Pamela. "My mother was an alcoholic and our house was always a mess. I wanted to make up for that by having the American Dream Life. I wanted to be the attentive mother my own mother wasn't because of her illness. My perfectionism was compounded because my husband was a pillar of the community and our children were adopted, and the agency *really* looked us over: I had to be perfect to prove to the whole world what a wonderful wife and mother I was.

"When the boys were toddlers I'd put them in white shoes, which I polished a couple times a day so they'd always be clean. I wouldn't let them play in the sandbox because I was afraid they would track sand into the house. Thank goodness I finally got into Al-Anon and learned to back off, to let my kids be themselves, to start listening to them. We went to family therapy when they were teenagers and that helped a lot, too. I totally missed my adolescence so I didn't know how teenagers were *supposed* to be. My youngest son can have a messy room now. I just keep the door closed so I don't see it."

It is important to keep in mind that one of the most valuable investments you can make in preparing for parenthood is to continue on the road of personal recovery. Resolving conflict from the past and letting old wounds heal help to break the cycle of family problems. Everything we learn about ourselves, whatever experience, strength, and hope we develop for ourselves, is going to count a great deal in our parenting efforts.

PARENTHOOD AS PROCESS

Parenthood is a process, not an event. Just as there are steps in a recovery process, there are steps or phases in the process of parenthood. Children's needs and their reactions change dramatically as they grow. Parents change too—they don't stop growing as individuals when their children start to grow. There are new challenges every day. And the challenge of a two-year-old is very different from the challenge of a twelve- or sixteen-year-old. Parents need to accept the fact that they may be much better at dealing with certain periods of a child's life than others. It's a very rare person who is equally adept at handling all childhood stages. Parents need to do the best they can when they can.

Sam, who talked about his difficulty in learning to become intimate, told me that he thought in most areas he was a good father, but he still wanted to work on becoming more comfortable expressing affection. "I was attracted to my wife and her family because they were so warm, but when my wife's parents would cuddle our children, I'd get very upset and say they were spoiling them. I'd be embarrassed and say things like, 'Leave them alone, they're okay.' I had never seen children being held just for the sake of being held. I didn't realize that hugging and kissing were normal."

WHAT'S NORMAL?

How does an ACOA figure out or define what normal is? We thought all families were like ours and now we have learned that ours may not have been "normal" at all. Since child development is not routinely taught in schools and all too often television portrays the perfect plastic family, there aren't many opportunities to learn about mainstream, everyday parenting. It's often helpful for parents to find out about the range of normal behavior; it's wider than most new parents suspect. It's helpful to remember that just as there are all kinds of grownups there are lots of kinds of toddlers and lot of kinds of teenagers. This may help you avoid making endless comparisons with other kids and being so hard on yourself—and your children.

Reading about child rearing and learning about the milestones, about age-specific behavior, and about how other families solve problems and respond to certain issues can be helpful. In addition you can attend PTA meetings. Many communities also have parenting discussion groups, adult classes, and workshops. They are often held in schools, Y's, or libraries, and are usually open to the general public. Participants do not have to be diagnosed, referred, analyzed, or looked over in order to register. And fees are generally minimal. Other parents are a good source of expertise, and increasingly fathers are participating in these programs too. Such groups give people an opportunity to learn more about how other families work, who decides what, how standards are established and enforced, what to do when the child won't go to sleep, what to do when a teenager becomes very shy or very aggressive, and so forth. As with any discussion group (including ACOA, Al-Anon, group therapy, etc.), feel free to take what you like and leave the rest. What works for the Jones family may not be right for you. But, by finding out what works for other parents and how they made their choices, you can often make more informed parental decisions.

COMMON PARENTAL PITFALLS

In addition to trying too hard to be too good, ACOA parents often encounter other difficulties in raising their children.

REFUSING HELP

Some ACOA parents insist that they can do it all, and do it alone. They don't like to ask other people to help them out. If you feel this way, you need to recognize that relatives, neighbors, and friends can form an informal support system that is extremely helpful in good times and vital in a crisis.

Sharing parenting problems with your own parents often has a special benefit: it can increase your understanding of what it was really like for your parents to be parents. (After all, no parent does *everything* wrong—whether it seemed that way at the time or not.) This sharing of parenting experience may help you forgive parents and get rid of old resentments from the past.

CREATING CRISES

Another pitfall for ACOA parents is that we often overreact to emotions that all children exhibit at some time or another. When we see our children disappointed or crying, it may depress and immobilize us. Or when a child is very impulsive and demanding, we may either fall apart or get extremely rigid about what must be done. Parents have to accept the ups and downs of children's feelings. We don't have to create a crisis out of what might just be a troublesome incident or a kid's bad day. ACOAs have to be careful not to try to fix things that aren't broken. Just because a child feels upset one minute doesn't mean he or she will feel that way five minutes from now. You may not always be able to sit tight, but you need to be able, at least, to sit.

"I couldn't bear to watch my son be worried or upset," remembered Grace, a mother of two. "I wanted to rush in and do something, make decisions, tell him what was best for him. Many times my hand was on the telephone ready to spring into action and smooth things out with a teacher or a Little League coach. But now I'm learning how to step back a bit. I realize that if I don't stop trying to take charge of my kids' lives they won't be able to grow."

GETTING OVERINVOLVED

Sometimes parents who feel that they were neglected as children go to the other extreme and become excessively active with their own children. You may think if a few hours a day of playing or reading with the child is good, then a few more hours must be better. Not so. Or the mother whose own mother never showed up at school plays may find herself at school day in and day out—helping the teacher, making scenery, cleaning the fish tank. A contribution to the functioning of a school is always appreciated; but, after a certain point, it sends a message to the child that the outside world and the strangers in it are not safe and that mommy is always needed. This neither builds the child's self-confidence nor fosters his or her autonomy.

BALANCING BOUNDARIES

Creating a safe, enriching home environment, one that balances trust in the outside world and intimacy within the family, is often difficult for parents who grew up without that sense of security. We have to be open and talk about our feelings. We need to know what appropriate parental responsibilities are and be able to carry them out in a consistent, direct, and loving way. Obviously, a nonviolent, nonabusive, protecting environment in which children feel it is safe to express their thoughts and feelings is of primary importance.

But parents also need to allow their children some privacy. They have to learn to step back a little; not every alone time is a dysfunctional withdrawal. Children need their separate space too. It's sometimes better to say very little or not to say anything at all when your child wants to be alone. Children need to establish their own feelings, opinions, and activities without always waiting for mom's or dad's opinions, suggestions, or approval.

PARENTS AT PLAY

As parents, we have to be able to nurture ourselves as well as our children. Adult children of alcoholics often have very little history or memory of playing together as a family. When we get to be parents, we don't always know how to have family fun. We may have forgotten those rare times when our families really did have a good time together. By learning to play with our children we can reawaken forgotten memories and nurture the child within.

Especially with younger children, almost any activity that the family can do together can prove enjoyable. No matter what the age, for instance, most people—kids included—like "going and seeing" activities. Trips to the zoo, ballgames, picnics in the park, and sightseeing drives can be a lot of fun for everyone. Don't fret too much over picking the one activity guaranteed to appeal to everyone the most; sometimes childhood memories of the unplanned activities are those most cherished.

Your family doesn't even have to go anywhere to have fun. Playing cards or a board game at a kitchen table, watching a special film on television together and making popcorn during the commercials, or singing a song together can be entertaining family play.

FINDING FAMILY FUN   First, think back to some of the highlights of your childhood and then make a list of ten or so of the times that were the most fun. Next, think about the activities that your family enjoyed together and make a list of the best times you had together. Then think also about the things you always hoped your family would do—perhaps the things you saw other families doing or heard about in school —and make a wish list. Which of the activities can you do now? Which can you plan for your own children, grandchildren, or even your friends' kids?

You may think about taking a child on an all-day outing. Two generations can expand their worlds by sharing an experience together. You can give a child your undivided attention and the affection all human beings need. And children can often give adults insight into their own lives. Children can teach you about directness, spontaneity, and a marvelous sense of wonder that can be very contagious. Children need adult friends, and adults can certainly benefit from young friends. You don't even have to be a parent to learn to play and relax with the younger generation.

Learning to play with your children can provide warmth and spontaneity that often extends to other areas of your lives as well. It's important to establish and maintain family traditions and rituals so children will have a positive sense of a special event. It is never too late to play with your family. A sixty-year-old man takes his son and grandson on a day canoe trip once a year, a fifty-year-old woman takes her mother on an outing to the ice-cream parlor every two weeks, a forty-three-year-old woman takes her nieces shopping for clothes and school supplies, and a couple in their seventies plan family reunions every year.

FAMILY FUNCTIONS

Planning family functions to include extended family is a good way to promote a larger support system for your children. Family reunions can give children the chance, for instance, to meet distant cousins and get attention from aunts, uncles, and grandparents. However, many of us are understandably wary of including in this extended family alcoholic family members who haven't yet achieved sobriety.

"It's a very sad thing, but in all the sixteen years I was married I never allowed my mother to come to our house unescorted," said Sam. "I didn't want my kids to be exposed to her craziness. It's really too bad because they never had the experience of grandparenting from my side of the family. My dad died before they were born and my mother certainly couldn't relate to them."

You may not feel comfortable about exposing your children to the disease that created so many problems in your life. If you feel uncomfortable about it, don't do it. Don't feel obligated to include actively alcoholic parents in your family gatherings. Like Sam, you may want to forbid the alcoholic to visit his or her grandchildren at all until he or she joins a recovery program. Or you may want to limit the alcoholic's visits to times when he or she is sober. Or you may feel most comfortable explaining your parent's disease to your children and making no demands at all on the alcoholic. You shouldn't protect your children from the truth, but you should protect them from having to suffer the shame and humiliation that you suffered. Ultimately, it's a very personal decision. But it's your decision, and you and your spouse have every right to make and enforce that decision.

CHILDREN AND CHEMICALS

Almost all parents today are concerned about preventing their children from getting into trouble with alcohol and other chemicals. ACOA parents may have more cause to worry because they not only have to watch out for the recurrence of old family patterns and physiological predispositions, but also be on guard for denial. Most adult children of alcoholics grew up thinking, "It can't happen to me." But we know that it very often does.

Alcoholism has an extremely high family incidence rate, and more than one member in a family is likely to be an alcoholic or drug addict. Children of alcoholics are four times as likely to become alcoholics as the rest of the population. And your children, the grandchildren of alcoholics, run almost as high a risk.

"It won't happen to my kids" is another myth of adult children, particularly of ACOAs who have recovered from their own addictions, who feel that they have already broken the cycle. They feel they have a tremendous amount of information and experience that might prevent alcoholism. It might. It also might not. Statistically, the risks remain just as high. At some point, you will have to make your children aware of these risks.

There are no hard and fast rules, no magic formulas about how and when to tell children about the alcoholism in the family. A good head and good fortune may have more to do with how the children turn out than all of those good intentions that parents have. The best way to approach any anxiety about parenthood is for us to have our own recovery programs in good working order, and the possibility of your child's drug or alcohol abuse is no exception. Your own recovery will better prepare you to decide how, when, and where you will raise these issues and provide the tools your children need to grow up wisely and safely.

Betty, an administrative assistant in her fifties, recalled: "I worried a lot about my children becoming alcoholics or drug addicts since both their parents and a history of four generations of alcoholism preceded them. I made them go to Alateen and I set very strict limits about when they had to be home at night. My daughter told me years later that she was glad I was so strict and that it really showed her how concerned I was. I tried to give them love and support along with discipline and hoped that they didn't experience my actions as punitive."

The foundation of prevention is the improved communication patterns that generally develop between parents in recovery and their children. Parents have to learn what to tell their children on the subject and how to tell it so that they'll *hear*. Increasingly, there are drug education programs going on in the schools. If you discover your children *are* abusing drugs or alcohol, however, you must take decisive action:

- You and your spouse have to form a unanimous voice, agreeing on what is and what isn't acceptable behavior. If drinking and drugging occur in or outside the home, your children need to hear strong, calm, consistent messages about the consequences of such behavior.
- Avoid getting into enabling positions by being overresponsible. Don't take on the responsibilities that are expected of your child.
- If your child gets into trouble because of drinking or drugging, try not to bail him or her out. For instance, if your teenage son has an accident while drinking and wrecks his car, don't pay to get it repaired or replaced. He doesn't need wheels, he needs grounding.
- Talk openly about the substance abuse in your own family and how you or others were helped (if they were). Outline the recovery options open to your children. Depending on a child's age, you can put your child into treatment and/or require attendance at AA meetings. If your child is seventeen or older, though, you may simply have to detach—if all attempts at intervention fail.
- Get additional help for yourself and your other children from a family-treatment counselor with expertise in the field of alcoholism and drug abuse.

POSITIVE PARENTING

Parenting is probably the biggest job an adult child of an alcoholic will ever have. There are moments of intense pleasure and intense pain, moments of extreme closeness and extreme distance. Parenting can greatly enrich our own lives as we discover new problems and new solutions. Ultimately, our own attitudes will shape the quality of this opportunity for growth and development.

As you accept the challenge parenting offers, you'll need to ask yourself:

What are my expectations in this situation?
Are they realistic?
If not, how can I change them to a plan that is more reasonable?

By providing reasonably firm guidance, expressing your values and beliefs, and encouraging your children to take on responsibilities appropriate to their ages, you can build the foundation your children need.

By nurturing a sense of adequacy and projecting it to your children, you can affirm your courage in the parental realm. In exposing your vulnerabilities, you can be strong and open. Parenting can help you become more accepting, responsible, and loving.

Many ACOAs have taken steps to break through their own circles of pain and unhappiness. As parents, you may have become very sensitive to the pain of the people you love. This sensitivity, and your other resources and strengths, can be imparted to your children to make them better able to handle difficulties without fleeing from them. Lessons of living a decent and balanced life, coupled with support and encouragement and love, can prevent your own children from growing up in houses of fear. Affection, reliability, responsibility, and predictability—the things that you may have missed in your own family—can be your gifts to your children. These are the messages that children will get, nonverbally as well as verbally. As ACOAs, we need to trust that who we are as human beings is infinitely more important than what we tell our children. What children see is what they get.

When we believe in ourselves as human beings, we can believe in ourselves as parents. Parenting needn't—shouldn't—be by the book; it should be by courage and love and understanding. ACOAs have every quality they need to be successful in accepting the challenge of parenting.

EPILOGUE
—
A PERSONAL PATH TO RECOVERY

Many strategies for change have been described in this book. I hope that these strategies help you see that you *can* change and grow beyond survival. Perhaps these descriptions of the actual life experiences of adult children can convince you that you are not alone and that help is available if you want or need it. You deserve recovery.

The one path that has just briefly been touched upon, the one that has been more implicit than explicit, is the spiritual path. It is central to all other paths and is, I think, the most important one for ACOA recovery. Spirituality helps adults deal with emotional issues both from the past and in the present. It promotes a healing experience that fosters love and understanding. Underlying all other routes of recovery, spirituality has been the cornerstone of all Twelve Step programs since beginning with Alcoholics Anonymous over fifty years ago.

The concept of spirituality, because of its personal yet universal nature, is the most difficult one to convey. Many adult children of alcoholics believe it is the key to their recovery. It has certainly been the key to mine. For that reason, I conclude this book with a brief account of my own spiritual journey.

Spirituality is hard to define because it has so many different meanings for different people. It is an emotional rather than an intellectual experience, and therefore it is uniquely individual. In many circles, particularly scientific ones, it is often suspect for these reasons.

My view of spirituality is my own. It's not a path of personal development that I advocate for anyone else. It is, simply, the path I have chosen. For many years, I never gave much thought to things of the spirit. I did not consider myself spiritual or religious; I did not even understand that there is a difference between spirituality and religion. As a skeptic, an agnostic, the matter was not something I concerned myself with. I lived my life willfully, compulsively, and, for the most part, unhappily. And, like many adult children of alcoholics, I certainly didn't think I needed help from anyone. I was defiantly self-sufficient and righteously self-centered. I thought I could do it all, all alone.

Some years ago, however, I found I could no longer deny that my life was falling apart. People thought I was quite successful—that I had an exciting life and interesting friends. But, though this was true, and things looked good from the outside, I was a mess on the inside. I had serious emotional and physical problems, and I was in utter despair. I didn't know what was wrong, and I didn't know which way to turn.

It was the most painful time of my life. I felt defeated; I could no longer maintain the illusion that I was in control of my life. Fortunately, I asked for and received help from people who seemed to understand me better than I understood myself. I admitted and accepted the fact that I was out of control. It was not until a year later that I was able to see that by admitting my powerlessness I had reclaimed my life. And it turned out to be a better life than I would ever have dreamed was possible.

With indisputable clarity, I became aware that I had been cared for when I could not take care of myself. This realization transformed my life, and it was the beginning of my spiritual journey. At that moment —when I was finally able to surrender my willfulness—I knew there was a power higher than myself in which I could put my trust. After all those years of desperately trying to control my life, and most of the people in it, I saw that I had no control at all. I could do whatever I thought was the best thing to do, but I could not control the results. And the big surprise was that it wasn't so terrible. In fact, it was a huge relief. It completely changed my perception of my life: all those things that had seemed so important were not important after all. What mattered to me most was what was going on in my inner life, not in the outside world.

It gradually became clear to me that my expectations of myself had been unrealistic, unnecessary. I didn't have to be other than what I was; I didn't have to do everything I used to feel compelled to do; I didn't have to please all the people I had thought I had to please.

I could simply be. How spiritually connected I felt at any given point was dependent upon how I chose to be in the world. I didn't need to run my life or run from it. I could enjoy and live each day that particular day.

I did not find my spiritual path by looking for it. I found it by being open to it. That attitude of openness is now the barometer of my spirituality. When I am anxious, angry, or afraid, I do not have it. I know I am on the spiritual path when I am being as open, honest, and caring as I can possibly be.

Spirituality is that inner resource that influences my entire life. It comes down to a fundamental choice: I can live in faith or I can live in fear. I know that I cannot experience both feelings at the same time. When I am afraid, I have no faith. When I have faith, I have no fear. I try to keep it that simple.

SELF-TESTS FOR ACOAs

THE COA QUIZ

The COA Quiz (from *Alcoholism & Addiction* magazine) can give you some clues about whether and how you may have been most affected by growing up with an alcoholic parent.

Give yourself ten points for each of the following statements if it is often true of you or sounds like you as a child.

1. I take care of other people, but no one takes care of me.
2. No matter what happens, I feel I get blamed for it.
3. Usually it's best when no one notices me.
4. I'll do almost anything to get a laugh.
5. It's really hard for me to figure out what I want in relationships.
6. People praise me for all I've done but I never feel I've done enough.
7. I think I'm just no good.
8. I'm more comfortable with computers than people.
9. I usually change the subject when people get excited.
10. I'm not sure what people want me to say when they ask about my feelings.
11. It's hard for me to be close to people.
12. It's probably my fault my family has so many problems.
13. People say I could achieve more, but I don't have the self-confidence.

254

14. Sometimes I wish someone would just tell me what to do.
15. I work hard at getting approval.
16. I always try to do the correct thing.
17. Most of my friends get in trouble.
18. My animals are my best friends.
19. I'm really attracted to strong people.
20. Angry people scare me.
21. My job involves teaching or healing other people.
22. As soon as I am old enough I'm leaving home.
23. I procrastinate a lot.
24. It's hard for me to sit still—I'm usually hyper.
25. I feel different from other people.
26. People think I'm a nice person but my spouse complains I won't get close.
27. If everyone would leave me alone, I'd be O.K.
28. It's hard for me to relax with someone else around.
29. When I was a kid, I was the class clown.
30. If I don't give in to others, I feel guilty.

SCORING

If you answered yes to 1, 6, 11, 16, 21, and 26 you are probably the oldest child, the only child, or the oldest girl or boy in your family.

If you tended to agree with 2, 7, 12, 17, 22, and 27 you are more likely to be the second child or the second sister or brother in your family.

A predominance of yes answers to 3, 8, 13, 18, 23, and 28 would indicate that you are the middle child.

Identifying with answers 4, 9, 14, 19, 24, and 29 suggests the likelihood that you were the last born.

OVERALL SCORE

An overall score of over 100 indicates a strong identification with typical traits of adult children of alcoholics, though you may find you are not in the birth order indicated. If you find you don't agree with many statements, you may still recognize the behavior of someone close to you.

The good news is that you can clarify these characteristics if you want to, and a good source of help is support groups such as Al-Anon and Children of Alcoholics.

CAST—CHILDREN OF ALCOHOLICS
SCREENING TEST

This test (written by Dr. John W. Jones) can help people of all ages recognize and identify what is or was going on in their homes.

Check the answers below that best describe your feelings, behavior, and experiences related to a parent's alcohol use. Take your time and be as accurate as possible. Answer all 30 questions by checking either "Yes" or "No."

	Yes	No
1. Have you ever thought that one of your parents had a drinking problem?	—	—
2. Have you ever lost sleep because of a parent's drinking?	—	—
3. Did you ever encourage one of your parents to quit drinking?	—	—
4. Did you ever feel alone, scared, nervous, angry, or frustrated because a parent was not able to stop drinking?	—	—
5. Did you ever argue or fight with a parent when he or she was drinking?	—	—
6. Did you ever threaten to run away from home because of a parent's drinking?	—	—
7. Has a parent ever yelled at or hit you or other family members when drinking?	—	—
8. Have you ever heard your parents fight when one of them was drunk?	—	—
9. Did you ever protect another family member from a parent who was drinking?	—	—
10. Did you ever feel like hiding or emptying a parent's bottle of liquor?	—	—
11. Do many of your thoughts revolve around a problem-drinking parent or difficulties that arise because of his or her drinking?	—	—
12. Did you ever wish your parent would stop drinking?	—	—
13. Did you ever feel responsible or guilty about a parent's drinking?	—	—
14. Did you ever fear that your parents would get divorced due to alcohol misuse?	—	—
15. Have you ever withdrawn from and avoided outside activities and friends because of embarrassment and shame over a parent's drinking problem?	—	—
16. Did you ever feel caught in the middle of an argument or fight between a problem-drinking parent and your other parent?	—	—

Yes No

17. Did you ever feel that you made a parent drink alcohol? ___ ___
18. Have you ever felt that a problem-drinking parent did not really love you? ___ ___
19. Did you ever resent a parent's drinking? ___ ___
20. Have you ever worried about a parent's health because of his or her alcohol use? ___ ___
21. Have you ever been blamed for a parent's drinking? ___ ___
22. Did you ever think your father was an alcoholic? ___ ___
23. Did you ever wish your home could be more like the homes of your friends who did not have a parent with a drinking problem? ___ ___
24. Did a parent ever make promises to you that he or she did not keep because of drinking? ___ ___
25. Did you ever think your mother was an alcoholic? ___ ___
26. Did you ever wish you could talk to someone who could understand and help the alcohol-related problems in your family? ___ ___
27. Did you ever fight with your brothers and sisters about a parent's drinking? ___ ___
28. Did you ever stay away from home to avoid the drinking parent or your other parent's reaction to the drinking? ___ ___
29. Have you ever felt sick, cried, or had a knot in your stomach after worrying about a parent's drinking? ___ ___
30. Did you ever take over any chores and duties at home that were usually done by a parent before he or she developed a drinking problem? ___ ___

TOTAL NUMBER OF "YES" ANSWERS ___ ___

WHAT ARE THE SIGNS OF ALCOHOLISM?

This test (by the National Council on Alcoholism) will help you identify signs of addiction and the progression of the disease in yourself. It might indicate to you whether you or a member of your family may need help.

1. Do you occasionally drink heavily after a disappointment, a quarrel, or when the boss gives you a hard time?
2. When you have trouble or feel under pressure, do you always drink more heavily than usual?
3. Have you noticed that you are able to handle more liquor than you did when you were first drinking?
4. Did you ever wake up on the morning after and discover that you

could not remember part of the evening before, even though your friends tell you that you did not pass out?

5. When drinking with other people, do you try to have a few extra drinks when others will not know it?
6. Are there certain occasions when you feel uncomfortable if alcohol is not available?
7. Have you recently noticed that when you begin drinking you are in more of a hurry to get the first drink than you used to be?
8. Do you sometimes feel a little guilty about your drinking?
9. Are you secretly irritated when your family or friends discuss your drinking?
10. Have you recently noticed an increase in the frequency of your memory blackouts?
11. Do you often find that you wish to continue drinking after your friends say they have had enough?
12. Do you usually have a reason for the occasions when you drink heavily?
13. When you are sober, do you often regret things you have done or said while drinking?
14. Have you tried switching brands or following different plans for controlling your drinking?
15. Have you often failed to keep the promises you have made to yourself about controlling or cutting down on your drinking?
16. Have you ever tried to control your drinking by making a change in jobs, or moving to a new location?
17. Do you try to avoid family or close friends while you are drinking?
18. Are you having an increasing number of financial and work problems?
19. Do more people seem to be treating you unfairly without good reason?
20. Do you eat very little or irregularly when you are drinking?
21. Do you sometimes have the shakes in the morning and find that it helps to have a little drink?
22. Have you recently noticed that you cannot drink as much as you once did?
23. Do you sometimes stay drunk for several days at a time?
24. Do you sometimes feel very depressed and wonder whether life is worth living?
25. Sometimes after periods of drinking, do you see or hear things that aren't there?
26. Do you get terribly frightened after you have been drinking heavily?

If you answered "yes" to any of the questions, you have some of the symptoms that may indicate alcoholism. "Yes" answers to several of the questions indicate the following stages of alcoholism:

Questions 1–8—Early Stage
Questions 9–21—Middle Stage
Questions 22–26—The beginning of the Final Stage

TEST FOR ALCOHOLISM
IN A SIGNIFICANT OTHER

This test (developed by Donald and Nancy Howard) will offer you guidance in helping to determine if someone close to you has a serious drinking problem.

	Yes	No
1. Do you worry about your spouse's drinking?		
2. Have you ever been embarrassed by your spouse's drinking?		
3. Are holidays more of a nightmare than a celebration because of your spouse's drinking behavior?		
4. Are most of your spouse's friends heavy drinkers?		
5. Does your spouse often promise to quit drinking without success?		
6. Does your spouse's drinking make the atmosphere in the home tense and anxious?		
7. Does your spouse deny a drinking problem because he/she drinks only beer?		
8. Do you find it necessary to lie to employer, relatives, or friends in order to hide your spouse's drinking?		
9. Has your spouse ever failed to remember what occurred during a drinking period?		
10. Does your spouse avoid conversation pertaining to alcohol or problem drinking?		
11. Does your spouse justify his or her drinking problem?		
12. Does your spouse avoid social situations where alcoholic beverages will not be served?		
13. Do you ever feel guilty about your spouse's drinking?		
14. Has your spouse driven a vehicle while under the influence of alcohol?		
15. Are your children afraid of your spouse while he or she is drinking?		
16. Are you afraid of physical or verbal abuse when your spouse is drinking?		
17. Has another person mentioned your spouse's unusual drinking behavior?		

	Yes	No
18. Do you fear riding with your spouse when he or she is drinking?	___	___
19. Does your spouse have periods of remorse after a drinking occasion and apologize for behavior?	___	___
20. Does drinking less alcohol bring about the same effects in your spouse as in the past required more?	___	___

The staff of the Family Training Center has served thousands of families in the past several years and based on these experiences suggest the following scale in answering the above twenty questions.

> If you have answered "Yes" to any two of the questions, there is a definite warning that a drinking problem may exist in your family.
> If you have answered "Yes" to any four of the questions, the chances are that a drinking problem does exist in your family.
> If you have answered "Yes" to five or more, there very definitely is a drinking problem in your family.

RATING YOUR CHILD'S POTENTIAL FOR RESISTING ALCOHOL OR SUBSTANCE ABUSE

Parents want to prevent chemical abuse and to intervene early should a problem be on the horizon. This test (by the Fairfield-Formica Chemical Awareness Program for Parents) can clarify what might be going on in many areas of a child's development that could relate to future alcohol or drug abuse.

> This rating scale has been designed to help parents assess the relative resistance of their children to the abuse of alcohol and/or drugs.

> After each statement, circle the number from 0 to 5 which indicates how closely the statement describes your child.

> 0 = Not at all like my child
> 5 = Exactly like my child

A. *Personal Factors*

1. My child is even tempered and not given to emotional outbursts.   0 1 2 3 4 5
2. My child can work and concentrate on a task in spite of frustrations or distractions.   0 1 2 3 4 5
3. My child is self-directed and not easily influenced by others.   0 1 2 3 4 5

4. My child is generally resistant to illness and tolerates physical distress well.   0 1 2 3 4 5

5. My child has no history of alcohol/substance abuse in his/her immediate or extended family.   0 1 2 3 4 5

6. My child likes the person he/she is and shows pride in his/her accomplishments.   0 1 2 3 4 5

7. My child has good judgment and correctly anticipates the consequences of his/her actions.   0 1 2 3 4 5

8. My child gets along well with other children.   0 1 2 3 4 5

9. My child's behavior and interests reflect positive social values.   0 1 2 3 4 5

10. My child is able to express feelings honestly and directly.   0 1 2 3 4 5

11. My child is aware of the dangerous consequences of alcohol/substance abuse.   0 1 2 3 4 5

12. My child has a broad range of positive interests.   0 1 2 3 4 5

Section A Subtotal   _____

B. *Family Factors*

13. My child is an active member of his/her family with responsibilities and privileges appropriate for his/her age.   0 1 2 3 4 5

14. My child's friends, interests, and activities are important and known to me.   0 1 2 3 4 5

15. My child is encouraged to express his/her feelings without fear of rejection or disapproval.   0 1 2 3 4 5

16. My child is not exposed to the alcohol/substance abuse of another family member.   0 1 2 3 4 5

17. My child lives in a happy home, where there are warmth, cooperation, and acceptance.   0 1 2 3 4 5

18. My child lives in a family which strongly believes in the importance of personal growth and development, and communicates these values clearly.   0 1 2 3 4 5

19. My child lives in a family which sets clear standards about children not using alcohol or drugs and enforces these standards consistently.   0 1 2 3 4 5

Section B Subtotal   _____

C. *Environmental Factors*

20. My child's friends have a positive influence upon his/her behavior. 0 1 2 3 4 5

21. My child enjoys being home and spending time with his/her family. 0 1 2 3 4 5

22. My child's free time is spent productively. 0 1 2 3 4 5

23. My child's school provides adequate educational and social programs. 0 1 2 3 4 5

24. My child's community provides programs designed to provide a positive environment for children. 0 1 2 3 4 5

25. My child's friends are not involved in using alcohol/drugs. 0 1 2 3 4 5

Section C Subtotal _____

SIGNS OF SUBSTANCE ABUSE

The following checklist contains a number of factors that have been associated with the presence of adolescent alcohol/substance abuse. If you find that you have answered *yes* to more than a few questions, it's possible your child is abusing drugs and you may want to get information on what you can do.

1. Have you recently noticed changes for the worse in your child's

   a. general health? yes no
   b. appearance? yes no
   c. sleep & eating behavior? yes no
   d. emotional stability? yes no
   e. general level of responsibility? yes no

2. At school, has your child been

   a. receiving lower grades? yes no
   b. absent more frequently? yes no
   c. dropping extracurricular activities? yes no
   d. getting into trouble? yes no
   e. changing his/her friends? yes no
   f. talking about dropping out? yes no

3. At home, has your child

   a. been arguing with you over his/her use of drugs? yes no
   b. been spending more time alone? yes no
   c. been caught stealing money from you? yes no

    d. been unwilling to introduce his friends to you?   yes no

    e. shown a preoccupation with "partying"?   yes no

4. Has your child

    a. been caught lying about his/her drug use or other behavior?   yes no

    b. shown unpredictable mood swings?   yes no

5. Have you

    a. found yourself making excuses for your child's irresponsible behaviors?   yes no

    b. found physical evidence of substance abuse?   yes no

    c. felt yourself getting more and more out of touch with your child's friends and interests?   yes no

TWENTY-FOUR STAGES OF GROWTH FOR SURVIVORS OF INCEST

Discovering and coming to terms with the traumas of sexual abuse offers a greater chance of becoming whole. The road to recovery is laid out in this list (by Karen Lison, based on the work of John Dean).

1. I acknowledge that something terrible happened. I know it is not my imagination.
2. I am aware on some level that something was done to me—I was a victim of incest or sexual abuse during my childhood.
3. I recognize that I am, in fact, a survivor, in the sense that I am alive, and have chosen life over self-inflicted death.
4. I recognize and begin to deal with feelings of being "contaminated" or "damaged."
5. I feel angry about being used and abused.
6. I experience rage at my nonprotecting parent (usually mother).
7. I discuss the abuse thoroughly with therapist.
8. I have told a nonfamily member about the abuse.
9. I have told a family member who previously did not know.
10. I completely reexperience and begin to deal with feelings appropriate for each incident of abuse.
11. I begin to give up my sense of responsibility for the abuse occurring.
12. I begin to recognize that I was probably acting appropriately at the time the abuse occurred. (That is, my reactions were appropriate, the abuse was not!)

13. I am able to understand how the molestation has affected my current relationships and behavioral patterns.
14. I am able to diminish my resistance to talking about the abuse, although maybe not the details of it, with others.
15. If there was a part of the molestation that was sexually pleasurable to me, I am coming to terms with the fact of that pleasure and I am dealing with the guilt surrounding it.
16. If there were aspects of the molestation that I perceived as positive (such as a feeling of being special in the family), I am beginning to understand and deal with these feelings.
17. I perceive the connection between the molestation and current relationships and am developing some control around the connection.
18. I recognize that I have a choice as to whether or not I confront my perpetrator(s).
19. I am beginning to understand what I desire from relationships, whether sexual or nonsexual.
20. I am able to enjoy intimacy.
21. I have developed a sense of self and my self-esteem has increased.
22. I have developed a sense of being somewhat at ease with the subject of my molestation and that of others.
23. I recognize that I have a choice as to whether or not I forgive my perpetrator(s).
24. I am in touch with past anger, but anger is not currently a constant part of my feelings in such a way that it negatively influences my other feelings, my functioning, and my relationships with others.

EATING DISORDERS QUESTIONNAIRE

Getting help for an eating disorder early offers the best chance for recovery. Eating disorders often show up in families that have had trouble with chemical substances. This questionnaire (by Judi Hollis) will let you know the warning signs of the possible development of serious illness.

	Yes	No
Do you feel guilty about eating?	—	—
Are you prone to consume large quantities of junk food?	—	—
Do you hide food or hide from others while eating?	—	—
Do you eat to the point of nausea and vomiting?	—	—
Are you sometimes repelled by food?	—	—
Do you relish preparing foods even if you don't eat?	—	—
Have you forced vomiting?	—	—

	Yes	No
Do you take many laxatives to control weight?	___	___
Do you weigh in on a scale more than once a week?	___	___
Have you found yourself unable to stop eating?	___	___
Have you taken on fasting to control weight?	___	___
Do you know your eating pattern is abnormal and embarrassing?	___	___
Do you eat until your stomach hurts?	___	___
Does eating cause you to fall asleep?	___	___
Do certain occasions require certain foods?	___	___
In your lifetime have you lost more than 50 pounds?	___	___
Does a "good" restaurant serve large portions?	___	___
Do you eat snacks before going out to eat with others?	___	___
Do you eat standing up?	___	___
Do you "inhale" your food?	___	___
Do you become irritated at postponed eating?	___	___
Have you heard others call food "too rich" and felt confused?	___	___
Do you awake from sleep to eat?	___	___
Does your wardrobe vary three sizes or more?	___	___
Does eating sometimes make you hungrier than not eating?	___	___
Do you feel like an object as others describe your body?	___	___
Have you felt people should "love me, love my fat"?	___	___
Do you usually clean your plate whether hungry or not?	___	___
Is your eating rather continuous?	___	___
At a party, do you spend most of your time at the snack table, or do you consciously avoid the food area?	___	___
Have you tried more than one fad diet?	___	___
Do you make fun of yourself before others can?	___	___
Do you feel exhilarated when you control food?	___	___
Are you afraid to be "normal"?	___	___
When you know certain foods are on the shelf, do they "call" to you?	___	___
Do you buy clothes either too big or too small?	___	___
Do your friends eat as you do and are they embarrassed?	___	___
Do you postpone joys with "wait till I control my weight"?	___	___
Do others see your shape differently than you do?	___	___

ORGANIZATIONAL CHARTERS AND FINDINGS
___

ALCOHOLICS ANONYMOUS
___

In its preamble, AA explains what the organization is and is not:

Alcoholics Anonymous is a fellowship of men and women who share their experience, strength and hope with each other that they may solve their common problem and help others to recover from alcoholism.

The only requirement for membership is a desire to stop drinking. There are no dues or fees for AA membership; we are self-supporting through our own contributions. AA is not allied with any sect, denomination, politics, organization or institution; does not wish to engage in any controversy; neither endorses nor opposes any causes. Our primary purpose is to stay sober and help other alcoholics to achieve sobriety.

AA's road to recovery is taken in Twelve Steps, set forth thus:

1. We admitted we were powerless over alcohol—that our lives had become unmanageable.
2. Came to believe that a Power greater than ourselves could restore us to sanity.
3. Made a decision to turn our will and our lives over to the care of God, *as we understood Him.*
4. Made a searching and fearless moral inventory of ourselves.
5. Admitted to God, to ourselves, and to another human being the exact nature of our wrongs.

6. Were entirely ready to have God remove all these defects of character.
7. Humbly asked Him to remove our shortcomings.
8. Made a list of all persons we had harmed, and became willing to make amends to them all.
9. Made direct amends to such people wherever possible, except when to do so would injure them or others.
10. Continued to take personal inventory and when we were wrong promptly admitted it.
11. Sought through prayer and meditation to improve our conscious contact with God *as we understood Him*, praying only for knowledge of His will for us and the power to carry that out.
12. Having had a spiritual awakening as the result of these steps, we tried to carry this message to alcoholics, and to practice these principles in all our affairs.

AL-ANON

The organization's declaration about itself reads:

Al-Anon is the only worldwide organization that offers a self-help recovery program for the families and friends of alcoholics whether or not the alcoholic seeks help or even recognizes the existence of a drinking problem. Members give and receive comfort and understanding through a mutual exchange of experiences, strength and hope. Sharing of similar problems binds individuals and groups together in a bond that is protected by a policy of anonymity. Al-Anon is not a religious organization or a counseling agency. It is not a treatment center nor is it allied with any other organization offering such services. Al-Anon Family Groups, which includes Alateen for teenage members, neither express opinions on outside issues nor endorse outside enterprises. No dues or fees are required. Membership is voluntary, requiring only that one's own life has been adversely affected by someone else's drinking problem.

Detachment: Alcoholism is a family disease. Detachment, a recovery tool for the family in Al-Anon, helps members to help themselves. In Al-Anon we learn that individuals are not responsible for another person's disease or recovery from it. We let go of our obsession with another's behavior and begin to lead happier and more manageable lives, lives with dignity and rights; lives guided by a Power greater than ourselves.

In Al-Anon, we learn:

- Not to suffer because of the actions or reactions of other people.
- Not to allow ourselves to be used or abused in the interest of another's recovery.

- Not to do for others what they should do for themselves.
- Not to manipulate situations so others will eat, go to bed, get up, pay bills, etc.
- Not to cover up for another's mistakes or misdeeds.
- Not to create a crisis.
- Not to prevent a crisis if it is in the natural course of events.

Detachment is neither kind nor unkind. It does not imply evaluation of the person or situation from which we are detaching. It is simply a means for us to recover from the adverse effects of the disease of alcoholism upon our lives.

NACOA

The charter statement of the National Association for the Children of Alcoholics describes its twelve goals:

- To increase public and professional awareness, understanding, and recognition of the needs of COAs of all ages.
- To advocate accessible services addressing the unique problems arising from being the child of an alcoholic.
- To protect the rights of children to live in a safe and healthy environment.
- To involve the entire community, especially the schools, human services, mental health, medical, religious, and law-enforcement professions.
- To help existing alcoholism programs initiate primary and comprehensive services for COAs staffed by professionals specifically trained to meet the needs of COAs.
- To support school-based programs which acknowledge and address the problems of COAs.
- To create a network which will promote the exchange of information and resources.
- To encourage clinical and biomedical research related to COA issues.
- To advocate funding from public and private sources.
- To encourage training for professionals in issues related to COAs.
- To develop professional guidelines for those who work with COAs.
- To offer support to professionals who are themselves COAs.

NACOA has established the following facts about children of alcoholics:

- An estimated 28 million Americans have at least one alcoholic parent.
- More than half of all alcoholics have an alcoholic parent.

- One of three families currently reports alcohol abuse by a family member.
- Children of alcoholics are at the highest risk of developing alcoholism themselves or marrying someone who becomes alcoholic.
- Medical research has shown that children born to alcoholics are at the highest risk of developing attention-deficit disorders, stress-related medical problems, fetal alcohol syndrome, and other alcohol-related birth defects.
- In up to 90 percent of child-abuse cases, alcohol is a significant factor.
- Children of alcoholics are also frequently victims of incest, child neglect, and other forms of violence and exploitation.
- COAs often adapt to the chaos and inconsistency of an alcoholic home by developing an inability to trust, an extreme need to control, an excessive sense of responsibility and denial of feelings, all of which result in low self-esteem, depression, isolation, guilt, and difficulty in maintaining satisfying relationships. These and other problems often persist throughout adulthood.
- Children of alcoholics are prone to experience a range of psychological difficulties, including learning disabilities, anxiety, attempted and completed suicide, learning disorders, and compulsive achieving.
- The majority of people served by employee assistance programs are adult COAs.
- The problems of most COAs remain invisible because their coping behavior tends to be approval-seeking and socially acceptable. However, a disproportionate number of those entering the juvenile justice system, courts, prisons, and mental-health facilities, and referred to school authorities are COAs.

THE CHILDREN OF ALCOHOLICS FOUNDATION, INC.

The Children of Alcoholics Foundation, Inc. has compiled research data that indicates problems that many children of alcoholics manifest at three life stages:

As youngsters, children of alcoholics may have physical problems, including headaches, tiredness, and stomach aches, although no specific illnesses are detected. Also, they may have tics, nausea, enuresis, sleep problems, asthma, and sensory problems with noise, bright lights, heat, and cold more often than other children. Young children of alcoholics may evidence such problems as emotional detachment, dependency, aggression, confusion of personal identity, and lower self-esteem. Some young children from alcoholic families become exceedingly responsible and take on parental roles toward their siblings and others. Teachers report that children of alcoholics are more likely to be hyperactive or delinquent. They have difficulty concentrating or forming trusting relationships.

For Adolescents: Teenage children of alcoholics are twice as likely to have psychiatric treatment for conduct disorders, anxiety or depressive symptoms, or to abuse alcohol and other drugs. Children of alcoholics are three times more likely to be expelled from school, or drop out due to early marriage, pregnancy, institutionalization, or military enlistment. Some teenage children of alcoholics appear more resilient and are top-ranking "mini-adults" who perform all functions well, but seem to experience no personal satisfaction in their successes. Recent studies indicate a relationship between bulimia and parental alcoholism. Preliminary reports show a relationship between parental alcoholism and adolescent suicide, and that parents of those who attempt suicide use significantly more alcohol than other parents.

For Adults: Adult children of alcoholics use health services more frequently than others. Sons of alcoholics make more hospital visits, require more surgery and ambulatory care, and make more visits to physicians for drug and alcohol abuse. Daughters of alcoholics make more visits to gynecological services. Adult children of alcoholics may have serious problems with anger and hostility and may experience more personal and social problems at younger ages, including loss of employment due to alcoholism and arrests while drinking. Adult children of alcoholics begin drinking and become alcoholic at earlier ages. They are more likely to experience greater enjoyment during early drinking occurrences, which later result in an associated worsening of mood, tendency to get sick after intoxication, and significantly more alcoholism symptoms. In its short history, the Children of Alcoholics Foundation, Inc. has achieved the following:

- Created a national education and public-awareness program about problems that alcoholism causes families. "The Images Within: A Child's View of Parental Alcoholism" is a dramatic display of artwork donated by children of alcoholics throughout the country. The five hundred drawings, stories, letters, and poems have been widely acclaimed by educators, medical professionals, community and business leaders, legislators, and media. The art has been collected and shown in New York, Rhode Island, Massachusetts, Minnesota, Texas, and California and the national tour will conclude with an exhibition in Washington, D.C.
- Developed an alcohol education and prevention program for school-aged youngsters by involving students in the art shows and taking steps to transfer the show for use in school settings. Through use of the art exhibit, young people learn about family alcoholism, and teachers are better able to discuss teenage drinking habits and risks with students.
- Promoted widespread interest in research by sponsoring a landmark

meeting of eminent scientists to develop an agenda of research needs and opportunities for children of alcoholics. The success of this conference prompted a similar conference on prevention research and has resulted in three important Foundation publications on research.

- Launched a health-education program for use by medical practitioners and other health-care professionals. Components of this program include workshops, materials for patients in waiting rooms, and the creation of an original drama on the plight of children living with parental alcohol abuse.
- Assembled the first national directory of available resources to provide referral information and help for children of alcoholics. Commissioned a survey of large corporation and employee-assistance programs to discover their knowledge, attitudes, and ways they can be motivated to help adult employed children of alcoholics and young children of alcoholic employees.

According to the Children of Alcoholics Foundation, Inc., one out of every eight Americans is the child of an alcoholic. Of the twenty-eight million children of alcoholics in the U.S., seven million are under the age of eighteen. We know that:

- Alcoholism runs in families.
- Sons of alcoholic fathers are four times more likely to become alcoholics.
- Daughters of alcoholic mothers are three times more likely to become alcoholics.
- Children of alcoholics are often grandchildren of alcoholics.
- Daughters of alcoholics are more likely to marry alcoholics.

How Do Children of Alcoholics Feel?

- Guilty and responsible for parental drinking and unaware that alcoholism is a disease which they can't cause, control, or cure.
- Invisible and unloved, since family life revolves totally around the alcoholic parent.
- Insecure, due to consistent inconsistencies in parental behavior, attitudes, and rules.
- Fearful that the alcoholic parent will become ill, have an accident, or die.
- Embarrassed by the public behavior of alcoholic parents.
- Ashamed because of the stigma society attaches to alcoholism and the need to keep it a family secret.
- Frightened by family conflict, violence, and abuse.

How Do Children of Alcoholics React? As youngsters, children of alcoholic parents may be more likely to:

- Have learning difficulties, do poorly in school, be truant or delinquent.
- Have fewer friends.
- Suffer psychosomatic illnesses.
- Be victims of neglect, child abuse, or incest.

As teenagers, children of alcoholic parents may be more likely to:

- Be expelled from school or drop out due to early marriage, pregnancy, institutionalization, or military enlistment.
- Abuse alcohol or other drugs.
- Have serious behavior problems, anxiety, or depression.
- Attempt suicide.

As adults, children of alcoholics may be more likely to:

- Have problems with interpersonal relationships.
- Experience difficulties in the workplace.
- Overuse medical facilities.
- Become alcoholic, suicidal, or mentally ill.

As youngsters the children of alcoholics may be superstars but develop serious problems in adulthood. Later on as a result of parental alcoholism, these "fast track" adults may function well but experience no joy or satisfaction from success and be prime candidates for heart attacks, stroke, ulcers, or depression.

RESOURCE ORGANIZATIONS

When seeking information on treatment for addictions or problems related to dysfunctional families, start with the local telephone book or contact an agency that is a central clearinghouse for services in the local area. The addresses and telephone numbers listed here are those of the national headquarters of selected organizations. Some of them provide hotline counseling; others offer referrals to services in your area as well as informational and educational materials.

Al-Anon Family Group
  Headquarters
1372 Broadway (at 38th Street)
7th Floor
New York, New York 10018
800-245-4656; in New York area
  212-302-7240

Callers receive information about Al-Anon meetings in their area; a catalog of literature and video tapes is offered free of charge; literature is sent at low fees. Also sponsors Alateen.

Alateen

Call Al-Anon cited above. Refers to groups for ages 11 to 18 whose lives are affected by alcoholism.

National Association of Children
  of Alcoholics (NACOA)
31706 Coast Highway
South Laguna, California 92677
714-499-3889

Offers lists of publications, assists in the formation of state chapters, and provides educational and informational material for all ages at no charge. Holds regional conferences and an annual national convention.

Children of Alcoholics
  Foundation
200 Park Avenue
31st Floor
New York, New York 10166
212-949-1404

Offers packet of general information free of charge; referrals to groups and treatment programs throughout the country; special reports available at low fee.

Alcoholics Anonymous—General Service Office (A.A.)
468 Park Avenue South
New York, New York 10016
212-686-1100

Refers callers to A.A. meetings in their areas; catalog of literature is free; pamphlets, books, and video tapes are available at low cost.

National Council on Alcoholism (NCA)
12 West 21st Street
New York, New York 10010
212-206-6770

Refers callers to their affiliates across the country; free catalog of many publications that can be purchased.

National Clearinghouse for Alcohol Information (NCALI)
P.O. Box 234
Rockville, Maryland 20852
301-468-2600

Prepares reference materials on a variety of frequently requested topics concerning alcoholism research and treatment; offers printouts of titles with summaries. No fee.

National Institute on Alcohol Abuse and Alcoholism (NIAAA)
Parklawn Building, 5600 Fishers Lane
Rockville, Maryland 20852
301-468-2600—same as Clearinghouse cited above

Disseminates wide variety of information on alcoholism treatment and research.

Narcotics Anonymous—World Service Office (NA)
P.O. Box 9999
Van Nuys, California 91409
818-780-3951

Refers callers to the NA office or groups in their area; free order form for low-cost literature on addiction and how N.A. works.

Nar-Anon

Holds meetings for family members who are involved in drug abuse; check local listings.

National Institute of Drug Abuse (NIDA)
Parklawn Building, 5600 Fishers Lane
Rockville, Maryland 20852
Information Office—301-443-6245

For help:
800-662-HELP (800-662-4357)
Day and evening hotline offering referrals to treatment centers, Twelve Step groups, and general information on drugs. Free pamphlets.

For employers:
800-843-4971
Informational hotline 9 A.M. to 8 P.M. for employers concerned about drug intake and drug testing of employees.

For literature:
National Clearinghouse for Information
P.O. Box 416
Kensington, Maryland 20895
Write for free catalog.

National Cocaine-Abuse Hotline
800-COCAINE (800-262-2463)

24-hour crisis line of Fair Oaks Hospital, Summit, N.J., offering general information about cocaine and referrals to treatment facilities, Twelve Step groups, and, in some areas, individual therapists.

Cocaine Anonymous—National
Office
P.O. Box 1367
Culver City, California 90232
213-559-5833

Hotline gives referrals to Twelve Step groups.

National Self-Help Clearinghouse
33 West 42nd Street
New York, New York 10036
212-840-1259

Refers callers to the Clearinghouse resource in their area; offers the Self Help Reporter for $10 per year and a booklet, How to Start a Self Help Group, for $6.

American Anorexia/Bulimia
Association, Inc.
133 Cedar Lane
Teaneck, New Jersey 07666
201-836-1800

Offers callers referrals to clinicians specializing in eating disorders; newsletter costs $25 per year (5 issues), free reading lists.

Overeaters Anonymous—
National Office
4025 Spencer Street
Suite 203
Torrance, California 90504
213-542-8363

Refers callers to meetings in their area; free introductory literature.

O-Anon

Holds meetings for family members with certain eating disorders; check local area.

National Child Abuse Hotline
Childhelp USA
P.O. Box 630
Hollywood, California 90028
800-4-A-CHILD (800-422-4453)

Concerned with the treatment and prevention of child abuse; operates national 24-hour hotline offering crisis counseling by professionals, referrals to services in local area; provides literature to parents under stress, for children from the age of two, and for the professional practitioner. Fees are charged for some literature, others free.

Parents United
Institute for the Community as
Extended Family (ICEF)
P.O. Box 952
San Jose, California 95108
408-280-5055

Takes calls from professionals seeking to establish Parents United programs in their areas. Parents seeking help should call the National Child Abuse Hotline—800-4-A-CHILD—cited above.

National Committee for
Prevention of Child Abuse
332 South Michigan Avenue
Suite 950
Chicago, Illinois 60604
312-663-3520

Offers packet of general information on the issue of child abuse—no charge.

Parents Anonymous—National Office
6733 South Sepulveda Blvd.
Suite 270
Los Angeles, California 90045
800-421-0353

Telephone crisis counseling, referral to services in local area, literature free to parents; $5 to others.

Incest Survivors Resource
  Network, International, Inc.
P.O. Box 911
Hicksville, New York 11802
516-935-3031

Trained incest survivors assist agencies in planning and delivering staff training, workshops, or conferences. Videotapes, referrals.

V.O.I.C.E.S. in Action
P.O. Box 148309
Chicago, Illinois 60614
312-327-1500

S.I.G.H. (Survivors of Incest
  Gaining Health)
20 West Adams
Suite 2015
Chicago, Illinois 60606
Contact: Karen C. Lison

Offers a national network of support and communication for survivors of incest.

Gamblers Anonymous
National Council on Compulsive
  Gambling
444 West 56th Street
Room 3207S
New York, New York 10019
212-765-3833

Disseminates information and educational materials on gambling as a psychological addiction; refers to treatment facilities and to Twelve Step groups. Literature is free; *Journal of Gambling Behavior* (a quarterly) is $34 to individuals and $88 to institutions per year.

Gam-Anon

Holds meetings for family members of problem gamblers; check local listings.

Drugs Anonymous

Formerly Pill-Anonymous—has no national headquarters. Look for groups in your area.

Debtors Anonymous

Has no national office; check local area for groups or for Shopaholic or Spendthrifter groups.

Students Against Suicide
P.O. Box 115
South Laguna, California 92677
714-496-4566

According to the Self-Help Resource Book this organization "runs groups that seek to create awareness of teen suicide and to implement programs to eliminate teen suicide." Networks with Safe-Ride and MADD.

RECOMMENDED READING

The books and articles the author referred to in developing this book are listed by categories of special emphasis. The reader who wishes to explore one of these areas of interest may find these references helpful, but should not be limited to the works selected for inclusion here.

ADULT CHILDREN OF ALCOHOLICS

Reading about the experiences of other ACOAs and learning more about how the problems and issues are described helps to give words to feelings and to encourage those who are unfamiliar with this field to embark on a journey of personal recovery. Clinical practitioners will find that becoming more familiar with ACOA experiences offers them an increased understanding of their clients.

Ackerman, Robert J. *Children of Alcoholics.* Holmes Beach, Florida: Learning Publications, 1983.

———, ed. *Growing in the Shadow.* Pompano Beach, Florida: Health Communications, 1986.

Bepko, Claudia, with Kreston, Jo Ann. *The Responsibility Trap.* New York: Free Press, 1985.

Black, Claudia. *It Will Never Happen to Me!* Denver: M.A.C. Printing and Publications Division, 1981.

Curtin, Paul H. *Tumbleweeds: A Therapist's Guide to Treatment of ACOAs*. Rockaway, N.J.: Quotidian, 1985.

Dean, Amy E. *Once Upon a Time*. Center City, Minnesota: Hazelden, 1987.

Deutsch, Charles. *Broken Bottles, Broken Dreams: Understanding and Helping the Children of Alcoholics*. New York: Teachers College, 1982.

Dulfano, Celia. *Families, Alcoholism and Recovery—Ten Stories*. Center City, Minnesota: Hazelden, 1982.

Elkin, Michael. *Families Under the Influence: Changing Alcoholic Patterns*. New York: W. W. Norton, 1984.

Fossum, Merle A., and Mason, Marilyn J. *Facing Shame*. New York: W. W. Norton, 1986.

Gravitz, Herbert L., and Bowden, Julie D. *Guide to Recovery—A Book for ACOAs*. Holmes Beach, Florida: Learning Publications, 1985.

Hornick, Edith Lynne. *You and Your Alcoholic Parent*. New York: Association Press, 1974.

Kritsberg, Wayne. *The Adult Children of Alcoholics Syndrome: From Discovery to Recovery*. Pompano Beach, Florida: Health Communications, 1985.

Krupnick, Louis B., and Elizabeth. *From Despair to Decision*. Minneapolis: CompCare, 1985.

McConnell, Patty. *A Workbook for Healing: Adult Children of Alcoholics*. New York: Harper & Row, 1986.

Middleton-Moz, Jane, and Dwinell, Lorie. *After the Tears*. Pompano Beach, Florida: Health Communications, 1986.

Norwood, Robin. *Women Who Love Too Much*. New York: Pocket Books, 1986.

Scales, Cynthia G. *Potato Chips for Breakfast*. Rockaway, N.J.: Quotidian, 1986.

Seixas, Judith S. *Living with a Parent Who Drinks Too Much*. New York: Greenwillow Books, 1979.

Seixas, Judith S., and Youcha, Geraldine. *Children of Alcoholism: A Survivor's Manual*. New York: Harper & Row, 1985.

This New Day. Rockaway, N.J.: Quotidian, 1985.

Wegscheider, Sharon. *Another Chance: Hope and Health for the Alcoholic Family*. Palo Alto, California: Science & Behavior Books, 1981.

Wegscheider-Cruse, Sharon. *Choicemaking*. Pompano Beach, Florida: Health Communications, 1985.

Woititz, Janet Geringer. *Adult Children of Alcoholics*. Pompano Beach, Florida: Health Communications, 1983.

———. *Marriage on the Rocks*. New York: Delacorte Press, 1979.

———. *Struggle for Intimacy*. Pompano Beach, Florida: Health Communications, 1985.

ALCOHOLISM

Learning more about the disease of alcoholism and its treatment provides a foundation for ACOAs to look at their experiences and those
of their families.

Al-Anon. New York: Al-Anon Family Group Headquarters, 1372 Broad-
way.
Alcoholics Anonymous. New York: Alcoholics Anonymous World Services,
1976.
Alcoholism Intervention: How to Get a Loved One into Treatment. Mill Neck, N.Y.:
Charles D. Smithers Foundation, undated.
Bean, Margaret H., and Zinberg, Norman E., eds. *Dynamic Approaches to
the Understanding and Treatment of Alcoholism.* New York: Free Press, 1981.
Cermack, Timmen L., M.D. *Diagnosing and Treating Co-Dependency.* Minne-
apolis: Johnson Institute, 1986.
Cheever, Susan. *Home Before Dark.* Boston: Houghton Mifflin Company,
1984.
*Columbia University College of Physicians and Surgeons Complete Home Medical
Guide.* New York: Crown, 1985.
Cook, David; Fewell, Christine; Riolo, John, eds. *Social Work Treatment of
Alcohol Problems.* New Brunswick, N.J.: Publications Division, Rutgers
Center of Alcohol Studies, 1983.
Each Day a New Beginning. Center City, Minnesota: Hazelden, 1981.
Ford, Betty. *A Glad Awakening.* New York: Doubleday, 1986.
Johnson, Vernon E. *I'll Quit Tomorrow.* San Francisco: Harper & Row,
1980.
———. *Intervention.* Minneapolis: Johnson Institute Books, 1986.
Kaufman, Edward, and Pauline N. *Family Therapy of Drug and Alcohol Abuse.*
New York: Gardner Press, 1979.
Kurtz, Ernest. *Not-God! A History of Alcoholism.* Center City, Minnesota:
Hazelden, 1979.
Mann, Marty. *Marty Mann Answers Your Questions About Drinking and Alcohol-
ism.* New York: Holt, Rinehart and Winston, 1970.
———. *Marty Mann's New Primer on Alcoholism.* New York: Holt, Rinehart
and Winston, 1981.
Milan, James, and Ketcham, Katherine. *Under the Influence: A Guide to the
Myths and Realities of Alcoholism.* New York: Bantam Books, 1981.
Molloy, Paul. *Where Did Everybody Go?* New York: Warner Books, 1981.
Pinkham, Mary Ellen. *How to Stop the One You Love from Drinking.* With
Families in Crisis, Inc., New York: G. P. Putnam's Sons, 1986.

Pursch, Joseph A., M.D. *Dear Doc. . . .* Minneapolis: CompCare, 1983.

Rachel V. *A Woman Like You.* San Francisco: Harper & Row, 1985.

Reddy, Betty. *Alcoholism—A Family Illness.* Illinois: Lutheran Center for Substance Abuse, 1977.

Robe, Lucy Barry. *Co-Starring Famous Women and Alcohol.* Minneapolis: CompCare, 1986.

Twelve Steps and Twelve Traditions. New York: Alcoholics Anonymous World Services, 1980.

Zimberg, Sheldon; Wallace, John; Blume, Sheila B. *Practical Approaches to Alcoholism Psychotherapy.* New York: Plenum Press, 1985.

EATING DISORDERS

Some people who grow up in dysfunctional families, or those in which a compulsive behavior was active, have difficulties with both alcohol and food. By identifying early warning signs and seeking treatment, resolution of the eating-disorder problem is optimized. Some experts believe that the path to recovery is similar to that for alcoholism and overlapping in some cases.

Arenson, Gloria. *Binge Eating.* New York: Rawson Associates, 1984.

Boskind-White, Marlene, and White, William C., Jr. *Bulimarexia: The Binge/Purge Cycle.* New York: W. W. Norton, 1983.

Bruch, Hilde, M.D. *The Golden Cage.* Cambridge: Harvard University Press, 1978.

Hollis, Judi. *Fat Is a Family Affair.* Center City, Minnesota: Hazelden, 1985.

Kinoy, Barbara P., ed. *When Will We Laugh Again?* New York: Columbia University Press, 1984.

Siegal, Michelle, and Brisman, Judith. *Surviving an Eating Disorder.* New York: Harper & Row, forthcoming 1988.

SEXUAL ABUSE

A subject that is receiving urgent attention recently but is still hidden to a large extent. Survivors are often found in alcoholic families. Reading can help survivors feel that they are less alone and give them the courage to seek support.

Armstrong, Louise. *Kiss Daddy Goodnight: A Speakout on Incest.* New York: Pocket Books, 1978.

Bass, Ellen, and Thornton, Louise, eds. *I Never Told Anyone.* New York: Harper & Row, 1983.

Bass, Ellen, and Davis, Laura. *The Courage to Heal.* New York: Harper & Row, forthcoming 1988.

Mrazek, Patricia Belzley, and Kempe, C. Henry, eds. *Sexually Abused Children and Their Families.* New York: Pergamon Press, 1981.

Sgroi, Suzanne M. *Handbook of Clinical Intervention in Child Sexual Abuse.* Lexington, Massachusetts: Lexington Books, 1981.

PARENTING

What's normal? A question everyone asks at times, but especially prominent in the concerns of ACOAs. By learning about how children behave at different ages and how problems are defined today by both experts and parents, parents can gain insight and confidence as well as target problems early on.

Bank Street College of Education. *Raising a Confident Child.* New York: Pantheon Books, 1984.

Galinsky, Ellen. *Between Generations: The Six Stages of Parenthood.* New York: Times Books, 1981.

Gordon, Thomas. *Parent Effectiveness Training.* New York: Peter H. Wyden, 1970.

Gruenberg, Sidonie Matsner, ed. *The New Encyclopedia of Child Care and Guidance.* Garden City, New York: Doubleday, 1967.

Miller, Alice. *For Your Own Good.* New York: Farrar, Straus, Giroux, 1979.

Miller, Gordon Porter. *Teaching Your Child to Make Decisions.* With Bob Oskam. New York: Harper & Row, 1984.

Scharlatt, Elisabeth L., ed. *Kids Day In and Day Out: A Parent's Manual.* New York: Simon and Schuster, 1979.

Sears, William, M.D. *Creative Parenting.* New York: Everest House, 1982.

Spock, Benjamin. *Raising Children in a Difficult Time.* New York: W. W. Norton, 1974.

Wilson, Earl D. *A Silence to Be Broken.* Portland, Oregon: Multnomah Press, 1986.

FAMILY SYSTEMS

How people work together in a family and how their own families influence their current behavior and relationships is fascinating from many points of view. By looking at the individual within the context of other relationships and events, we can sometimes move away from blame and on to the future.

Beavers, W. Robert. *Successful Marriage: A Family Systems Approach to Family Therapy*. New York: W. W. Norton, 1985.

Bowen, Murray. *Family Therapy in Clinical Practice*. New York: Jason Aronson, 1978.

Carter, Elizabeth A., and McGoldrick, Monica, eds. *The Family Life Cycle: A Framework for Family Therapy*. New York: Gardner Press, 1980.

Foley, Vincent D. *Introduction to Family Therapy*. Orlando, Florida: Grune & Stratton, 1986.

Kübler-Ross, Elisabeth. *On Death and Dying*. New York: Macmillan, 1969.

Lerner, Harriet Goldhor. *The Dance of Anger*. New York: Harper & Row, 1985.

McGoldrick, Monica, and Gerson, Randy. *Genograms in Family Assessment*. New York: W. W. Norton, 1985.

Napier, Augustus Y., and Whitaker, Carl, M.D. *The Family Crucible*. New York: Bantam Books, 1980.

Satir, Virginia. *Peoplemaking*. California: Science & Behavior Books, 1972.

Worden, William. *Grief Counseling and Grief Therapy: A Handbook for the Mental Health Practitioner*. New York: Springer, 1982.

Zimmerman, William. *How to Tape Instant Oral Biographies*. New York: Guarionex Press, 1979.

INDEX

Boundaries, blurred, 38–39
Bulimia, 42–43

Calmness, 144–146
Change
  commitment to, 82–83
  effects of, on family, 217–220
  embracing the process of, 81–87
  safe place for, 88–103
  of view, 86–87
  wanting, 84
  working together for, 104–116
Chaos, 144–146
Chemicals. See Substance abuse
Child within, the, 132–135
  caring for, 133–135
  connecting with, 133–134
  developing sympathy for, 134
  freeing, 132
  having fun, 136
  writing to, 134–135
Childhood
  loss of, 132–133
  roles, 47–50
Children of alcoholics
  characteristics of, 96–97
  chemicals and, 247–248
  facts about, 268–269
  growing up in control, 15–16
  growing up in denial, 9–12
  growing up normal, 5–8
  growing up perfect, 12–15
  growing up too soon, 13–14
  hidden fears in, 20–31. See also specific
    fears
  hidden feelings in, 18–19. See also
    specific feelings
  myths of, 54–55
  resistance in, to alcohol or drug abuse,
    260–263
  responsibilities and, 13
  roles of, 47–50
  screening test for, 256–257
  setting impossible standards, 14–15
  unscathed, 49
  vulnerability in, 19–20
Children of Alcoholics Foundation, 103,
    273–274
  achievements of, 270–271
  facts from, 271–272
  organization of, 269–272
  three life stages, problems at, 269–270
Choice Making (Wegscheider-Cruse), 35–
  36
Clinging vine, role of, 188–190
COA Quiz, 254–265

COA Review: The Newsletter about Children of
    Alcoholics (Perrin), 100–102
Cocaine Anonymous, 275
Co-dependency
  in alcoholic families, 35–37
  characteristics of, 37–41
Commitment, 207
Communication, skills in, 206–207
Compulsive eating, 42–43
Confrontation, fear of, 27
Control
  of future, 156–157
  growing up in, 15–16
  intimate relationships and, 205
  loss of, 61–63
  of others, 147–161
  of relationships, 147–149
  relinquishing, 149–150
Cooperation, 172
Courage, 174–175
Crises
  creating, 243–244
  management of, 171

Debtors Anonymous, 276
Denial
  alcoholic, 63–65
  breaking down, 11–12
  growing up in, 9–11, 20
Depression, signs of, 125
Detachment, 92–94
  a recovery tool, 267
Disapproval, fear of, 26
Distance, false sense of, 213–217
Domestic violence, 43–46
Doom, impending, fear of, 28–29
Drug abuse. See Substance abuse
Drugs Anonymous, 276

Eating disorders, 42–43. See also specific
    disorders
  questionnaire for, 264–265
  recommended reading, 280
Empathy, with others, 173
Enabling behavior, 33–35

Family(ies)
  alcoholic
    behavior patterns in, 6–7, 32–33
    blurred boundaries in, 38–39
    childhood roles in, 47–50
    co-dependency in, 35–41
    eating disorders in, 42–43
    emotional blackouts in, 37–38
    enabling behavior in, 33–35
    isolation in, 39–41